Intervention Strategies for Children With Emotional or Behavioral Disorders

Marvin L. Dice, Jr., Ph.D.
Harris-Stowe State College
St. Louis, Missouri

SINGULAR PUBLISHING GROUP, INC.
San Diego, California

Singular Publishing Group, Inc.
4284 41st Street
San Diego, California 92105-1197

® 1993 by Singular Publishing Group, Inc.

Typeset in 10½/12 Garamond by House Graphics
Printed in the United States of America by McNaughton & Gunn

Library of Congress Cataloging-in-Publication Data
Dice, Marvin L.
    Intervention strategies for children with emotional or behavioral
disorders / Marvin L. Dice.
       p.   cm.
    Includes bibliographical references and index.
    ISBN 1-56593-166-1
    1. Problem children—Education—United States. 2. Classroom
management—United States. 3. Behavior modification—United States.
I. Title.
LC4802.D53   1993
371.93'0973—dc20   93-22671
                                                                           CIP

Intervention Strategies for Children With Emotional or Behavioral Disorders

For my late father, Mr. Marvin L. Dice
and my mother, Mrs. Victoria P. Dice.

Contents

Preface

This methods textbook is primarily for prospective teachers of children who have emotional or behavioral disorders. It is comprehensive and includes interventions that beginning teachers need to understand to address the many problems they will encounter in their classrooms. Because emotional or behavioral disorders are frequently present in other special education populations as well as in nonspecial education populations such as head-injury victims, "crack babies," and other "at-risk" children, students of psychology, health care providers, parents, and private providers should find this book useful also.

Chapter 1 provides the reader with current information defining emotional or behavioral disorders and describing how children with these problems are currently classified. Chapter 2 describes Individual Educational Programs (IEPs) and the major service delivery options that are available to special students. Chapter 3 describes how to design an assessment-based academic, social, and emotional curriculum for children with emotional or behavioral disorders. In Chapter 4, the seven principal conceptual models which influence intervention are summarized and illustrated.

When beginning teachers walk into the classroom to teach for the first time, they often have little idea of what to do and where to begin. Because this tragedy occurs so often, the reader is offered a complete description of Hewett's classic engineered classroom. This developmental approach and general principles of behavior management are outlined in Chapter 5.

Because beginning teachers often attempt to help students by using ineffective power-oriented authoritarian methods, Chapter 6 describes several major methods for developing effective facilitative interpersonal skills.

Chapter 7 identifies and describes respondent and operant strategies associated with the behavioral intervention. The material related to respondent strategies will be especially helpful to prospective teachers who find themselves working with children who have personality problems.

Chapter 8 describes methods that prospective teachers can use to help children understand how thoughts influence feelings and behavior. In this chapter, the major strategies for teaching children to monitor and modify the thoughts which are causing them to feel bad and have behavior problems are enumerated.

Chapter 9 emphasizes the belief that effective teachers either integrate or combine interventions. In this chapter, the reader is offered practical suggestions for how to either select or combine interventions while using the method of science to solve classroom problems.

Chapter 10 is designed to help teachers deal with children who are in crisis. Prevention and intervention approaches are outlined and the Life Space Intervention is emphasized because of its focus on teaching children to develop inner controls.

Finally, an Appendix is included to assist teachers, paraprofessionals, and private providers in identifying and locating materials and resources that can be put to use in the classroom.

My sincerest hope for this book is that its use will help solve a few of the many problems of children with emotional or behavioral disorders.

Acknowledgment

During the various stages of the preparation of this book, I was offered invaluable support, encouragement, and assistance. To the many students and teachers who offered suggestions about what should be included in this methods text, I am extremely grateful. To my long-standing friends, Joe Meindl, Dick Oldfield, and Frank Lippert, who respectively challenged me to practice the use of the scientific method, integrate and combine interventions, and hold to the courage of my convictions, I am forever indebted. Among the many colleagues who encouraged me and provided much of the support necessary for me to complete this project, I would particularly like to thank Eileen O'Brien, Michael Lowenstein, and Betty Schultze. Also, I am grateful to Al Walker, the Vice-President of Academic Affairs, who lent his support to this project and to Jack Burke, Patricia Barton, Earl Murphy, Sam Oliveri, Terry Werner, and Armetta Whitmore who served on the Sabbatical Leave Committee which granted the semester leave which contributed so greatly to the initial draft of this manuscript. In addition, I would like to extend my gratitude to the various anonymous expert consulting reviewers and especially to Richard Simpson, all of whom reacted to and reviewed different parts of the manuscript during its various stages of development. Additionally, I am grateful to Mike Bender, Marie Linvill, Angie Singh, and Randy Stevens of Singular Publishing Group for their assistance in the various phases of the project. Too, I thank Karen Ryan and Sidney Miranda of The Print Connection for the many figures and tables which they produced so artfully and with such ease. Finally, I want to thank my wife Laurie for her patience and warmth during the many long hours I labored in the preparation of this text.

1

Introduction to Children with Emotional or Behavioral Disorders

This chapter discusses children who have emotional or behavioral disorders. First, the problems and issues surrounding terminology and definition are outlined. Second, a brief historical background is provided to set the stage for current public policy and practice. Next, the current and a proposed new definition of children who are emotionally or behaviorally disordered are set forth. Finally, classification is discussed and the American Psychiatric Association's qualitative classification system and Quay's well known quantitative dimensional classification system are described.

Terminology

To date, a number of terms have been used to identify and describe children who have emotional or behavioral problems. These terms include behavior disorders, emotional disturbance, social maladjust-

1

ment, serious emotional disturbance, emotional disorders, and many others. Although these terms generally represent behavior problems which can be grouped into the two broad and often overlapping categories—externalizing (acting out) and internalizing disorders (withdrawal) (Hardman, Drew, Egan, & Wolf, 1993)—they do not identify clearly different types of disorders. Instead, the different labels represent preferences for terms and different theoretical orientations (Hallahan & Kauffman, 1991). Because the terminology in the field of special education is variable and changing, the use of the term "emotionally/behaviorally disordered" (E/BD) has been selected to describe the problems of children discussed in this text.

Problem of Definition

To serve children with disabilities who are emotionally or behaviorally disordered (E/BD), educators have had to develop a definition, but the problem of developing a universally acceptable definition of E/BD appears to be enduring and complex. Perhaps the most salient reason for this difficulty is that E/BD in most instances is not a disease in the medical sense, in the way tuberculosis is, but is instead a somewhat culturally created disability. That is, E/BD does not exist outside of a cultural context. In fact, the assignment of the label E/BD to a student depends a great deal on the perception of significant authority figures whose responsibility it is to make such a determination. The inherent subjectivity of most definitions increases the probability that error in referral and identification will occur. Hallahan and Kauffman (1991) list several factors that make it difficult to arrive at a good definition of emotional or behavior disorders.

1. "Lack of an adequate definition of mental health and normal behavior" (p. 174).
   This is because all children exhibit some of the characteristics of mental illness occasionally. Therefore mental illness has to be determined by the degree to which a particular child exhibits characteristics of the definition.
2. "Differences among conceptual models" (p. 174).
   This means that any understanding of normal or abnormal development as well as treatment is ultimately based on a particular paradigm, and competing conceptual models result in competing definitions of behavior disorders.

3. "Difficulties in measuring emotions and behavior" (p. 174).
   Because there are no valid and reliable tests for measuring behavior disorder and because few norms exist for determining how much or how little of a specific behavior is indicative of behavior disorders, the diagnosis of behavior disorders has to be made on a subjective clinical basis.
4. "Relationship between behavioral disorders and other handicapping conditions" (p. 174).
   Often when behavior disorder is combined with another handicapping condition it becomes impossible to tell which condition is the primary one and to what degree one handicapping condition contributes to another.
5. "Differences in the functions of socialization agents who categorize and serve children" (p. 174). Educators, police officers, officials of the juvenile court, psychologists and other professionals create definitions according to the service they render (Hallahan & Kauffman, 1991).

Background

The mandate to serve children with emotional or behavioral disorders occurred in 1975 when Public Law (PL) 94-142, The Education for All Handicapped Children Act, guaranteed a free appropriate public education for all disabled children. The impetus for PL 94-142 which serves E/BD children as well as other groups of disabled children can be traced to 1961 when President John F. Kennedy commissioned a panel on mental retardation to search for a solution to the problems of the mentally retarded and the country learned that Rose, one of the Kennedy sisters, was mentally retarded. In 1963, President Kennedy addressed the Congress and the nation, asking to begin a national effort to assist individuals with mental illness as well as mental retardation.

Congressional Action

Congressional action occurred first with PL 85-926, which provided aid to universities and colleges to prepare teachers and administrators in mental retardation, and next with PL 88-164, which extended PL

85-926 to include E/BD and all other handicapped children. PL 85-926 was to foreshadow a series of legislative action on behalf of exceptional children.

Legislative Action

Later, within a different branch of government, landmark decisions on behalf of plaintiffs were taking place in right-to-treatment and right-to-education litigation which would prove irrevocable. Right to treatment generally referred to the right of someone who had been deprived of liberty through institutionalization to receive a treatment program directed toward the reason for that deprivation, for example, an individual who had been placed in an institution for the mentally ill had, the plaintiff argued, the right to be treated for mental illness. Right to education referred to the right to have access to nonrestrictive educational programming (Repp, 1983). Similar litigation continues today on behalf of exceptional children.

Public Law 101-476

Today PL 101-476, **The Individuals With Disabilities Education Act (IDEA),** which modified slightly the earlier PL 94-142, mandates **free, appropriate, public** education for **all** disabled children. Under IDEA in 1990, the list of disabilities which made students eligilble for public special education and related services was expanded to include traumatic brain injury and autism.

Definition

Although problems abound, the definition included in PL 101-476, which identifies the E/BD students that special educators are to serve, uses the term "seriously emotionally disturbed" and defines it as follows:

   (i) The term means a condition exhibiting one or more of the following characteristics over a long period of time and to a marked degree, which adversely affects educational performance.
      A. An inability to learn which cannot be explained by intellectual, sensory, or other health factors.

B. An inability to build or maintain satisfactory interpersonal relationships with peers and teachers.

C. Inappropriate types of behavior or feeling under normal circumstances.

D. A general pervasive mood of unhappiness or depression.

E. A tendency to develop physical symptoms or fears associated with personal or school problems.

(ii) The term includes children who are schizophrenic or autistic.[1] The term does not include children who are socially maladjusted unless it is determined that they are seriously emotionally disturbed.

This current definition has received a great deal of criticism. Many professionals view the inclusion and exclusion clauses as inappropriate or unnecessary. They explain that the clause "which adversely affects educational performance" omits children who have no academic problems and as such eliminates many E/BD children (Morse, 1985; Smith, Woods, & Grimes, 1988). Also, the clause "the term includes children who are schizophrenic or autistic" appears to be unnecessary as psychotic children would certainly be included in the original definition by virtue of exhibiting at least one of the five characteristics.

The Exclusion of Socially Maladjusted Students

Finally, the clause "does not include children who are socially maladjusted unless it is determined that they are emotionally disturbed" has caused the most controversy. It has been interpreted variously to: (a) exclude all children except those who have personality problems (Slenkovich, 1983), include all who are socially maladjusted as this group would almost certainly exhibit many of the five characteristics listed in the definition to a marked extent over a long period of time (Bower, 1982), and exclude that category of children who have been identified as socialized aggressive (Quay, 1987) under this dimensional category because they identify with a delinquent subculture (Center, 1990).

Perhaps Wood (1990) defines the controversy surrounding the exclusion of socially maladjusted students most succinctly in an

---

[1] Under IDEA in 1990, the list of disabilities which made students eligible for public special education and related services was expanded to include autism, thereby removing it from "other health impaired" where it had been placed after its earlier removal from the category of "seriously emotionally disturbed."

editorial in a special issue of *Behavioral Disorders*. He explains that for some,

> "socially maladjusted" means "conduct disorders" as defined by the American Psychiatric Associations's Diagnostic and Statistical Manual III-R. Following the logic of their argument, most conduct disordered students currently being served should be "decertified,". . . . Their view has been supported by several state education agencies, several state associations of school psychologists, and some local school districts. Opponents of this viewpoint maintain that conduct disordered students are eligible. . . . Their view is that the variety of problems presented by subgroups of the emotionally and behaviorally disordered students require differential placement and programming but that no students with special needs should be excluded from service. . . . This viewpoint has been supported by the Council for Children with Behavioral Disorders and the Council of Representatives of the American Psychological Association (August 10, 1989) as well as by individual special educators. (p. 139)

A Proposed Definition

Because of the problems of the current federal definition, professionals have recently attempted to persuade the U.S. Congress to adopt a new one. In spring of 1992, the National Mental Health and Special Education Coalition recommended to Congress that the term "seriously emotionally disturbed" be replaced with the term "emotional or behavioral disorder" and proposed a new definition. However, because of the ongoing controversy regarding the proposed definition, Congress recently ordered the Department of Education to publish a notice of inquiry. The results of this inquiry will be analyzed by the Department of Education who will consider further action. In any case, this long-standing proposed definition which was circulated at the 1993 International Convention of the Council for Exceptional Children, follows:

(i) The term emotional or behavioral disorder means a disability characterized by behavioral or emotional responses in school programs so different from appropriate age, cultural, or ethnic norms that they adversely affect educational performance. Educational performance includes academic, social, vocational or personal skills. Such a disability—

    (A) is more than a temporary, expected response to stressful events in the environment;

    (B) is consistently exhibited in two different settings, at least one of which is school-related; and

(C) is unresponsive to direct intervention applied in general education or the child's condition is such that general education interventions would be insufficient.

(ii) Emotional or behavioral disorders can co-exist with other disabilities.

(iii) This category may include children or youth with schizophrenic disorders, affective disorders, anxiety disorders, or other sustained disorders of conduct or adjustment when they adversely affect educational performance in accordance with section (i).

Note that in the proposed new definition the term has been changed from "serious emotional disturbance" to an "emotional or behavioral disorder" to insure that the qualifier (seriously) is not overly restrictive nor unfair (Sweeney, 1993) and to indicate that the disorder may have either an internal emotional or an external behavioral aspect. Further, the clause "Educational performance includes academic, social vocational or personal skills" ensures that children are not omitted because their problems are nonacademic. In addition, the definition focuses on the child's responses in school settings and places these responses in the context of age appropriate and ethnically and culturally appropriate norms (Sweeney, 1993). Finally, the phrase "sustained disorders of conduct or adjustment" allows for the inclusion of some children and adolescents who are socially maladjusted.

Because the inclusion of children who are considered to be socially maladjusted in the federal definition continues to be a hotly debated issue, the adoption of this proposed new definition remains uncertain. Nevertheless, those who support the new definition hope that it will become the standard by which a greater number of children with special needs will be served.

Prevalence

There are many different and conflicting estimates of prevalence. Some are conservative. The U.S. Department of Education revised its prevalence estimate downward from 2% to 1.2% during the mid-1980s. Since then a prevalence estimate has not been published (Kauffman, 1989). Other estimates have been as high as 10% (Bower, 1981). Using population surveys, Achenbach and Edelbrock (1981) and Cullinan, Epstein, and Kauffman (1984) have reported prevalence figures ranging from 3 to 6%. Most professionals believe that the 2% prevalence figure reported earlier by the U.S. Department of

Education is low. There is general agreement that the male to female ratio of children with emotional or behavioral disorders is approximately 3 to 1.

Classification

Because classification is basic to all scientific work, categorizing emotional and behavioral disorders precisely and reliably will provide the basis for understanding these disorders and developing effective empirically supported interventions.

Quay (1979) distinguished between two basic types of classification, namely qualitative and quantitative classification. Qualitative classification systems, such as many psychiatric ones, are based on the observations of clinicians and are considered qualitative because of the inherent subjectivity of psychiatric or clinical observations. These systems therefore are viewed as less reliable and valid than quantitative systems. Quantitative classification systems such as behavioral or dimensional systems are said to be quantitative because they are based on the direct observation of specific behaviors and because an attempt is made to scientifically identify clusters of highly intercorrelated behaviors which comprise classification categories.

Although teachers are probably better served by understanding the categories of certain quantitative or dimensional systems because of superior reliability and validity, a general consideration of the framework and some of the terminology associated with the American Psychiatric Association's qualitative system is recommended. This classification system is put forth in their revised *Diagnostic and Statistical Manual of Mental Disorders* (DSM III-R).

DSM III-R

Three comprehensive qualitative systems for classifying "mental disorders" of childhood were published in 1966 by the Group for the Advancement of Psychiatry (GAP), in 1969 by the World Health Organization (International Classification of Diseases, ICD-9), and in 1987 by the American Psychiatric Association (DSM III-R).

DSM III-R, which is the most recent revision of the American Psychiatric Association, will be considered for the purpose of demonstrating how "mental disorders" of childhood have been organized. However, be aware that these clinical classifications are not always satisfactory criteria for eligibility under the federal law for services for the seriously emotionally disturbed. For example, the clinical diagnosis of attention deficit disorders does not make one eligible for federal services. In addition, some clinical conditions, for example, autism, are no longer classified as a serious emotional disturbance under PL 101-476. Autism is currently a separate and new disability. Finally, psychiatric classification has little relevance for classroom management and instruction. Nervertheless, a familiarity with the terminology in DSM III-R is advised because it often appears in psychological and psychiatric evaluations (Kauffman, 1989).

The DSM III-R system consists of 17 major categories of mental disorders including 1 category of classification of mental disorders usually first evident in infancy, childhood, or adolescence. In addition, DSM III-R provides a multiaxial system of diagnosis which requires evaluation on five separate axes.

The first two axes and V codes (conditions not attributable to a mental disorder that are a focus of attention or treatment) include all diagnostic categories and as such diagnosis can be made from both axes. The disorders on axes I generally begin after adolescence, whereas the disorders and axes II generally begin in childhood or adolescence and persist into adult life. The separation between axes I and II ensures that in the evaluation of adults every consideration is given to the possibility of axes II developmental disorders. In evaluating children, the axes I-II distinction stresses the need to consider disorders related to the development of cognitive social and motor skills (American Psychiatric Association, 1987). A brief outline of the five axes including examples for each axis follows.

Axis I: Clinical syndromes—obsessive compulsive disorder
Axis II: Personality and developmental disorders—Tourette's disorder
Axis III: Physical Disorders—cocaine dependence
Axis IV: Psychosocial stressors—death of spouse
Axis V: Global Assessment of Functioning (GAF)
           Current GAF—30
           Highest past year GAF - 61

As can be seen in the example given, axes I and II provide the framework for the diagnosis, that is, the individual diagnosed has received the primary diagnosis "obsessive compulsive disorder," but consideration has also been given to the associated developmental disorder "Tourette's disorder." Axis III has been used to indicate any current physical disorder or condition that is potentially relevant to understanding or treating the condition, for example, cocaine dependence. Although axes IV and V are optional, axis IV provides a scale for assessing the degree to which certain contributing factors have placed additional stress on the client, for example, death of a spouse, and axis V provides a means for rating a person's overall psychological, occupational, and social functioning by comparing his or her current global assessment of functioning (GAF) with his or her highest GAF during the past year. In this example, the GAF 30 is on a continuum that start at 90 with absent or minimal symptoms and becomes progressively worse as the numerals decrease. A GAF 30 implies that currently this patient is considerably influenced by delusions and hallucinations.

For teachers of children with emotional or behavioral disorders, most psychiatric information will be associated with the DSM III-R axis II. What follows therefore in Table 1-1 is a list of the diagnostic categories associated with axis II.

The major categories and subclasses of mental disorders in DSM III-R that are of interest to educators of students who are emotionally or behaviorally disordered are subclasses IB1, IB2, and major categories II and III. Currently, however, because of the controversy in the definition of SED related to the clause "does not include children who are socially maladjusted," subclass IIB1 group type for now remains in question because some authorities view this group as socially maladjusted and not as emotionally disturbed.

To get an impression of what a clinician might review in DSM III-R to make a diagnosis, a sample from DSM III-R of subclass B of major category III is provided in Figure 1-1. Note that the subcategories of Avoidant Disorder, especially the subcategory of Differential Diagnosis, contribute substantially to assisting the clinician in determining the correct diagnostic category.

Finally, it should be clear that the diagnostic criteria of DSM III-R are written in such a way as to require substantial clinical judgment in determining the correct diagnosis.

The Quay Dimensional Approach

In contrast to the qualitative approach offered in DSM III-R, Quay's 1983 dimensional classification system stands as an outstanding example of the quantitative approach. Based on the statistical technique of factor analysis, Quay (1983) has identified clusters of behaviors that are highly intercorrelated, that is, the behaviors identified under each category generally occur in the presence

TABLE 1-1. DSM III-R diagnostic categories for disorders usually first evident in infancy, childhood, and adolescence.

I. DEVELOPMENTAL DISORDERS
  A. Mental Retardation
      1. Mild mental retardation
      2. Moderate mental retardation
      3. Severe mental retardation
      4. Profound mental retardation
      5. Unspecified mental retardation
  B. 1. Autistic disorder
      2. Pervasive developmental disorder not otherwise specified
  C. 1. Specific Developmental Disorders
          a. Developmental arithmetic disorder
          b. Developmental expressive writing disorder
          c. Developmental reading disorder
      2. Language and speech disorders
          a. Developmental articulation disorder
          b. Developmental expressive writing disorder
          c. Developmental receptive language disorder
      3. Motor skills disorder
          a. Developmental coordination disorder
      4. Other Developmental Disorders
          a. Developmental disorder not otherwise specified

II. DISRUPTIVE BEHAVIOR DISORDERS
  A. Attention-Deficit Hyperactivity Disorder (ADHD)
  B. Conduct Disorder
      1. Group type
      2. Solitary aggressive type
      3. Undifferentiated type
  C. Oppositional Defiant Disorder

III. ANXIETY DISORDERS OF CHILDHOOD OR ADOLESCENCE
  A. Separation Anxiety Disorder
  B. Avoidant Disorder of Childhood or Adolescence
  C. Overanxious Disorder

IV. EATING DISORDERS
  A. Anorexia Nervosa
  B. Bulimia Nervosa
  C. Pica
  D. Rumination Disorder of Infancy
  E. Eating Disorder Not Otherwise Specified

V. GENDER IDENTITY DISORDERS
  A. Gender Identity Disorder of Childhood

(continued)

TABLE 1-1. *(continued)*

    B. Transsexualism
    C. Gender Identity Disorder of Adolescence or Adulthood, Nontranssexual Type
    D. Gender Identity Disorder Not Otherwise Specified

VI.   TIC DISORDERS
    A. Tourette's Disorder
    B. Chronic Motor or Vocal Tic Disorder
    C. Transient Tic Disorder
    D. Tic Disorder Not Otherwise Specified

VII. ELIMINATION DISORDERS
    A. Functional Encopresis
    B. Functional Enuresis

VIII. SPEECH DISORDERS NOT CLASSIFIED ELSEWHERE
    A. Cluttering
    B. Stuttering

IX.   OTHER DISORDERS OF INFANCY, CHILDHOOD, OR ADOLESCENCE
    A. Elective Mutism
    B. Identity Disorder
    C. Reactive Attachment Disorder of Infancy or Early Childhood
    D. Stereotype/Habit Disorder
    E. Undifferentiated Attention-Deficit Disorder

Source: From *Diagnostic and Statistical Manual of Mental Disorders-Revised* (3rd ed., p. 3-4) by American Psychiatric Association, 1987, Washington, DC: American Psychiatric Association. Copyright 1987 American Psychiatric Association. Adapted by permission.

313.21 AVOIDANT DISORDER OF CHILDHOOD OR ADOLESCENCE

The essential feature of this disorder is an excessive shrinking from contact with unfamiliar people that is of sufficient severity to interfere with social functioning in peer relationships and that is of at least six months duration. This is coupled with a clear desire for social involvement with familiar people, such as peers the person knows well and family members. Relationships with family members and other familiar figures are warm and satisfying. The diagnosis is not made if the disturbance is sufficiently pervasive and persistent to warrant the diagnosis of Avoidant Personality Disorder.

A child with this disorder is likely to appear socially withdrawn, embarrassed, and timid when in the company of unfamiliar people and will become anxious when even a trivial demand is made to interact with strangers. When social anxiety is severe, the child may be inarticulate or mute, even if his or her communication skills are unimpaired.

Figure 1-1 *(continued)*

Associated Features. Children with this disorder are generally unassertive and lack self-confidence. In adolescence, inhibition of normal psychosexual activity is common. The disorder rarely occurs alone: children with this disorder usually have another Anxiety Disorder, such as Overanxious Disorder.

Age at onset. The disorder typically appears during the early school years, within the context of increased opportunities for social contact. It may, however, develop as early as two and a half years, after "stranger anxiety," as a normal developmental phenomenon, should have disappeared.

Course. The course seems variable: some children improve spontaneously, whereas others experience an episodic or chronic course. How often this disorder becomes chronic and continues into adulthood, as a Social Phobia, Generalized Type, or Avoidant Personality Disorder, is unknown.

Impairment. Age-appropriate socialization skills may not develop. The impairment in social functioning is often severe.

Predisposing factors. There is some evidence that Specific Developmental Disorders involving language and speech may predispose to the development of this disorder.

Complications. The most serious complication is failure to form social bonds beyond the family, with resulting feelings of isolation and depression.

Prevalence. The disorder is not common.

Sex ratio. The disorder is apparently more common in females than in males.

Familial pattern. There is some evidence that Anxiety Disorders may be more common in the mothers of children with the disorder.

Differential Diagnosis. Socially reticent children are slow to warm up to unfamiliar people, but after a short time can respond, and suffer no impairment in peer interaction. In **Separation Anxiety Disorder**, the anxiety is focused on separation from the home or major attachment figures rather than on contact with unfamiliar people per se, but both disorders may be present. In **Overanxious Disorder**, anxiety is not focused on contact with unfamiliar people, but, again, both disorders may be present. In **Major Depression** and **Dysthymia**, social withdrawal is commonly present, but is generalized. In **Adjustment Disorder with Withdrawal**, the withdrawal is related to a recent psychosocial stressor and lasts less than six months.

The diagnosis is not made if the disturbance is sufficiently pervasive and persistent to warrant the diagnosis of **Avoidant Personality Disorder**.

(continued)

Diagnostic Criteria for 313.21 Avoidant Disorder of Childhood or Adolescence

A. Excessive shrinking from contact with unfamiliar people, for a period of six months or longer, sufficiently severe to interfere with social functioning in peer relationships.

B. Desire for social involvement with familiar people (family members and peers the person knows well), and generally warm and satisfying relations with family member and other familiar figures.

C. Age at least 2½ years.

D. The disturbance is not sufficiently pervasive and persistent to warrant the diagnosis of Avoidant Personality Disorder.

Figure 1-1. Sample from DSM III-R. From *Diagnostic and Statistical Manual of Mental Disorders—Revised* (3rd ed., p. 60-61) by American Psychiatric Association, 1987, Washington, DC: American Psychiatric Association. Copyright 1987 American Psychiatric Association. Reprinted by permission.

of other behaviors in the same category and not with behaviors named in other categories. Also, the behavioral data for these clusters were obtained from reports in case histories (Hewitt & Jenkins, 1946) and from behavior rating scales (Achenbach & Edelbrock, 1984; Quay & Peterson, 1987). To get a sense of Quay's quantitative dimensional classification system, the major behavioral dimensions and some of the associated behaviors that characterize each dimension follow (Quay & Peterson, 1987):

I. Conduct Disorder—engages in attention getting behavior, "shows off"; disturbs and "annoys" others, provokes "fights"; "has temper tantrums."

II. Socialized Aggression—engages in group thievery; "loyal to delinquent friends"; skips school with friends; has friends who often get into trouble; has inadequate moral development and often gets into trouble with the law.

III. Attention Problems/Immaturity—"Short attention span," can't concentrate, easily distracted; impulsive, responds without thinking; moves slowly, acts tired.

IV. Anxiety/Withdrawal—"Self-conscious," overly sensitive, gets hurt feelings; afraid; "anxious"; often sad or dysphoric.

V. Psychotic Behavior—"Repetitive speech"; has delusions and hallucinations; engages in repetitive behaviors.

VI. Motor Excess—Is hyperactive, "unable to sit still"; talks too much; appears unable to relax.

Children with Emotional or Behavioral Disorders

To more fully understand children who have emotional or behavioral disorders, each of Quay's major dimensions will be described in greater detail. What should be understood, however, is that although for many children most of their behavioral characteristics will align with either one specific dimension or another, some children will exhibit behavioral characteristics in several dimensions.

Conduct Disorder

Although normal children fight, hit, scream, cry, and do most of the things disturbed children do, conduct disordered children exhibit aggressive acting out behavior to a much greater degree. They are not popular with their peers, and some of these externalizing children appear to be able to harm others deliberately without feeling remorse. The unsocialized aggressive behavior that these children exhibit is characterized by physical and verbal aggression. Although different terms are used to describe these aggressive children, the central features of conduct disorders are well established. Additionally, this disorder appears at an earlier age and is more common than socialized aggression. Quay's (1986) specific behavioral symptoms of conduct disorders are associated with: (a) physical and verbal aggression, (b) noncompliance, (c) intrusiveness, (d) lack of self-control, and (e) impaired interpersonal relationships (p. 36). The behavioral symptoms associated with conduct disorders are:

1. Physical/Verbal Aggression—fighting others, hitting, bullying, impertinent, impudent
2. Noncompliance—disobedient, defiant, negative, uncooperative
3. Intrusiveness—attention-seeking, boisterous, disruptive
4. Lack of self-control—temper tantrums, irritable, irresponsible
5. Impaired relationships—dishonest, lying, callous (p. 36)

Clearly, the behavioral symptoms associated with conduct disorders involve behaviors in which the rights of others are directly violated.

Socialized Aggression

Like conduct disorder children, children who exhibit the socialized aggressive pattern of behavior show aggressive behavior to a much greater degree than normal children. However, unlike conduct disordered children, these children are often popular with their peers and conform to the norms and rules of their own often delinquent subculture. Whereas children who exhibit the socialized aggressive pattern are not technically delinquents, because delinquency is a legal term, the socialized pattern is connected to delinquent activities carried out in a peer group-context. Additionally, socialized aggression is less common than conduct disorders and occurs more frequently in later childhood and adolescence. The specific behavioral symptoms involve primarily delinquent activities which occur within the context of the peer group. Some of the primary behavioral symptoms (Quay, 1986) associated with this category are:

1. group stealing
2. truancy from home and school
3. staying out at night
4. admitted disrespect for moral values and laws
5. gang membership
6. group loyalty (p. 36)

Although socialized aggression involves primarily delinquent activities, delinquency which is a legal term, cannot be equated directly to socialized aggression. In the case of socialized aggression, behaviors which directly violate the rights of others may or may not be involved. Unlike the "overt antisocial behaviors" associated with conduct disorders, many of the behaviors associated with socialized aggression are referred to as "covert antisocial behaviors" because they are nonviolent and do not involve confronting another person directly (McMahon & Forehand, 1988).

Attention Problems-Immaturity

The children described here have problems that are similar to the problems experienced by children who are placed in the special education category of learning disabilities. Their problems are cognitive and integrative, that is, they experience problems in thinking and remembering as well as in impulse control and frustration tolerance. They have difficulty organizing and interpreting visual and auditory stimuli, have frequent shifts of mood, and often exhibit a sense of helplessness. Their deficits are often conceptualized as a learning deficiency and their behaviors are often similar to those of younger children.

Anxiety-Withdrawal

Although all children act withdrawn and anxious occasionally, the children discussed here are typically self-conscious and hypersensitive and are often characterized as having social skill deficits. They are often social isolates who retreat into fantasy, become depressed or fearful, and complain of physical ailments that keep them from participating in normal activities (Hallahan & Kauffman, 1991). Anxiety-withdrawal is well documented and described by Quay and Peterson (1987) as a behavioral dimension characterized by a number of behaviors that are usually transitory. Additionally, children who exhibit these behaviors have a better prognosis than children who exhibit behaviors associated with either unsocialized or socialized aggression. Some of the behavioral symptoms (Quay, 1987) associated with anxiety-withdrawal are:

1. feelings of inferiority and inability to succeed
2. "self-conscious"
3. "easily embarrassed"
4. shyness
5. bashfulness
6. anxiousness and fearfulness
7. feelings of being unloved
8. "depressed"
9. reluctant to try new things for fear of failure
10. "hypersensitivity" (easily hurt feelings)

Note that many of these behavioral symptoms have traditionally been associated with the label "neurotic" in the psychodynamic literature.

Psychotic Behavior

Children with psychotic behaviors have a severe degree of pathology. Their assessment of the world and their place in it appear to be grossly impaired. In fact, Prior and Werry (1986) state that the degree of impairment experienced by these children is so great as to render "the interpretation of oneself, of the world, and of one's place in it, . . . so seriously at variance with the actual facts of the matter as to interfere with the everyday adaptation and to strike the impartial observer as incomprehensible" (p. 156). Although attempts to validate the broad-band psychotic disorder dimension (Quay & Peterson, 1987) have not been completed, there appears to be clinical evidence suggesting that there are two separate psychoses of childhood. These are infantile autism and childhood schizophrenia (Prior & Werry, 1986).

Infantile Autism

Infantile autism is called autistic disorder in DSM III-R and is classified as a serious pervasive developmental disorder which begins in infancy or childhood and is characterized by an impairment in social interaction, verbal and nonverbal communication, and a restricted repertoire of activities and interests. Most often the diagnosis is made before the age of 3 years, and the cause appears to be brain damage that affects the areas of the brain concerned with language and social understanding (Prior & Werry, 1986). According to DSM III-R, "the essential features of this disorder constitute a severe form of Pervasive Developmental Disorder with onset in infancy or childhood" (p. 38).

Childhood Schizophrenia

Though childhood schizophrenia is uncommon, the onset of this disorder usually occurs in adolescence or early adulthood and refers to psychotic behavior characterized by loss of contact with reality and bizarre thought processes and behavior. With the exception of developmental variations, childhood schizophrenia is identical to adult schizophrenia (Prior & Werry, 1986). This is perhaps why the authors of DSM III-R have chosen not to include a separate category of childhood schizophrenia which they had included in the earlier DSM III. Instead, they note that schizophrenia can occur in childhood or adolescence. According to DSM III-R:

> The essential features of this disorder are the presence of characteristic psychotic symptoms during the active phase of the illness and functioning below the highest level previously achieved (in children or adolescence, failure to achieve the expected level of social development), and a duration of a least six months that may include characteristic prodromal or residual symptoms. (p. 187)

It should be clear that the diagnostic criteria of schizophrenia are very different than the criteria for autistic disorder. Rutter and Schopler (1987) have distinguished between autism and schizophrenia as follows:

Autism	**Schizophrenia**
rarely runs in families	often runs in families
delusions and hallucinations are rare	delusions and hallucinations are frequent
continuing symptoms	normal behavior interrupted with psychotic behavior
seizure in 25% of children	children rarely have seizures

Motor Excess

Children with these behaviors are often called **hyperactive, attention-deficit disordered (ADD)**, or **attention deficit hyperactivity disordered (ADHD)**, and their problems have frequently been associated with excess activity. Although explanations for this excess activity vary, their problems typically include restlessness, unpredictability, flightiness, distractibility, impulsiveness, irritability, and destructiveness. Additionally, it is important to note that according to Loeber (1985, cited in McMahon & Forehand, 1988) some investigators view excess activity as a principal factor in the development of conduct disordered children.

Summary

Children and adolescents with emotional or behavioral disorders exhibit many behavior problems that span a wide range from disorders that are primarily external to those that are primarily internal. Because of the great variability of problem behavior found in this population, a number of different terms have been used to identify and describe E/BD children. Agreement regarding an appropriate definition of the population described by these different terms has been equally difficult. The terminology used in the current federal definition is different than the terminology used in a proposed new definition. These different terms and their accompanying different definitions reflect the changes this area of special education continues to experience. Classification, which is basic to science, provides the basis for understanding emotional or behavioral disorders. Although teachers will come in contact with terminology used in the various revisions or editions of the American Psychiatric Association's DSM III-R, psychiatric or qualitative classification which lacks reliability and validity has not been especially useful to them.

Quantitative classification sytems are more helpful to teachers because of their reliability and validity. Quay's dimensional approach divides the broad dimensions of externalizing and internalizing behaviors into the more specific categories of conduct disorders, socialized aggression, anxiety withdrawal, problems of attention/immaturity, psychotic behavior, and motor excess.

Review Questions

1. Why is it so difficult to define emotional and behavioral disorders?
2. Why have the authors of the proposed new definition changed the term from "serious emotional disturbance" to "emotional or behavioral disorder"?
3. Why is it important to have a classification system for emotional and behavioral disorders?
4. What is the difference between quantitative and qualitative classification systems?
5. In using the DSM III-R multiaxial system, what axes provide the framework for the diagnosis?
6. What section of DSM III-R is used to classify the disorders of children and adolescents?
7. In what ways are conduct disorders and socialized aggression different?
8. In what ways are attention problems-immaturity and anxiety-withdrawal different?
9. In what ways are infantile autism and childhood schizophrenia different?

Learning Activities

1. Because of the subjectivity of most definitions of emotional or behavior disorders, the assignment of the label "E/BD" to a student depends to a great extent on what professionals perceive as truly disordered. Divide into small groups of eight or ten, and generate a list of five descriptions of behaviors that have a high probability of being labeled disordered, for example, "Ten year old Mark does not talk to anyone except the teacher." After the five descriptions have been written, divide once again so that half of you can develop a

rationale for labeling while the other half develops a rationale for not labeling. You should take no more than 10 to 15 minutes for each of the descriptions, and the rationale must be based on the current federal definition. For each of the five descriptions, your subgroup then debates the merits of either labeling or not labeling, in front of the class.

2. Put your group's five descriptions of potentially disordered behavior on the blackboard. Using the Quay Dimensional Approach and the diagnostic categories of DSM III-R in Table 1-1, each group attempts to classify the descriptions of behavior into the appropriate categories of each classification system. Next, each group develops a rationale for the classification of those descriptions that were difficult to categorize. Finally, your group presents its classification decisions and the rationale for these decisions to the entire class.

2

Educational Services

This chapter discusses educational services. First, the services required in PL 101-476 in an individual education program are described. Second, the continuum of service placement options described in Deno's long-standing classic cascade system are outlined. Next, the roles that teachers must play at each level of the cascade system, to meet the needs of children with emotional or behavioral disorders (E/BD), are described. Finally, a description of emerging alternative educational services is provided to emphasize recent trends in attempting to integrate and coordinate general education, special education, and community services.

Individual Education Programs

One of the requirements of PL 101-476 is that all children with disabilities receiving special education services must be provided with an individual education program (IEP). The concept of individualization of instruction and of the accountability for this instruction are inextricably tied to right-to-education and right-to-treatment court cases. All of these court decisions have suggested that there should be standards for service providers. This recognition carries with it the need for individualized instruction formally required in PL 94-142.

Additionally, although IEPs differ in level of detail, the diagnostic evaluation which results in the identification of a student as emotionally or behaviorally disordered typically includes medical, psychological, social, and educational data and must be completed by a group of professionals of which at least one is a specialist qualified to teach students with the disability under consideration. Also, after parental permission for the evaluation is obtained, all components of the evaluation must be completed in 65 days (Pullen & Kauffman, 1987), and the IEP must be signed by the responsible parties. The signatures of the special education teacher, an administrative representative of the special education program, and one of the student's parents are the minimum number of signatures required. Table 2-1 is an abbreviated sample of an IEP.

Components of the IEP

Each IEP includes the specific components described below.

The Student's Present Level of Performance

This implies that the IEP will contain assessment data that are reliable and valid and of sufficient breadth to cover the major areas of educational need. Although some norm-referenced data may be helpful, the most useful data related to the student's present level of educational performance are obtained through direct observation and informal criterion-referenced assessment. Some of the areas often included in this section of the IEP are intelligence quotient; speech, vision, and hearing; academic skills; and social and emotional behavior.

Annual Goals

This implies that a determination is made of what the student can accomplish during the school year. These goals are expressed in broad terms and cover academic and social and emotional behavior, for example, to improve math skills by one grade level, to reduce the number of playground fights, and to identify and label the primary emotions. Generally, procedures are based on the direct observation

TABLE 2-1. An abbreviated example of an IEP for a student with emotional and behavioral disorders.

INDIVIDUALIZED EDUCATION PROGRAM

Student: Calvin Sacken
Birthdate: April 20, 1978
District: Jefferson County
School: Emerson Middle School
Grade: Eighth
Teacher: Ms. Herzog
Placement: Emotional/Behavioral Disorders

Current Level of Performance:

    Calvin's intellectual development is somewhat below average for his age. Although he has a full scale WISC-III in the low normal range, his academic skills as assessed formally on the Woodcock-Johnson-R indicate that his academic performance is significantly below ability level. Informal measures support this conclusion.

    Calvin's social and emotional behavior is characteristically aggressive and impulsive. He has few friends and lacks age-appropriate social skills.

Performance data:

Intelligence: WISC-III Full scale 90
Speech: Normal
Vision: Normal
Hearing: Normal
Academic Skills: Reading 4.8, English 4.5, Math 4.0, Science 5.0, Social
                Studies 4.5, Spelling 5.1
Social Behavior: Overly aggressive, oppositional, immature
Emotional Behavior: Excessive anger, pouts, tantrums

Long-Term Goals

1. To improve reading skills by one grade level.
2. To improve math skills by one grade level.
3. To reduce inappropriate agression.
4. To develop age-appropriate social skills.
5. To acquire basic rational-emotive skills.

Short-Term Objectives

1. To pronounce correctly new words on sight.
2. To use context clues to pronounce words correctly in text.
3. To multiply correctly two-digit numbers with carrying.
4. To decrease hitting and teasing others.
5. To identify some of his own primary emotions.

Placement: Resource room—math, reading, social and emotional behavior

Initiation of Services: September 7, 1992

(continued)

25

TABLE 2-1.   *(continued)*

Duration of Services: One year

Reevaluation: September 6, 1995

Committee Members: Signature

   Dr. White, Principal   _____

   Dr. Schultze, Counselor   _____

   Mr. Gelderman, BD Teacher   _____

   Mrs. Gandy, Parent   _____

   Mr. Clark, School Psychologist   _____

I agree with this plan to place my child in special education.

_____   _____
Signature   Date

of a student's behavior, for example, direct observation or curriculum-based evaluation, provide meaningful information, and encourage social validation (Kauffman, 1993). Since these procedures include an informal criterion-referenced assessment component, they are particularly helpful in making decisions about what the precise annual goals are to be. Principles of curriculum design can then be formulated to implement daily instruction.

Short-Term Objectives

The short-term objectives should be tied to annual goals, and each annual goal should have several short-term objectives. Short-term objectives represent approximate subgoals, for example, to be able to correctly add two two-digit numerals without regrouping and be achievable in shorter periods of time, for example, a month or so. Short-term objectives can best be derived through direct observation by fractioning down the long-term goal into subskills or obtained from curriculum outlines. Although short-term objectives are required for the IEP, they are not sufficiently detailed to use for teaching purposes. These have to be fractioned down further to develop instructional objectives in order to begin teaching. This additional fractioning down process, which occurs as the result of task analysis, is helpful in the development and design of curricula.

Special Education and Related Services

This section of the IEP must specify the type of program the student will participate in, for example, the program for students with emotional or behavioral disorders and the type of service delivery model under which the services will be made available, for example, the resource room. The requirement to make services available in the least restrictive environment will have a bearing on the type of service delivery model selected. Additionally, any related service, for example, speech therapy or the services that a child psychologist might provide once a week, should be identified in this section.

Participation in Regular Education Programs

This section specifies the extent to which students will participate in a regular education program. Often this participation depends on consultive support services. Also, the type of service delivery model selected, for example, resource room or class within a class, will affect the degree of participation.

Initiation and Duration of Services

The IEP should identify the date on which services will begin and the period of time during which the special education services will continue. Because a triennial re-evaluation must be conducted, the duration specified for services cannot exceed 3 years.

Evaluation Plans

Although the evaluation of student progress should be ongoing, progress toward the goals and objectives of the IEP must be formally assessed once a year. Ideally, however, frequent assessments of the student's performance through direct observation should be used to measure student achievement and modify the program as needed.

The Promise of the IEP

According to several authors, the spirit of IEPs is not being upheld (Reiher, 1992; Repp, 1983; Smith & Simpson, 1989). Repp (1983) reported that after collecting data from a number of residential facilities for children with disabilities, many considered 8 to 10 objectives per client per year was sufficient. After analyzing 214 IEPs of students with emotional or behavioral disorders from three metropolitan school districts, four rural special education cooperative programs, and one small city school district, Smith and Simpson (1989) found procedural faults in over 50% of the IEPs inspected. Among the concerns they expressed were whether special class placement was justified in instances where the class average was less than one behavioral and less than one social/emotional goal. In addition, they expressed concern over the lack of integrity that existed when either an annual goal was identified in the absence of a need or a need was indicated in the absence of a goal. Reiher (1992) found a similar lack of agreement between areas of deficit and IEP goals and objectives.

Regardless of the difficulty involved in upholding the spirit of the PL 101-476, future educators of children with emotional and behavioral disorders will have to face the challenge of developing substantive IEPs.

Service Delivery Systems

Because special education implies an education that is specifically tailored to the unusual needs of children with disabilities, several service delivery placements are available to address the unique needs of E/BD students. The different placement options vary according to the degree to which E/BD students are: (a) integrated with nonexceptional students and (b) served by the special education teacher. The type of service delivery model used has been influenced by PL 101-476, which requires that students with disabilities be placed in the least restrictive environment (LRE) appropriate. This requirement is based on the philosophy that students with disabilities have contact with the normal learning environment to the greatest extent possible to meet their learning needs. A student placed in a residential facility may be in the LRE if that is the only environment that can clearly meet her needs.

Deno (1970) presented what is now viewed as a classic model of service delivery, namely a cascade system of special education services that can be applied to all disabilitiy conditions. What makes Deno's system so enduring is that it is shaped like an hourglass to indicate the differences in the numbers of students with disabilities served at each level and to emphasize that the system can be viewed as a diagnostic filter, that is, disabled students should be served at the upper levels of the system if possible and only moved downward to the lower levels to the extent necessary. This diagnostic aspect of the cascade system anticipated the LRE clause in PL 94-142 by several years. Deno's cascade system, which every special educator should know about, includes seven levels and is shown in Figure 2-1. Following is a description of each level of Deno's classic cascade system of special education services.

Level I: Regular Class With/Without Support

This level includes exceptional children who are able to function with or without medical or counseling support therapies. The regular teacher is skilled at meeting many of the individual needs of students. He can select and use the appropriate instruction methods and/or materials. Sometimes the regular classroom teacher may need the support of other professionals such as the counselor or school psychologist. The students being served are totally integrated into the regular classroom.

Level II: Regular Class Attendance Plus Supplementary Instructional Services

This arrangement is comprised of children who are able to function in the regular class with the help of additional instructional services. These consultive support services may be provided either directly or indirectly to students with disabilities. The special education teacher may provide crisis intervention services directly to students with disabilities or may support the regular teacher by taking over some of her duties, while the regular teacher works with students with disabilities. The special educator may support the regular teacher by providing her with instruction in various management techniques or in demonstrating the use of methods, materials, or equipment. The students being served are totally integrated into the regular classroom.

Level III: Part-Time Special Class

At this level students attend the special class part of the time and spend the remainder of their school day in the regular class. This is

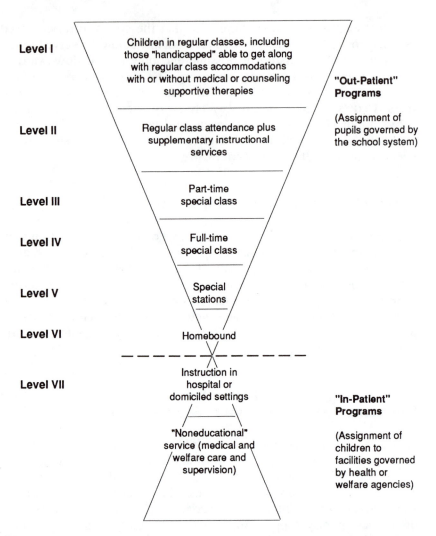

Figure 2-1. The cascade system of special education service. From "Special Education As Developmental Capital" by E. Demo, 1970, *Exceptional Children, 37,* 235. Copyright 1970 by The Council For Exceptional Children. Reprinted by permission.

both a direct and indirect service delivery system and is often referred to as the resource room. The resource teacher usually teaches children individually or in small groups in the resource room, but also acts as a consultant or specialist to the regular teacher. In this capacity, the resource teacher may demonstrate instructional techniques or advise the regular teacher on instructional and management strategies.

The students being served under this plan usually have mild to moderate problems and spend most of their time in the regular classroom.

Level IV: Full-Time Special Class

In this placement, students spend most of the day segregated from their nonexceptional peers in a special education classroom. Sometimes they are integrated with nonexceptional peers for music, physical education, and other activities in which they can participate meaningfully. Because these students have moderate to severe problems, the full-time special class often has a teacher assistant or aid to help the teacher. The special class teacher may need to consult with regular teachers, but her main responsibility to other professionals is to plan and coordinate some of the activities of her assistant and to consult with support personnel such as the school psychologist and counselor.

Level V: Special Stations

In this placement, students spend the whole day in a special day school specifically designed for a category of exceptionality, for example, emotional or behavioral disorders. The disabilities of these students are usually severe or profound, and they are unable to function in a regular school program. Generally, the special school is physically separate from the regular school and is staffed by professionals from a variety of disciplines, for example, special educators, social workers, psychologists, physical therapists, recreational therapists, and so on.

Level VI: Homebound

These children receive instruction in their home. This usually occurs when a more permanent placement is not immediately available and is only for a brief time. The child is visited regularly by the special or itinerant teacher who offers instruction in the area of greatest need and provides support by acting as a liaison between the home and school settings.

Level VII: Instruction in a Hospital or Residential Setting

In this setting, students receive 24-hour care at a facility away from their home. Sometimes these children make periodic visits home or spend weekends at home. Students in residential settings are usually profoundly disabled, whereas children in hospital settings may or may not be so seriously disabled, depending on the reason for their hospitalization, for example, hospitalization may be ordered as the result of a serious psychotic relapse or for the purpose of serving a mildly E/BD student who has pneumonia.

Level VIII: Noneducational Service

In this setting, children are assigned to facilities that are governed by health or welfare agencies. These noneducational services include medical and welfare care and supervision.

Teacher Roles

In this section, the various roles and characteristics which teachers of children who are emotionally or behaviorally disorders must possess at each educational level of the cascade system are discussed.

Level I

At this level, the special education teacher is not needed because children with disabilities are able to manage under the supervision of the regular teacher.

Level II

At this level, the special education teacher must become knowledgeable about the regular education program. This includes understanding the regular class curriculum, methods, and materials. The special education teacher must have good interpersonal skills and be able to help the regular teacher adapt materials to the needs of mildly disturbed children. A principal duty of the special education teacher is to attempt to understand the perspective of the regular teacher as it applies to student problems. This implies a capability of informally assessing the regular teacher through conversation and interview and of possessing knowledge regarding the use of informal data collection methods which can be used for intervention purposes.

Level III

At this level, a special education teacher should possess the same skills required at level II plus greater familiarity with the specialized curriculum that she will use directly with students. In the part-time special class or resource room, the teacher directly plans and implements academic, social, and emotional interventions. Also, because students will spend more than half of their time in the regular classroom, the special teacher coordinates instructional planning with the regular teacher. This implies the need to conference with regard to assignments, grades, and management techniques. Often forms are used to help regular and special teachers coordinate their activities in such areas as instructional objectives, classwork, and projects as well as to provide feedback about social and emotional behavior.

Levels IV and V

At levels IV and V, students are placed full-time in a self-contained classroom. Although they may be programmed into regular education settings occasionally, the special teacher has almost complete responsibility for designing and delivering services to these children. Because these children are moderately to severely disordered, teachers working in full-time special classes or special stations usually have a teacher's aide to assist them. Although teachers at this level should possess many of the skills described at earlier levels of the cascade, their role is primarily to provide intervention to children who have serious academic, social, and emotional problems while supervising and making use of the assistance provided by their aide.

Level VI

At this level, special education teachers for the emotionally and behaviorally disorder will seldom be needed. When they are needed, their primary purpose is to provide instruction in areas where the need is greatest and to coordinate activities between school and home. These teachers should have a thorough knowledge of the curriculum and possess good interpersonal skills.

The Regular Education Initiative

Although Deno's continuum of services model describes how most E/BD students currently receive services, many leaders have argued for changes in educational policies which would more completely integrate general and special education. Radical proponents of integration have argued for the inclusion of all students in regular settings by insisting that the current system of service delivery is fragmented, insufficiently collaborative, and stigmatizing of students. They have called for a full partnership or merger between regular and special education, which has become known as the regular education initiative (REI), and sometimes full inclusion (Lipsky & Gartner, 1991; Stainback & Stainback, 1991; Will, 1986) which ultimately would entail the dissolution of special education as a separate system of educational services. Some writers have suggested that special education is discriminatory (Wang, Reynolds, & Walberg, 1988) and have described the special education system as a burden (Gartner & Lipsky, 1989). Currently, however, opinion is mixed with regard to the extent to which general and special education should be merged. Other proponents of integration, for example, argue that while E/BD students should be integrated into general education to the greatest extent possible, a continuum of a service placement model which includes pull-out programs, for example, some of the ones described in Deno's cascade system, should be maintained to efffectively serve students (Fuchs & Fuchs, 1991; Kauffman, 1991).

Emerging Alternative Educational Services

Regardless of the position one supports concerning the extent to which general and special education should be integrated, many alternative educational services have emerged as a result of efforts to facilitate the integration of regular and special education. One well known model program which has been designed for integrating students with disabilities with general education peers is called the Adaptive Learning Environments Model (ALEM). The major features of this model that facilitate the adaptation of instruction to student differences include: (a) individualized progress plans, (b) a diagnostic-prescriptive monitoring system, (c) an instructional and management system, (d) a program delivery system, (e) a data-based development program, (f) a school and classroom organizational support system, and (g) an active program of family involvement. This program has been supported by research which has documented that effective implementation can lead to positive changes in regular classrooms in a wide variety of school settings (Wang, Peverly, & Catalano, 1987). The following alternative educational services attempt to make regular school classrooms and communities serve the differing needs of the greatest number of diverse students possible.

Collaborative Consultation

Collaborative consultation perhaps represents the foundation on which alternative educational services are based (Curtis & Meyers, 1988). This is because collaborative consultation enables a variety of personnel with diverse expertise to creatively address mutually defined problems (Idol, Paolucci-Whitcomb & Nevin, 1986). It creates the possibility for a new mix, with each participant alternating between the consultant and consultee role as this becomes warranted by differing expertise (Thousands, Villa, Paolucci-Whitcomb, & Nevin, 1992). Although anyone can provide consultation, the collaborative model encourages special education teachers, general education teachers, other school professionals, and parents to work together to jointly prevent or remediate academic and social problems that occur in the general school program (Idol, 1988).

In addition, because collaborative consultation is based on (a) team ownership of the problem, (b) a recognition of developmental differences, (c) the application of reinforcement principles, and (d) data-based decision making (Idol, Paolucci-Whitcomb, & Nevin, 1986), collaborative consultation appears to be a promising approach to meeting the needs of many disabled students in general education settings. Nevertheless, to be effective, consultants must (a) possess facilitative interpersonal skills, (b) have a strong foundation in the area of knowledge specific to the consultant, (c) possess expertise in problem solving, and (d) be knowledgeable of system theory (Curtis & Meyers, 1988.)

Support Facilitation

Closely aligned with collaborative consultation, support facilitation requires that individuals be able to develop networks that encourage collaboration among many individuals. However, unlike collaborative consultants, who have acquired technical mastery of a process, for example, assessment or curriculum planning, the support facilitator focuses on developing a network of support options. One such support network may require the expertise of a collaborative consultant (Stainback & Stainback, 1990). Some of the emerging roles of a support facilitator are to:

1. establish an integration task force
2. seek extra support, for example, a teacher's aide
3. establish a peer support committee
4. organize teacher and student assistance teams
5. serve as a team teacher
6. serve as a curriculum analyst
7. locate specialists
8. work with families
9. locate curriculum and equipment
10. foster professional peer collaboration
11. help modify traditional language, for example, terminology associated with disabled students
12. stress the importance of communication systems, for example, find ways for students who speak a foreign language to send and receive messages (Stainback & Stainback, 1990).

Regardless of what roles the support facilitator puts into place, support facilitation is essential to the achievement of inclusive quality education in regular settings.

Pre-Referral Intervention

Like the first two alternative educational services, pre-referral interventions attempt to enhance general education's capability for meeting the needs of diverse student populations. In addition, pre-referral interventions direct assessment and intervention to difficult-to-teach nonhandicapped students in an attempt to reduce or completely eliminate the need for students to be formallly referred to special education. The rationale for pre-referral interventions is based on the belief that (a) too many students are being identified as handicapped and (b) that this over-representation of identified students represents the failure of general education to deal with a heterogeneous population (Fuchs & Fuchs, 1988).

To prevent arbitrary and precipitous teacher referrals, pre-referral teams collaborate to assess problems and develop strategies for working with children exhibiting academic and behavioral problems. Although pre-referral consultation models may differ, for example, some may be more behavioral than others, the goal is for the consultant and the general education teacher to collaboratively design, modify, and evaluate the intervention. The hope for this alternative service is that general education will become increasingly able to effectively meet the needs of diverse and difficult students.

Peer-Assisted Learning

Because of the prevailing opinion that general education has had difficulty meeting the needs of children who function at different levels of ability, peer-assisted learning (PAL) has emerged as an alternative educational service. In peer-assisted learning, at least two students interact in learning situations which have been guided or structured by a teacher for the purpose of promoting the academic or social and emotional growth in some or all of the students involved (Miller & Peterson, 1987).

Most often, instruction occurs in two broad areas: (a) peer tutoring and (b) cooperative group learning (Hawryluk & Smallwood, 1988). In peer tutoring, the teacher usually structures the activities or lessons and the older, more competent student provides individualized instruction. Sometimes, however, the tutor and learner's roles are reversed. The classroom teacher and the tutor must work in close consultation so that the teacher can closely monitor students who are working as peer tutors (McDonnell, Wilcox, & Hardman, 1991). Peer tutoring is sometimes referred to as cross-age tutoring (Zins, Curtis, Garden, & Ponti, 1988).

In cooperative group learning (CGL), students collaborate in learning exercises to stimulate learning and achieve group approval and rewards. These groups are typically heterogeneous so that students with disabilities and those without disabilities can benefit by the increased opportunity to engage actively in academic tasks. Although teachers may select varying methods of implementing CGL, most approaches can be classified as either group tutoring or group investigation (Sharan, 1980). In group tutoring, students assist each other in learning material, for example, spelling words, whereas in group investigation, students explore a topic, engage in creative or critical thinking, or share information which is integrated into a group project (Hawryluk & Smallwood, 1988).

In any case, PAL has emerged as an alternative educational service for meeting the needs of diverse groups of students.

Mandated Alternative Educational Services

Since the national mandate under PL 94-142 in 1975 to educate students with disabilities, several recent alternative educational services similar to IEPs have been mandated. Like many emerging alternative educational services, these services attempt to coordinate and integrate school, community, and home.

Individual Family Service Plans

Because of the recognition that the early years are critical to the overall development of children, Individual Family Service Plans (IFSP) which bridge the gap between state and local education agencies and the community are developed cooperatively by parents and educators to assure that infants and toddlers under the age of 3 receive needed services. This incentive was established under PL 99-457, which amended the education of the handicapped act in 1986. While PL 99-457 assured that young 3- to 5-year-old children received a free, and appropriate education that includes an IEP, it also encourages states to implement programs that include an IFSP to meet the needs of toddlers and infants. The IFSP is similar to the IEP except that it is broadened to include all members of the family and specifies how each is to be involved. Although the identification of children with emotional and behavioral disorders is a difficult task (Kauffman, 1993), early intervention has the potential to make many of these children normal (Lovaas, 1987).

Regardless of their overall success with specific children, IFSPs have emerged as a recent alternative educational service which promotes and coordinates collaboration between the school and community.

Adult Transition Plans

Because the transition from school to work and adult life is difficult for disabled students and especially difficult for E/BD students (Hallahan & Kauffman, 1991), PL 101-476 has required that each student's IEP include a transition statement by the time students are 16 years of age. Accordingly, transition plans are being drafted which enhance the opportunities for success following school by showing the linkages between different agencies and the agency's responsibilities to the students leaving school. According to Ianacone and Stodden (1987), service providers " must intervene at three levels, that is, (1) transition preparation, (2) transition linkage from a preparatory environment to the receiving environment, and (3) access and participation within the receiving environment" (p. 4). Because E/BD students often exhibit irritating socially unacceptable behavior which makes it difficult for them to be helped and accepted by their employers and coworkers (Hallahan & Kauffman, 1991), it is critical that transition plans coordinate services between the schools and adult service agencies, for example, vocational rehabilitation services, social services, and mental health services (Hardman, Drew, Egan, & Wolf, 1993).

Although emerging alternative services bode well for providing help for children with emotional and behavioral disorders, there are significant barriers to achieving appropriate interagency coordination (Forness, 1988). According to Forness (1988), "conflicting or vague policies around who pays, who serves, and who is ultimately responsible for what happens to a child can result in children with serious emotional disturbance 'falling through the cracks' of differing jurisdictions" (p. 130). However, because of the recent interest in interagency collaboration and coordination, as well as the call for federally mandated therapeutic and support services for these children, the future appears brighter (Forness, 1988).

Summary

Because of the requirement in PL 101-476 to provide special education students with an IEP, it would appear that more students with emotional or behavioral disabilities are receiving instruction that is individually tailored to the student's needs. Although there is some question of whether the spirit of IEPs is being upheld in terms of the lack of annual goals programmed and/or the agreement between deficit areas and goals, educators are now being challenged to make themselves accountable for individualized instructional programming.

The requirement of PL 101-476 to place students in the least restrictive environment (LRE) appropriate has ensured Deno's classic cascade system of special education services a permanent place in special education history. This continuum of services delivery model with eight levels of special education services suggests that students should be served at the least restrictive upper levels of the system if possible and only moved downward to the extent necessary. Teachers of children who are emotionally or behaviorally disordered must play various roles and possess different characteristics at each level of the cascade system.

Primarily because of the regular education initiative (REI) in which proponents have argued for the placement of disabled students in regular education classrooms, alternative educational services which encourage a rich and diverse learning partnership between regular and special education have emerged. A major element in the newly emerging alternative services is collaboration between regular and special education teachers, other school professionals, parents and students, and various agencies which provide help for children with emotional or behavioral disorders.

Review Questions

1. Who must sign the IEP?
2. After parental permission for a diagnostic evaluation is obtained, how long do the professionals responsible for the evaluation have to complete it?
3. What are the components of the IEP?
4. How is the most useful educational data related to the student's present level of performance obtained?
5. How can you distinguish between annual goals and short-term objectives?
6. How often must a student's progress toward the goals and objectives of the IEP be assessed?
7. What is the maximum time between the initial diagnostic evaluation and the re-evaluation?
8. Why is Deno's cascade system designed like an hour-glass?
9. What are the major roles the special education teacher must perform at levels II through V of the cascade system?
10. Distinguish between collaborative consultation and support facilitation.
11. What is the purpose of pre-referral intervention?
12. Describe the two broad areas of peer-assisted learning.
13. Compare individual family service plans with adult transition plans

Learning Activities

1. Using the IEP format depicted in the illustration in Figure 2-1, divide into groups of five to six members and jointly make a mock IEP of a hypothetical student with emotional and behavioral disorders. Make certain that there is a logical relationship between each of the components, for example, a student who is below average on the Wechsler Intelligence Scale for Children-III (WISC-III) probably will be below ability on the Woodcock-Johnson-R. After reaching consensus on each IEP component, present your mock IEP to the class.

2. Divide into groups of five to six members. Select a level from Deno's cascade system of special education services and give six concrete examples of duties that a special teacher might perform. For example, in level III, the special education teacher might design a form to help coordinate instructional planning with the regular teacher. Each group is to select a different level and no group is to select level I. Present each of the six concrete examples to the class.

3. Divide into groups of five or six members and design a form to help coordinate activities with the regular teacher. Areas in which such forms might be developed include classwork, projects, social and emotional behavior, and the scheduling of reinforcement.

3
Designing Educational Programs

B ecause emotionally or behaviorally disordered (E/
BD) students are characterized by problems "which
adversely affect educational performance," special
educators must design educational interventions that address both
academic and social or emotional behavior competence. Although
there are many approaches designed to address the needs of children
and youths with emotional or behavioral disorders, (e.g., developmen-
tal/cognitive, remedial/behavioral, functional), what is often found
lacking in classrooms is a well designed comprehensive functional
educational program or plan of instruction. Such a program can be
developed, but only through the difficult and sometimes tedious work
of directly assessing each student's individual academic and social
behavioral characteristics. This chapter provides a description of a
plan for the comprehensive assessment of academic and social/
emotional behavior and the development of an academic and social/
emotional behavior curriculum based on this assessment.

Academic Assessment

Academic assessment is greatly aided by ensuring that teachers are
able to determine exactly what students can and can't do in each of

the subjects in the curriculum. This determination is based on the teacher's ability to fractionate the curriculum into instructional objectives.

The Academic Curriculum Profile

The starting point for academic assessment is often the development of an academic curriculum profile. This process is facilitated when someone knowledgeable about the administration of a standardized achievement test such as the Woodcock-Johnson-R Tests of Achievment or the Peabody Individual Achievement Test-Revised administers such a test or several such tests and collects the resultant data. Most standardized achievement tests that cover several content areas will provide some clues about students' strengths and weaknesses. Usually, these tests will provide an age and grade level equivalent as well as a standard score and percentile ranking. Although standardized achievement tests will not always give all of the assessment data needed for instruction, they will provide sufficient information to develop an academic curriculum profile. Figure 3-1 illustrates an Academic Curriculum Profile which was derived from administering the Peabody Individual Achievement Test-Revised. On this standard score profile, the subject's results are compared to the age group from the standardized sample. The bold vertical line at the standard score of 100 is the mean for the age group and the other bold vertical lines are standard deviations from the mean.

Formal Assessment

The next step in the assessment of academic skills is to conduct an indirect formal assessment of each subject area in the curriculum. This is facilitated by administering a standardized diagnostic test for each academic area profiled, for example, the Key Math Test-Revised might be used to survey the subskills of math. Most standardized diagnostic tests are designed to provide detailed information about the strengths and weaknesses students display in the subject area for which the test was written. Usually these tests contain information related to the subskills that comprise the subject areas. Although there is presently debate over the degree to which standardized diagnostic tests are helpful in developing intervention plans, they will

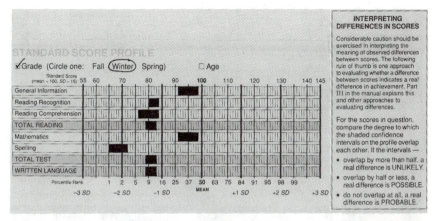

Figure 3-1. An illustration of an academic curriculum profile based on the Peabody Individual Achievement Test-Revised. From *Test Record, Peabody Individual Achievement Test-Revised,* (p. 25) by F. C. Markwardt, 1989, Circle Pines, MN: American Guidance Service. Copyright 1989 by American Guidance Service, Inc. Reprinted by permission.

provide some initial ideas about the subject area and about some of the strengths and weaknesses students possess in each subject area. Figure 3-2, which depicts a sample profile and area comparisons from the Key Math-R, provides an example of the various subskills that can be assessed by administering a formal diagnostic test which has been designed for a particular content area. On this score profile, Form A, which employs Fall norms, was administered. The Key Math-R manual recommends the use of a 90% confidence level for profiling the Total Test and area scores and a 68% confidence level for subtest scaled scores. The area comparisons indicate that Basic Concepts are of low to low average performance, but significantly higher than both Operations and Applications area scores.

Informal Assessment

The third step in the assessment of academic skills is to conduct a direct informal assessment of each academic area. This step is necessary to develop a well designed comprehensive functional intervention plan. Whereas the standardized diagnostic test will be of help initially, the best way to pinpoint precisely the specific skills that need to be taught is to assess each academic area directly. The

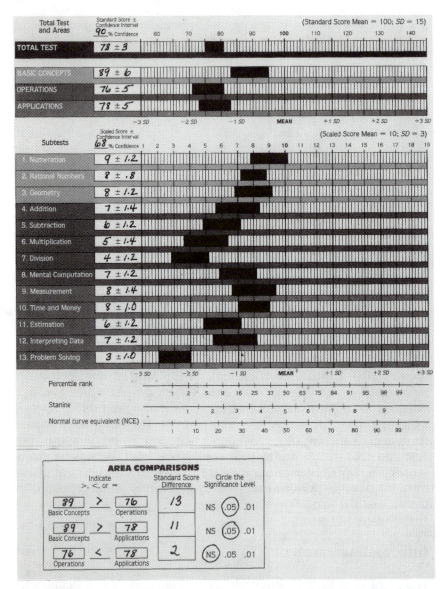

Figure 3-2. An illustration of a sample profile and area comparisons from the Key Math-R. From *Key Math Revised Individual Test Record,* Form A (p. 12) by A. J. Connoly, 1988, Circle Pines, MN: American Guidance Service. Copyright 1988 by American Guidance Service, Inc. Reprinted by permission.

starting point for direct assessment is sometimes called content analysis (Center, 1989). Content analysis is the process of analyzing a subject area into a discrete skill sequence. The process of content analysis usually begins by taking a long-term goal and identifying the subskills or objectives needed to achieve the long-term goal. The earlier step of administering a standardized diagnostic test of each academic area often will provide some of these subskills, that is, formal assessment and content analysis overlap. The number of subskills derived, however, depends entirely on the degree to which the fractioning down process apppears necessary in helping individual students master the subject area. Figure 3-3 illustrates a content analysis. The long-term goal, to master time, has been subdivided into two broad areas: clock skills and calendar skills. Clock skills has been

Content Analysis

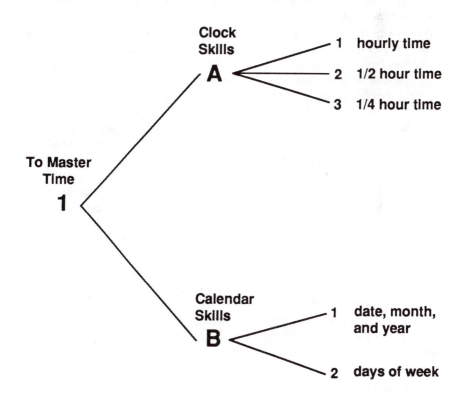

Figure 3-3. An illustration of content analysis which begins by taking a long-term goal and culminates in the establishment of short-term objectives.

subdivided into hourly time, 1/2 hour time and 1/4 hour time. Calendar skills is divided into date, month, year, and days of the week.

In content analysis, the long-term goal resembles the trunk of a tree, and the subgoals are often referred to as branches. The ending point for content analysis is the establishment of short-term objectives. It is important to note that the content analysis tree will not always have the same number of branches on each limb and that the number of limbs and branches will depend on the degree to which the fractioning down process is continued.

After having developed a sequence of suitable short-term objectives, the next stage of conducting a direct informal assessment requires fractioning down these short-term objectives into smaller teachable tasks or instructional objectives. This requirement, which is sometimes viewed as an extension of content analysis, is called task analysis (Center, 1989). Figure 3-4 illustrates a task analysis. The short-term objective to master hourly time has been subdivided into (a) moves hands on model clock to correct position and (b) writes and says hourly times from pictured clock. The objective, move hands on clock model to correct position, has been further subdivided into moves little hand to correct position and moves big hand to correct position.

In task analysis, the short-term objective is the trunk of the tree, and the branches are comprised of subobjectives. The ending point for task analysis is the establishment of instructional objectives that are used for individualized lesson plans. As in content analysis, the task analysis tree also will not necessarily have the same number of branches on each limb. However, for the task analysis to be complete, the ending point must be made up of instructional objectives, and the instructional objectives must be ones that will be of use with particular students. Although it is not difficult to find the content analyses for many different subject areas already completed, task analyses are difficult to find because they most often have to be designed individually for specific students. Therefore, it is advisable to find short-term objectives from content analyses that have already been completed. These are often found in curriculum guides and will cover many subjects. The short-term objectives from these can be used to begin task analyses for individual students. Figure 3-5 lists short-term objects for a functional reading curriculum sequence from kindergarten through sixth grade. Many of these skills could be task analyzed further.

Establishing Criteria

After completing a task analysis of each short-term objective, begin the assessment of each student which will direct intervention plans.

Task Analysis

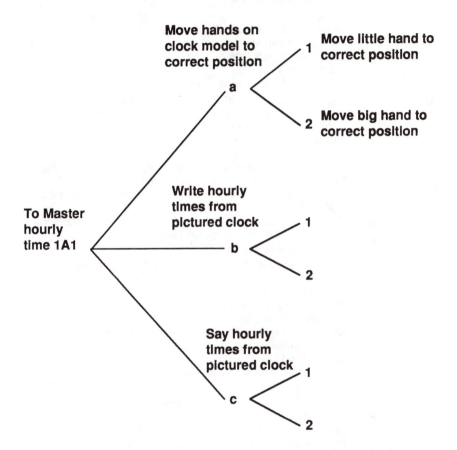

Figure 3-4. An illustration of task analysis which begins with short-term objectives and culminates in the establishment of instructional objectives.

The assessment which best complements task analysis and is used either implicitly or explicitly in all informal assessments is criterion-referenced assessment. This approach to assessment evaluates each particular skill against a functional criteria which you establish. There are two types of functional criteria: performance and consistency criteria.

Performance Criterion

The performance criterion is an accuracy measure in which a determination is made of the degree of accuracy required of the

GRADE	SKILLS ACQUIRED
Kindergarten	Identify sounds and pictures
	Express ideas in complete verbal sentences
	Understand meaning of words such as **above** and **far**
	Understand concepts of size, small, etc.
	Recognize and identify colors
	Organize objects into groups
	Match forms
	Understands beginning concepts of number
Grade 1	Recognize letters of alphabet; can write and give sound
	Auditory and visual perception and discrimination of initial and final consonants
	Observe left-to-right progression
	Recall what has been read
	Aware of medial consonants, consonant blends, diagraphs
	Recognize long sound of vowels; root words; plural forms; verb endings, **-s, -ed, -d, -ing;** opposites; pronouns **he, she**
	Understand concept of synonyms, homonyms, antonyms
	Understand simple compound words
	Copy simple sentences, fill-ins
Grade 2	Comprehension and analysis of what has been read
	Identify vowel diagraphs
	Understand variant sounds of **y**
	Identify medial vowels
	Identify diphthongs
	Understand influence of **r** on preceding vowel
	Identify three-letter blends
	Understand use of suffix **-er**
	Understand verb endings (e.g., **stop, stopped**)
Grade 3	Recognize multiple sounds of long **a** as in **ei, ay, ey**
	Understand silent **e** in **-le** endings
	Understand use of suffix **-est**
	Know how to change **y** to **i** before adding **-er, -est**
	Understand comparative and superlative forms of adjectives
	Understand possessive form using **s**
	Use contractions
	Identify syllabic breaks
Grade 4	Recognize main and subordinate parts
	Recognize unknown words using configuration and other word attack skills
	Identify various sounds of **ch**
	Recognize various phonetic values of **gh**
	Identify rounded **o** sound formed by **au, aw, al**

(continued)

	Use and interpret diacritical markings
	Discriminate among multiple meanings of words
Grade 5	Read critically to evaluate
	Identify diagraphs **gn, mb, bt**
	Recognize that **augh** and **ough** may have round **o** sound
	Recognize and pronounce muted vowels in **el, al, le**
	Recognize secondary and primary accents
	Use of apostrophe
	Understand suffixes **-al, -hand, -ship, -ist, -ling, -an, -ian, -dom, -ern**
	Understand use of figures of speech: metaphor, simile
	Ability to paraphrase main idea
	Know ways paragraphs are developed
	Outline using two or three main heads and subheadings
	Use graphic material
Grade 6	Develop ability for critical analysis
	Recognize and use Latin and Greek roots, such as **photo, tele, graph, geo, auto**
	Develop generalization that some suffixes can change part of speech, such as **ure** changing an adjective to noun **(moist-moisture)**
	Understand meaning and pronounciation of homographs
	Develop awareness of shifing accents

Figure 3-5. An illustration of a reading curriculum sequence for kindergarten through sixth grade. From *Informal Assessment in Education* (pp. 245-6) by G. Guerin and A. Maier, 1983, Mountain View, CA: Mayfield. Copyright 1983 by Mayfield. Reprinted by permission.

student in performing a particular task, for example, identifying 90% of the letters of the alphabet. Generally this criterion is set rather high to guarantee the acquisition of the skill and because students should be working on skills that are just slightly above their mastery level in the skill sequence. For most students, criteria generally are set somewhere between 70% and 95%.

Consistency Criterion

The consistency criterion, which complements the performance criterion, indicates how often the skill must be exhibited at the level of the performance criterion, for example, identifying 90% of the letters of the alphabet on three consecutive days. Consistency criteria are useful in analyzing trends, and they help ensure that performance is authentic and not accidental.

The Task

The next step in the assessment is to identify a task by which the student can demonstrate the degree to which he has mastered the instructional objective, that is, the behavior in the objective is listed as the task. For example, the student will vocally name the uppercase letters of the alphabet.

Directions

In this step, the directions, either to the teacher or to the student, and the conditions under which the behavior will occur are specified. The behavior in the objective will appear again in these directions. For example, the teacher might write in directions to the students, "I am going to show you different letters of the alphabet and ask you to say the name of each letter aloud. Okay, let's get started!" Or under directions to the teacher, the teacher might write "Present each of the letters visually on a 5 × 8 index card. Be sure to present them randomly." Occasionally there will be a need to have a direction component for both the student and the teacher. Most often, however, the conditions under which the behavior should occur can be described satisfactorily with one direction section only.

Materials

In this step, the material that will be used in conducting the assessment is identified. Implicit in this component is the identification of an additional condition under which the behavior will occur.

Figure 3-6 illustrates a criterion-referenced assessment plan for identifying the uppercase letters in the alphabet. The criterion-referenced assessment plan includes an instructional objective, a performance criterion, a consistency criterion, the student task, directions to the student, directions to the teacher, and materials. At this point, the final assessment process can begin. Several instructional objectives are available for every short-term objective in the curriculum sequence. A task with directions for the conditions under which the task will be implemented as well as a performance and consistency criterion for each instructional objective has been prepared. Begin the assessment of the student by asking for performance on the tasks associated with the instructional objectives that are tied to the short-term objectives in the curriculum sequence

Instructional Objective: The student will identify each of the uppercase letters
in the alphabet

Performance Criterion: 90%

Consistency Criterion: Four consecutive days

Task: The student will vocally name the uppercase letters of the alphabet

Directions to Student: "I am going to show you different letters of the
alphabet and ask you to say the name of each letter
aloud. Okay, let's get started."

Directions to Teacher: Present each of the letters visually on a 5 × 8 index
card. Be sure to present each randomly.

Materials: Twenty-six 5 × 8 index cards with one uppercase letter on each
card.

Figure 3-6. A criterion-referenced assessment plan for identifying the
uppercase letters in the alphabet.

where the student is presently functioning. Next, depending on how
the student performs, move up or down the sequence until an
identification can be made of the first skill in the hierarchy that the
student is unable to master. This will be the beginning point for
intervention, and the curriculum sequence should provide the
direction needed to continue to formulate individualized lesson plans.

Social/Emotional Behavior Assessment

Social/emotional behavior assessment is similar to academic assessment in that it requires that teachers measure skills precisely.
However, in the case of social/emotional behavior assessment, these
skill assessments are assessments of social and emotional behavior.
The beginning point for social/emotional behavior assessment is the
same as that for academic assessment, namely developing a profile.
However, for social/emotional behavior assessment, this profile must
be developed initially in a piecemeal fashion from information derived
from a number of different sources. This is because there is no single
universally endorsed indirect method which will provide the kind of
information necessary for developing a general social/emotional
behavior profile. Following is a review of the various assessment
sources for social/emotional behavior.

Anecdotal Records

Anecdotal records are often kept in the student's personal file. These
records may provide information about social and emotional behavior.

Sometimes narrative information identifies behavior patterns and emotional and social traits that persist. Teachers can begin a social behavior assessment by keeping their own anecdotal records.

Personality/Emotional Testing

Tests can be useful in obtaining an overall picture of social and emotional development. Although psychometrically sound assessment instruments have not been developed to assess personality, they can be used in conjunction with other measures to contribute to understanding a child's personality. One such test which has a wide clinical appeal and is useful for children ages 3 to 16 is the Personality Inventory for Children.

Some tests are projective, that is, the student is provided with an ambiguous stimulus or a deliberately vague situation and asked to describe what is occurring and to explain how they feel about it. These descriptions and the accompanying feelings are then interpreted. The Thematic Apperception Test (TAT) is an example of a projective test in which the authors use 20 pictures which are varied in content to purposely elicit fantasies that help clinicians understand personality (Karon, 1981).

Interviews

Interviews or self-reports constitute another approach to assessing social behavior. Interviews either directly or indirectly ask students to report about themselves and their problems. Interviews may be structured or unstructured. The unstructured interview is open ended and allows the interviewer sufficient flexibility to pursue whatever line of questioning he thinks is appropriate at the time. The unstructured interview allows for a great deal of variability between interviewers. The structured interview provides a format and often a sequence for the interview.

Additionally, the manner in which the interviewee and interviewer relate to each other is critical. Many believe that the use of Rogerian relationship tactics provides an important contribution to the outcome (Thurer & Hursh, 1981).

Self-Rating

Self-rating scales either ask students to rate themselves on a number of social behaviors or to select a response from a number of responses as the response they would exhibit in specific social situations. Morris and Kratochwill (1983) have explained that self-report measures can vary according to several dimensions: "specific vs. global measures, publicly observable vs. private events, relatively permanent characteristics vs. more transient aspects of performance, direct vs. indirect" (p. 98). While there have been criticisms of self-report measures in general (Bellack & Hersen, 1977), these measures offer the advantages of: (a) being relatively cost efficient and easy to administer, (b) possessing face validity for targeted behavior problems, (c) being relatively easy to score, (d) being applicable to a wide range of populations and target problems, and (e) being of use in obtaining data on multiple response indices (Jensen & Haynes, 1986).

Behavior Rating Scales and Sociograms

Some reports use individuals who know the student as the basis for obtaining data. For these reports one or both parents are asked to answer interview questions about their child. As mentioned earlier some interview schedules may be highly structured in format with predetermined questions and little flexibility, whereas others may consist of open-ended questions which allow for the exploration of many content areas. Sometimes knowledgeable persons are asked to complete a rating scale. The Revised Behavior Problem Checklist (RBPC) (Quay & Peterson, 1987), and the Child Behavior Checklist (CBCL) (Achenback, 1991; Achenback & Edelbrock, 1981, 1984), which can be used by both teachers and parents, are well known rating scales. Occasionally teachers rely on a sociogram approach in which students are asked to rank who they like the most and the least or to rate their peers on a roster for likability. The most common sociometric procedure used is that of partial ranking or peer nomination; however the rating sociometric procedure may be best suited for identifying children with few friends. It also ensures that every child is given equal consideration (Greenwood, Walker, & Hops, 1977). A third type of sociometric procedure, the paired comparison technique, presents the child with all possible pairs of pictures of her classmates and asks her to make a choice. High test-retest reliabilities have been reported with this method for preschoolers (Cohen & Van Tassel, 1978).

Direct Observation

Because a massive amount of information has accumulated regarding the use of direct observation for observing students directly in environments where the problems occur (Ollendick & Hersen, 1984), direct observation has become an important strategy for assessing overt observable behavior. Often, a three column running narrative or an A B C approach is used in which the teacher records the **antecedents** to a particular behavior, the **behavior**, and the **consequences** that follow the behavior. To do this, the teacher first writes a narrative which describes behavior continuously over a period of time. Next the narrative would be separated into three columns that list (a) the events that are antecedents to behaviors, (b) the behaviors that follow the antecedents, and (c) the events which are consequences to the behaviors. For example, in the following running narrative in which John's behavior is targeted, the antecedent is asking John to read; the behaviors are reading, bowing, and sitting; and the consequence is commenting approvingly.

> Mrs. Jones asks John to take out his reader and read the first two paragraphs on page ten. John gets his reader out, reads two paragraphs, bows, and sits down. Mrs. Jones comments approvingly on John's reading ability and turns to the blackboard.

In this example, the teacher might hypothesize that John's reading, bowing, and sitting behaviors might increase. By observing continuously over several brief periods of time, the teacher is able to acquire insight into the nature and cause of specific behaviors. This insight can be useful for designing interventions.

The Social/Emotional Behavior Profile

Once these various assessments have been conducted, sufficient information will be available with which to develop a general social/emotional behavior profile. This collected information can be organized with the intent of putting together a coherent picture of the social and emotional behavior of the student. If some of these assessment sources are not available, the task then becomes one of trying to piece together the best picture of the student that is possible with the limited data available. Figure 3-7 illustrates a social/emotional behavior profile.

Informal Assessment

The next step in the assessment of social/emotional behavior skills is to conduct a direct informal assessment of each social/emotional

Social Behavior Profile

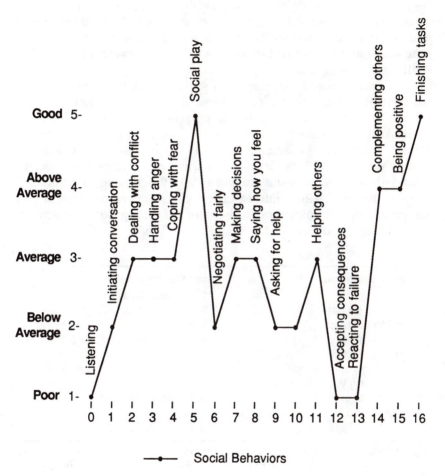

Figure 3-7. An illustration of a teacher-made social behavior profile based on several different assessment sources.

behavior in the social/emotional behavior profile. The starting point for this analysis may be either content analysis or task analysis depending on the level of behavioral specificity obtained thus far. In most cases a task analysis should be sufficient because of the number of social skills curricula that have already been developed. For example, the ACCEPTS program (Walker, McConnell, Holmes, Todis, Walker, & Golden, 1983) is comprised of 28 social skills divided into five categories, and the child (McGinnis & Goldstein, 1984) and adolescent (Goldstein, Sprafkin, Gershaw, & Klein (1980) "skill-streaming programs" include 60 and 50 prosocial skills, respectively. In addition, many of the rating scales used to obtain indirect assessment data are relatively precise and cover both inappropriate and appropriate behaviors. Figure 3-8 lists appropriate and inappropriate social and emotional behaviors which often appear in curriculum outlines and rating scales.

As with academic assessment, a social skill task analysis will need to generate instructional objectives that can be combined with criteria reference assessment for the purpose of evaluating a particular social behavior against a performance and a consistency criterion. Unlike academic assessment, social behavior assessment will not usually require a task, a direction, or a material component, because what is being tested is the student's daily functioning in naturalistic settings. Figure 3-9 illustrates a criterion referenced assessment plan for measuring the inappropriate behavior of hitting other students in class during school days.

Prosocial Behaviors	Inappropriate Behaviors
1. Listening	1. Hums in class
2. Giving a compliment	2. Cries a lot
3. Asking for help	3. Fidgets
4. Saying thank you	4. Overconforms to rules
5. Apologizing	5. Showing off
6. Knowing your feelings	6. Picks nose
7. Expressing your feelings	7. Steals
8. Sharing something	8. Preoccupied with sex
9. Negotiating	9. Truancy
10. Helping others	10. Uses alcohol or drugs

Figure 3-8. A list of appropriate and inappropriate social behaviors which can be used as a starting point for developing individual instructional objectives for a social behaviors curriculum.

Objective: Does not hit other students while in class during the school day

Performance Criterion: No more than two hits

Consistency Criterion: Four consecutive school days

Evaluation: Using event recording, take baseline of student's hitting behavior over five consecutive school days

Figure 3-9. An illustration of a criterion-referenced assessment plan for measuring inappropriate behavior.

With inappropriate behaviors, start in the curriculum sequence with behaviors that are most likely to interfere with the student's social adjustment and ability to learn and then, depending on success with these behaviors, move to behaviors that are less noxious. Figure 3-10 illustrates a criterion-referenced assessment plan for measuring appropriate prosocial behaviors.

With appropriate prosocial behavior, begin in the curriculum sequence where the student is presently functioning and, depending on how well she or he performs, move up or down the sequence accordingly until an identification can be made of the first skill the student is unable to master. For example, a student may recognize that she has emotions but not be able to label or identify them. This will be the beginning point for intervention and should help with the formulation of individualized lesson plans.

Lesson Plans

The task of designing educational assessment makes the job of developing lesson plans an easy one. Begin in either the academic or social/emotional curricular sequences with the first instructional objective the student is unable to master and develop a teaching intervention for that objective. The intervention components of the lesson plan specify the plan designed to bring about the acquisition of the skill on the part of the student. This is teacher input into the teaching/learning process. The second component in the lesson plan is a description of the student's output or response, that is, what must the student do in each phase of the lesson. This is the student's response or output. Sometimes the student is expected to perform and interact during instruction and at other times the student must practice a particular skill. The next component details the materials

---

Objective: The student will tell others that he or she likes something about them or about what they do

Performance Criterion: Two times per school day

Consistency Criterion: Four consecutive school days

Evaluation: Using event recording, take baseline of the student's compliment behavior over five consecutive school days

---

Figure 3-10. An illustration of a criterion-referenced assessment plan for measuring appropriate behavior.

needed for the lesson, for example, a set of vocabulary words written on index cards. Finally, an evaluation component similar to the criteria-referenced assessment described under the section "Academic Assessment" is needed to evaluate the lesson. Like the pre-test assessment, this evaluation should include an instructional objective and a performance and a consistency criterion. Figure 3-11 illustrates a lesson plan.

Instructional Objective:
> The student will identify the time represented on either the chalkboard, pictured clocks, or handouts when the hands indicate hourly, half hour, and quarter hour time.

Input/Intervention:
> Direct instruction using modeling and chalkboard will be the initial phase of instruction. The various times will be shown on the chalkboard and verbal explanation will be used to demonstrate the various times. Students will be reinforced through praise and bingo chips. In the next phase of instruction, model clocks will be provided for the student to manipulate. The final phase requires the student to mark the times shown on pictured clocks. Initially, student responses will be prompted and reinforced on a continuous schedule. Later, prompts will be faded and the reinforcement schedule stretched to a 1 to 15 schedule upon the mastery of the objective.

Output/Response:
> In the initial phase of the lesson, students will say the time for each chalkboard clock as directed. Later, the student will turn the hands on a model clock as directed. Finally, students will mark the time presented by pictured clocks in the spaces provided on handouts.

Materials:
> Chalkboard, clock models, and 20 pictured clocks on two handouts with clocks pictured at hourly, half hour, and quarter hour times.

Evaluation:
> The performance criterion will be a minimum of 90% accuracy. The consistency criterion will be four consecutive sessions. Mastery will require identifying the correct times shown on the pictured clocks depicted on the handouts. Prompting and reinforcing is not allowed. The 20 clocks depicted on the two handouts used for evaluation must occupy different locations on the handouts than the locations used for intervention.

Figure 3-11. An illustration of a lesson plan which flows logically out of the assessment process.

Summary

Although many approaches exist that are designed to address the needs of children and youth with emotional and behavioral disorders, often classrooms appear not to have a well designed comprehensive functional teaching plan. These plans or educational programs, however, can be designed to teach both academic and social or emotional behavior competence. The development of such educational plans requires a comprehensive assessment of academic and social/emotional behavior.

Academic assessment is aided greatly when teachers determine what students can and can't do in each subject in the curriculum. This determination is facilitated by the teacher's ability to fractionate the curriculum into instructional objectives. To do this, an academic curriculum profile is developed to indicate the student's academic strengths and weaknesses. Next, an indirect formal assessment of each subject area in the curriculum is conducted. Third, each academic area is fractioned down into instructional objectives by conducting a content and task analysis. Next, each instructional objective is given an accompanying functional performance and mastery criterion against which the student is assessed. Task, direction, and materials components are included to determine if the student has mastered each instructional objective.

Social/emotional behavior assessment is similar to academic assessment in that teachers need to measure skills precisely. However, in the assessment of social/emotional behavior, the skills assessed are not academic but social and emotional behaviors. Like academic assessment, the starting point for social/emotional behavior assessment is the development of a profile. This social/emotional behavior profile, however, is developed in a piecemeal fashion by putting together information from a number of different assessment sources. These sources include anecdotal records, personality and emotional testing, interviews, rating scales and sociograms, and direct observation. Once this information is collected and a social/emotional behavior profile is developed, a task analysis is conducted to generate instructional objectives. These objectives are combined with mastery or functional criteria which provide the basis for assessing the student's social/emotional behavior.

The task of designing educational assessment facilitates the design of educational programs. Teachers can begin in either the academic or social/emotional curricular sequences with the first instructional objective that the student was unable to master and develop a teaching intervention or lesson plan for teaching that objective.

Review Questions

1. How do you put together an academic curriculum profile?
2. What is the difference between formal and informal assessment?
3. In what ways can you differentiate between content and task analysis?
4. In what ways can you differentiate between performance and consistency criteria?
5. How can you develop a social/emotional behavior profile?
6. What do the three columns of a running narrative describe?
7. What are the advantages of self-rating scales?
8. Why is content analysis not necessary for the informal assessment of social and emotional behavior?
9. Why does social and emotional behavior assessment not require a task as academic assessment does?
10. In a lesson plan, how do the input and output components differ?

Learning Activities

1. Divide into small groups of five to six and do a task analysis of one of the skills identified in Figure 3-5, for example, the student will recognize unknown words using configuration and other word attack skills. Each small group is to select a different skill.

2. Each small group is to identify an instructional objective from the task analysis conducted in activity 1 and develop a criterion-referenced assessment plan. Your assessment plan should include: (a) an instructional objective, (b) a performance criterion, (c) a consistency criterion, (d) the task, (e) directions to student, (f) directions to teacher, and (g) materials. Each small group is to present the completed criterion referenced assessment plan to the class.

3. From the description of behavior that follows design a running narrative using three columns to list (a) the antecedents to responding, (b) the responses or behaviors which follow the antecedents, and (c) the events which are consequences to these behaviors.

John and Sally were playing together in the sandbox. John tried to get the shovel from Sally when it accidently hit her in the face. Sally began to cry. Mrs.

Jones walked over to Sally and said "You'll be Okay" and patted her head. John began to throw sand in the air. Mrs. Jones told John to settle down and took the shovel away. The recess bell rang.

Design your running narrative, that is, (a) the antecedent, (b) the behavior, and (c) the consequence for each of the three participants in the narrative above. Each group is to display its design on the blackboard.

4. Divide into groups of five to six and develop a lesson plan for social or emotional behavior similar to the one developed for academic behavior depicted in Figure 3-11. Your lesson plan should include: (a) an instructional objective, (b) an input/intervention component, (c) an output/response component, (d) a materials component, and (e) an evaluation component. Each group is to select a different emotional or social behavior. Each group is to present its lesson plan to the class.

4

Conceptual Models Which Influence Intervention

Because every strategy, technique, method, and approach is ultimately derived from some major theoretical framework on which it depends, the requirement of special educators to understand the major conceptual model of influence is imperative. Not only do these various points of view underpin methodology, but they also provide a structure for understanding normal as well as abnormal development. Because each model is based on different underlying assumptions about the nature of human development and learning, proponents of each model have devised different (a) definitions of deviance or abnormal behavior; (b) paradigms to explain development, learning, and functioning; and (c) interventions to remediate the problem of emotional and behavioral disorders. In addition, proponents of each theoretical orientation ascribe to a terminology which is unique. Sufficient familiarity with each conceptual model and the associated terminology should provide the student with a means for readily distinguishing between models. Additionally, these differing points of view will provide a means for personally identifying and helping the student to become aware of her own implicit assumptions about human development. What follows is a brief overview of the seven major conceptual models of influence. Each model is discussed in terms of (a) how deviance or abnormality is defined, (b) the major paradigms with which the model is associated, and (c) the general approaches to intervention which are derived from the model. Figure 4-1 is a template of each of the conceptual models that will be discussed.

The Psychodynamic Model

Definition of Deviance

Proponents of the psychodynamic model define deviance as intrapsychic conflict, unresolved conflict, or as a lack of integration among the mental structures of the mind (id, ego, superego). The mind is viewed as a nonphysical entity which derives from an energy source or "life force."

Major Paradigms

The major paradigms associated with this model include the theory of: (a) mental structures in which mind is viewed as comprising id, ego, and superego; (b) defense mechanisms, that is, mental devices by which the ego protects itself from material not acceptable to consciousness; (c) stages of development, that is, developmental steps which are invariant and normative; and (d) catharsis which suggests that the organism relieves or cleanses itself by purging or venting pent-up emotional material.

Interventions

The interventions associated with this point of view are largely based on the paradigm of catharsis. Among other requirements, these interventions imply that the child needs an accepting teacher, a permissive classroom environment, and the structuring of other environmental opportunities for purging pent-up emotions. Some of the more common and specific interventions include role play, psychodrama, drawing and painting, and physical activity. Aggressive

Models	Definition of Deviance	Major Paradigms	Interventions
Psychodynamic	Intrapsychic conflict	Mental structures Catharsis Defense mechanisms Stages of development	Permissive environment Role play, Drama Drawing, Painting Physical activities
Biophysical	Defect of anatomy physiology neurophysiology	Human behavior & physiology connected	Surgery, Diet control Biofeedback Drug therapy Physical exercise
Psychoeducational	Intrapsychic conflict pressures of daily living	Intra psychic material available to consciousness Insight leads to behavior change	Therapeutic discussion Identify problems Plan solution
Ecological	Lack of fit between culture violator culture bearer	Individual is inseparable part of social system Intractions are reciprocal	Developing skills Adjusting class expectations
Humanistic	Incongruence between self-structure experience	Self-acutalization Fully functioning person	Teacher is non-authoritarian Emphathetic, congruent Nonjudgmental
Behavioral	Learned inappropriate behaviors	Respondent conditioning Operant conditioning Three-term contingency Scientific method	Measurement Evaluation Behavior change techniques
Cogntive Learning	Irrational thinking Immature beliefs Errors of cognition	Perception and thinking influence behavior	Cognitive social skills training Rational-emotive therapy Cognitive social problem solving Cognitive self-monitoring Cognitive self-instruction Cognitive stress inoculation

Figure 4-1. An illustration of seven conceptual models of influence and their associated definitions of deviance, major paradigms, and interventions.

students, for example, may spend time punching a punching bag to release pent-up hostility.

In discussing the theory and practice of therapeutic intervention, Ginott (1959) explains what can be achieved through directing catharthic energies into the symbolically acceptable channels of playing, painting, modeling, puppetry, and discussion.

> A child who is angry with his father can stab or shoot a father doll. The aggressive child may symbolically destroy his parents, teachers, and therapist over and over again in his play and games, and learn from his own experiences that his impulses do not actually kill anybody. The neurotic child may discover that his innner impulses can be discharged into the playroom without dooming him, thus learning that his desires are not fatal and need not be so rigidly inhibited. (p. 77)

The Biophysical Model

Definition of Deviance

Proponents of the Biophysical Model define deviance as a defect of anatomy, physiology, or neurophysiology. Something in the constitutional or physical makeup of the organism is viewed as functionally or structurally defective and as such results in abnormal human behavior.

Major Paradigms

Human behavior is said to be inextricably associated with physiology. Genetic factors, brain damage or dysfunction, and metabolic processes are viewed as the underlying causes of a wide range of disorders, for example, depression, autism, hyperactivity, and psychopathology.

Intervention

The interventions associated with this point of view include surgery, physical exercise, dietary control, psychotropic drug therapy, and biofeedback. In discussing the role of biofeedback in psychotherapy, Green and Green (1983) report the following:

With many patients, . . . temperature training serves to help reorganize their lives, not because it is necessarily good to have warm hands but because of the feeling of self-mastery they get. That feeling if it could be put into mathematical terms would be called "an enabling function." It enables the patient to take postive action in a variety of ways. In other words, the gains from temperature training as well as from other kinds of feedback training, are not merely physical. (p. 225)

The Psychoeducational Model

Definition of Deviance

Proponents of the Psychoeducational Model view deviance as the result of underlying conflicts (as discussed under the section "psychodynamic model") in combination with the pressures of functioning in the home, school, and community.

Major Paradigms

Proponents of this point of view are aware that some human behavior is the result of unconscious motivation, but believe that humans possess much mental material which is also available to consciousness. Based on this understanding, they believe that insight can lead to changes in behavior and that behavior does not have to be modified directly for individuals to change.

Interventions

The interventions associated with this model generally get students to: (a) identify their behavioral problems and motivations, (b) observe the consequences of their actions, and (c) plan alternative action which result in more favorable consequences. The life-space intervention, a major intervention based on this model, includes therapeutic discussions.

In his early work with the clinical treatment of aggressive youth at Pioneer House, Dr. David Wineman describes a psychoeducational technique dubbed the "quilt-squeeze" in which an interview is conducted for the purpose of entering a value into ego awareness (Redl & Wineman, 1952):

Today was Bob's (head counselor) day off. Mike insisted upon going upstairs and waking him right after breakfast in order to get a toy plane that he had asked Bob to keep. His counselor told him that he would have to wait until Bob got up, but he was adamant and began to raise quite a fuss, saying he didn't care whether he was awake or asleep. He was going to have his plane and that was that. I put it to him this way: "Don't you think Bob deserves a chance to rest up a bit? After all, he works plenty hard around here just so you and the other guys can have a good time. Do you really think Bob should be treated as mean as being waked up on his day off?" Mike "gave" on this point amazingly well, saying, "I guess you're right, Dave." (p. 258)

The Ecological Model

Definition of Deviance

Proponents of this model view deviance as the result of a lack of "fit" between the culture violator (the individual exhibiting behaviors that violate the expectations of significant authority figures) and the culture bearer (the individual responsible for transmitting the norms and values of the culture). Therefore, deviance is not owned by the student, but resides in the relationship between the student and his environment, for example, the teacher.

Major Paradigms

Students are individuals who are inseparable parts of a complex social system which is comprised of the child, the family, the school, and the community. Interrelations between the student and other components of the social system, for example, the teacher, involve reciprocal interactions. The student and the teacher influence each other reciprocally as excitors and responders. Influence is a "two way street." Individuals who are viewed as abnormal are incongruent with their social system.

Intervention

Since deviance is defined as lack of fit or incongruence between the individual and those persons responsible for transmitting the norms of the culture, effective intervention requires teaching decisions designed to achieve congruence by helping students become harmonious with their environment. This implies that teachers help students become more congruent by either helping them to acquire needed skills or by adjusting teacher expectations and/or the classroom environment.

In describing the ecological perspective, Swap (1991) suggests considering the following:

> A setting in which I felt unhappy, stupid, and unproductive was a required geography class that I took in seventh grade. I found the teacher's voice so monotonous, the ominipresent maps so confusing, and the lists we were to memorize so boring that one day I started to giggle—and could not (would not?) stop. Other students found the giggling infectious, and soon most of the class were laughing, too. The teacher, quite annoyed, sent me out of the room to get a drink of water and wait in the hall until I could get control of myself. My "giggling fits" recurred periodically during the rest of the semester in that class. (p. 244)

Swap (1991) explains that her classroom experience illustrates the ecological model in several aspects. First, she states that "giggling" was the result of a unique interaction or incongruence which occurred between her and the environment, that is, the incongruence was not experienced by others at least to the same degree because it did not result in inappropriate behavior on the part of other students. Second, her behavior was incongruent with the expectations of the highly structured setting in which she was participating at the time, but might not have constituted a mismatch for another setting, for example, the lunchroom or a less structured classroom setting (Swap, 1991).

The Humanistic Model

Definition of Deviance

Proponents of this point of view define deviance as a lack of congruence between an individual's experience and her self-structure (Rogers, 1951). Experience can mean either inner experience such as feelings and emotions or outer experience such as activities or interests. Self-structure is the way in which an individual defines or views herself and is acquired initially from her parents or close family members. Individuals who define themselves in ways which are inconsistent or incongruent with their experiences are said to lack congruence. A lack of congruence will present itself in the form of disturbed emotions and/or deviant behavior.

Major Paradigms

The humanist approach which emphasizes self-direction, self-fulfillment, and free choice is based on the theoretical concept of self-actualization. The concept of self-actualization implies that children who are cared for in a loving and supportive environment, and who are free to make their own decisions and explore their own interests, will naturally and spontaneously find solutions to their problems and mature and develop into productive and fully functioning adults. An additional and central paradigm is the concept of the fully functioning person. The fully functioning person is said to be: (a) open to experience, (b) able to trust his or her own judgments, and (c) congruent. This implies the ability and desire to live in the moment and to restructure or redefine oneself continually on the basis of new experience.

Intervention

The interventions associated with this model focus on the relationship between the teacher and the student. In this relationship, the teacher is nonauthoritarian and acts more as a resource and catalyst for learning than as a director of activities. The teacher must acquire the necessary skills and abilities to foster the student's self-actualization. The teacher must: (a) learn to be empathetic, (b) be able to provide unconditional positive regard, and (c) be a congruent person himself. The classroom atmosphere that is largely fostered by this kind of teacher is open, nontraditional, and personal. Learning is viewed as self-directed, and most humanistically oriented teachers believe that younsters will acquire knowledge and learn to find solutions to their own problems if they are free to do so in a supportive, nurturing, and loving environment. Many of the basic concepts associated with counter theory, as well as with alternative, free, and open schools, overlap with the humanistic model of education. Rogers (1980) describes learning which occurs as the result of the application of this model as follows:

> If the purpose of teaching is to promote learning, then we need to ask what we mean by that term. Here I become passionate. I want to talk about learning.

But not the lifeless, sterile, futile, quickly forgotten stuff that is crammed into the mind of the poor helpless individual tied to his seat by the ironclad bonds of conformity! I am talking about learning—the insatiable curiosity that drives the adolescent boy to absorb everything he can see or hear or read about gasoline engines in order to improve the efficiency and speed of his "cruiser." I am talking about the student who says, "I am discovering, drawing in from the outside, and making that which is drawn in a real part of me." I am talking about any learning in which the experience of the learner progresses along this line: " No, no, that's not what I want"; Wait! This is closer to what I'm interested in, what I need"; "Ah, here it is! Now I'm grasping and comprehending what I need and what I want to know!" (pp. 18-19)

The Behavioral Model

Definition of Deviance

Deviance is best defined as mislearning or simply learning inappropriate behaviors. Behaviors are judged as deviant, inappropriate, or maladaptive if so judged by individuals who control the reinforcers in a particular environment. In a school setting, individuals who control the reinforcers would include most school personnel and especially teachers.

Major Paradigms

The major paradigms of this model are that most learning occurs as the result of either respondent conditioning/classical conditioning or operant conditioning. An additional paradigm is the requirement to analyze behavior in terms of the "three term contingency"—the antecedent, the behavior, and the consequence. A metaparadigm for this model, in attempting to understand human behavior, is the application of the scientific method which requires measurement and the analysis of independent and dependent variable relationships.

Intervention

Interventions include defining and measuring behavior, methods of directly recording behavior, the evaluation of behavior change, respondent extinction, counter conditioning, positive and negative reinforcement, extinction, shaping, scheduling, chaining, fading, and punishment. Whaley and Malott (1971) describe a behavioral appproach that was used by Dr. Patterson at the University of Oregon Psychology Clinic to condition study behavior in a hyperactive child:

> Earl . . . was easily distracted and worked for only short periods of time. Earl's hyperactivity took the form of talking, pushing, hitting, pinching, looking about the room and out the window, leaving his desk, tapping, squirming, and fiddling with objects. In addition, he was aggressive, pinched other children, and threw himself into groups of children, disrupting their work or play. . . .
>
> Dr. Patterson used M&M candies and pennies as reinforcers. . . . A small box containing a light bulb and a counter was placed on Earl's desk. Earl was told that at the end of each ten-second interval, if he had paid attention to his work for the entire time, the light would flash and the counter would count. Each time this happened he had earned one M&M or one penny and these would be given to him at the end of each lesson. The daily lessons lasted from five to thirty minutes. . . .
>
> The [other] students were told that some of the pennies and candy which Earl earned for working hard and paying attention to his lessons were to be shared with all of them and that they could help Earl earn more if they did not distract him when he was working. . . .
>
> At the end of each conditioning session when the score was announced, the students applauded Earl. They also frequently walked by his desk to check the counter and to see how many reinforcers he had earned and spoke approvingly to him. . . .
>
> Before conditioning started, Earl spent 25 percent of his time making disruptive or inattentive responses. By the end of the ten days of conditioning, he misbehaved less than 5 percent of the time. (pp. 28-29)

The Cognitive-Learning Model

Definition of Deviance

Proponents of this model view deviance as the result of immature beliefs, irrational self-talk or self-perceptions, and insufficient self-instruction or self-reinforcement which result in dysfunctional affect and behavior.

Major Paradigms

The cognitive learning model is based on the premise that perception, representation, and interpretation influence psychological adjustment idiosyncratically and that because of the operations of cognitive factors such as beliefs and reasoning processes, the individual's interaction with the world is largely self-determined (Bernard & Joyce, 1984). In addition, proponents of this model emphasize that a continuous reciprocal causal interaction occurs between individuals and their environments (Bandura, 1986; Thoresen & Mahoney, 1974). Unlike traditional psychoanalytic or behaviorist views, the cognitive learning model accords individuals a large amount of responsibility for creating their own emotional disturbance and for determining their destiny (Ellis, 1973).

Interventions

Interventions include teaching the students to: (a) generate solutions to individual problems; (b) use self-reinforcement, self-instruction, and self-talk to foster learning and solve academic problems; (c) learn new adaptive self-statements with new social behavior skills; (d) inoculate themselves from stress by employing self-instructional techniques; (e) retrain attributional thinking by providing feedback and manipulating success and failure; and (f) dispute irrational beliefs and self-statements.

Bernard and Joyce (1984) illustrate how a 17-year-old girl's jealousy of her friend can be treated by challenging her irrational beliefs and teaching her a more self-accepting view:

> **THERAPIST:** You seem pretty upset. What are your feelings right now?
> **CLIENT:** Well, I don't really know. It's not right, that's all.
> **THERAPIST:** What do you mean "It's not right? What's not right?"
> **CLIENT:** Just because the others suck up to the teacher, they never get into trouble or have to repeat their homework. They get all the good things. The teacher likes them and I'm a nothing!
> **THERAPIST:** Well, Jane, I can see there's some things that are upsetting you. But as we've discussed previously, it is your thoughts about the situation that are causing this; that are making you feel worthless and jealous of your friends.
> **CLIENT:** So what if I'm jealous. What does that change?
> **THERAPIST:** It can change your feelings because it's your thoughts about the situation that control your emotions. Now, who said the teacher had to like you as much or more than the others? Is there anything that says a teacher isn't human and can't like some people more than others? Is it absolutely 100% "awful" that the teacher doesn't like you?
> **CLIENT:** No, but . . . .
> **THERAPIST:** And even if your teacher doesn't think highly of you and your friends are better off, that might not be fun, but it's not the end of the world.

It doesn't mean you're less of a person or less worthy. You do other things well and you can learn to accept yourself for what you are.

CLIENT: That's true but it doesn't make things any easier for me.

THERAPIST: If you continue to think irrationally then it won't get any easier for you. If you're going to judge yourself on how much someone likes you and how much better off your friends are than you, then you'll waste so much energy being upset that you won't be able to do anything about changing your situation. Look at this objectively and you'll feel less upset.

CLIENT: I guess you're right. It's not so bad that this teacher doesn't like me. Other people like me. And my friends aren't always better off than me—and it wouldn't matter if they were!

THERAPIST: Why wouldn't it matter?

CLIENT: Because I'm not a worthless person just because somebody has more than me, or because somebody doesn't attend to me when I want them to.

THERAPIST: That's right. It doesn't matter how much attention and approval you get, it's not going to matter if you don't like yourself. And things aren't going to be the way you want at times, so you try to change them, or accept their existence.

CLIENT: Okay, I understand. Let me continue. It would be nice to do better, and if I try to get my homework done, I might have a more pleasant time in that class. And it would be better for me to concentrate on liking myself more instead of trying to get the teacher's attention. How's that for changing my irrational thoughts? (pp. 240-241)

Summary

Every method of intervention is derived from some major conceptualization. Conceptual models are based on different underlying assumptions about the nature of human development and learning. Proponents of each conceptual model have developed definitions of abnormal behavior, paradigms to explain behavior, and interventions to solve behavior problems. The seven major conceptualizations which influence intervention include the psychodynamic, biophysical, psychoeducational, ecological, humanistic, behavioral, and cognitive learning models. Familiarity with the seven major conceptual models can be helpful in facilitating a personal awareness of one's implicit assumptions regarding human behavior.

Review Questions

1. In what general ways do conceptual models influence one's choice of an intervention strategy?

2. How do proponents of the psychodynamic model define deviance or abnormality?
3. What would proponents of the biophysical model offer as potential causes of emotional and behavioral disorders?
4. What role does the teacher play in a classroom designed entirely around the humanistic model?
5. Based on the assumptions of the behavioral model how would one decide whether a student was emotionally or behaviorally disordered?
6. What is the most important concept underlying the cognitive-learning model in terms of its implications for teaching emotionally and behaviorally disordered children?
7. What is a metaparadigm for the behavioral model?
8. Why might someone use a nonbiophysical intervention when the behavior problem is caused by a biophysical disorder?
9. In what ways are the humanistic and cognitive-learning models similar?

Learning Activities

1. Divide into groups of five to six and as a group select a conceptual model. Each group is to select a different model. After reviewing the following information on a student assigned to your class, describe an intervention plan based on the conceptual model selected by your group. Each group is to present its intervention to the class.

Billy had blond hair and large freckles. He was small for a fifth grader and his clothes were usually torn and dirty. As one of nine siblings bused from a remote rural area, it was not difficult to understand his need for attention. What was hard to see was the way he sought it out. In fact, he was a master at getting attention. The problem, however, was that the attention he got was usually always painful. One tactic which almost always worked was to sneak up in back of one of his bigger and older classmates when they weren't expecting it and to make snorkeling sounds with his nose while calling them and their family names. Because the snorkeling sounds would reach a particularly irritating and specific pitch, they were often accompanied by wads of snot. This last irritant occurred regularly, especially when Billy had a cold. Because he excelled in this venture, he was usually punched and pounded several times by the larger boy, until the fight which he could never win was broken up.

Perhaps what was most disturbing about these incidents was that almost immediately after the blood was wiped from his face and the crying subsided, you could see the wheels in his mind turning as he began to plot his next plan of attack.

5

Classroom Management

T his chapter introduces the study of classroom management. Not only do experienced regular and special educators view management as a primary concern, but it is almost always stressed in evaluating teacher competence. Because many of today's schools are becoming "battle grounds" for teachers and students, the issue of managing students is becoming increasingly important. For these reasons, in the first half of the chapter, the major points of agreement among much of the general literature on classroom management is discussed. The second half of the chapter describes two major classroom management approaches for students with emotional or behavioral disorders.

Characteristics of Effective Teachers

Teacher characteristics are important in determining how successful a teacher will be in managing the classroom. One very important characteristic is the obvious one of being liked by students, which is determined by attributes such as a cheerful disposition, friendliness, emotional maturity, sincerity, and general mental health and personality adjustment. Also, there are many qualities which are important for managing a classroom that flow from underlying self-confidence and should enable you to: (a) remain calm in crisis, (b) listen actively without becoming defensive or authoritarian, (c) avoid win-lose conflicts, and (d) maintain a problem-solving orientation (Brophy & Putnam, 1979). Curwin and Mendler (1988) suggest that when a classroom rule violation occurs, the incident should be interpreted as an opportunity for students to see the effect of their behavior and their capability of making other choices, that is, these incidents can become opportunities for positive interaction and communication. Curwin and Mendler (1988) list the following nine principles for consequence implementation once a rule is broken:

1. Always implement a consequence: Be consistent
2. Simply state the rule and consequence
3. Be as physically close as possible when you implement a consequence: Use the power of proximity
4. Make direct eye contact when you deliver a consequence (this is dependent on ethnicity and culture)
5. Use a soft voice
6. Catch a student being good
7. Don't embarrass the student in front of his peers
8. Be firm and anger free when giving your consequence
9. Do not accept excuses, bargaining, or whining (pp. 95-9).

Teacher Preparation

One basic way of managing classroom problems is to prevent them from occurring, which can be influenced by preparation for instruction. Kounin (1970) found that the differences between successful and unsuccessful classroom managers had a lot to do with the planning and preparation they put into effective instruction. Also, the lessons of effective teachers were paced rapidly and smoothly and teachers who had management problems had lessons that lacked coherence. Additionally, Kounin (1970) found that when students were involved in seat work, the work had to be appropriately challenging and had to provide interest or variety. In general, Kounin's research implies that management problems are caused in part by delays or confusion (Brophy & Putnam, 1979). Good and Brophy (1991) appear to agree by suggesting that you can limit problems by: (a) creating smooth traffic patterns, (b) avoiding bottlenecks and lines, (c) maximizing student independence and responsibility, and (d) preparing backup activities. In fact, they have shown that the teacher's movement in the classroom influences the behavior of students (Good & Brophy, 1987). That is, increased movement by teachers in classrooms has been found to decrease inappropriate student behavior while simultaneously increasing positive interactions between students and teachers (Fifer, 1986).

The Classroom Atmosphere

Brophy and Putnam (1979) reflected on the classic study of Lewin, Lippitt, and White (1939, cited in Brophy, & Putnam, 1979) in which adults working with groups of 10-year-old boys were trained to act consistently in an authoritarian, democratic, and laissez-faire manner. In this study, the group of boys who had authoritarian leadership were the most efficient in meeting goals. The reason for recapturing this historic study was to compare it to the research of Baumrind (1971) who studied the leadership style of parents who were classified as authoritarian, authoritative, or laissez-faire. For Baumrind (1971) the difference between authoritarian and authoritative was extremely important because the authoritative "leader has a position of authority and responsibility, speaks as an experienced and mature adult and retains ultimate decision making power. Unlike authoritarian leaders, however, authoritative leaders solicit input, seek consensus and take care to see that everyone is clear about the rationales for decisions as well as the decisions themselves" (Brophy & Putnam, 1979, p. 195). In fact, Baumrind (1971) determined that compared to children raised by authoritarian or laissez-faire parents, children of authoritative parents were more self-confident and more autonomous for their age. The reason that Brophy and Putnam emphasized this research was because: (a) they believe that the term "authoritative" is preferable to the term "democratic" in that the kind of leadership most often termed democratic is not truly democratic, that is, the teacher has the ultimate responsibility for leadership, and (b) it provides a convincing argument to support authoritative over authoritarian and laissez-faire methods.

Finally, Curwin and Mendler (1988), who have also considered classroom atmosphere, list the following nine characteristics of a healthy classroom environment:

1. Trust is established
2. The learner perceives the benefit of changing his behavior
3. The learner is aware of different options and is allowed to make a growth choice
4. The evaluation of learning actively engages the learner
5. Learning facts and concepts are important, but incomplete goals for learners
6. Learning is conceived as meaningful
7. Learning is growth producing, actualizing, and therefore enjoyable
8. Learning is process- and people-oriented rather than product- or subject-oriented
9. Learning includes more than just the cognitive or affective domains (pp. 162-163).

Teacher Expectations

In several studies, what teachers expect of their students has been found to have a significant impact on their performance (Rosenthal & Jacobsen, 1968; Rubin & Balow, 1971). Children who were expected to fail appeared to be influenced by this expectation or prophecy, whereas children who were expected to succeed appeared to have a higher probability of succeeding. Although it is uncertain whether teacher expectations directly influence student behavior, it is probable that teachers do behave differently toward students they expect to succeed than they do toward students they expect to fail. This has caused some investigators to suggest that teacher expectations may influence teachers to set higher academic and social standards for some students than for others. Therefore, if the relationship between teacher expectations and behavior and student performance is correct, the question for teachers becomes one of determining how high to set one's standards.

In thinking about this question, Kirk (1972) has suggested that a great discrepancy between the student's ability and adult expectations for performance can contribute to behavior problems, that is, teacher expectations that are either too high or too low can be damaging. This implies that in special education programs for students with emotional and behavior disorders, reasonable expectations for students must be established. However, in an investigation of tolerance for deviance, Kauffman, Lloyd, and McGee (1989) found a high variability in teacher standards and tolerance. Perhaps one way to match teacher expectations with student performance is to jointly negotiate reasonable teacher expectations and reasonable student performance.

Teaching Behaviors

Good and Brophy (1987, 1991) believe that all teaching techniques must be compatible with a positive classroom environment and a good working relationship between each student and the teacher. This implies that through words and actions, teachers should communicate integrity, sincerity, concern for individual and collective student welfare, and positive attitudes and expectations about each student's learning potential as well as his willingness and ability to cooperate with you as well as with the other students. Brophy and Putnam (1979) suggest that effective management requires a set of classroom rules, but that the rules should be minimized and phrased qualitatively as aspects of behavior rather than specific do's and don'ts. The rules should also be flexible so that the teacher can adapt to situational differences, for example, "When you finish you can talk and move around, but not disturb those who are working" (p. 196) is flexible, whereas, "Remain silently in your seat when you finish" (p. 196) is inappropriately restrictive. Shores, Gunter, and Jack (1993) recommend eliminating the "don'ts" entirely by suggesting that teachers state classroom rules positively and provide positive consequences for following the rules. In addition, teachers should limit the amount of time spent talking and attending to a personal problem when conducting a lesson (Brophy & Putnam, 1979).

Additionally, Kounin (1970) has identified an important teacher characteristic associated with success in managing the classroom which he dubbed "withitness" (p. 74). Teachers with "withitness" are aware of what is going on in all parts of the classroom. A related characteristic which Kounin discusses is called "overlapping," that is, the ability to do more than one thing at a time (p. 74). In addition, Kounin believes that transitions between activities should be characterized by a sort of "smoothness" (p. 93).

Teaching and Learning Styles

Another aspect of teaching and learning that has received a great deal of attention is learning style. Different writers have proposed that individual students possess different learning styles. This has lead to the development of a various theories which purport to outline the major individual learning styles. The principal concept, however, is that a student with a particular learning style will have difficulty if the teaching style used by the teacher is incompatible with the student's learning style. Therefore, one of the most effective ways to influence learning is to attempt to match instruction with learning style. Curwin and Mendler (1988) have discussed learning styles which they believe can be divided into the three categories of dependent, collaborative, and independent. In the dependent learning style, the student views the teacher as an expert or authority who lectures and directs the student who then receives information, reinforcement, and esteem for exerting the efforts to master the assignment. In the collaborative learning style, the student views the teacher as a discussion leader or resource provider who sets the environment, co-leads the learning group, provides feedback, and facilitates peer exchange and social acceptance. Finally, in the independent style, the student views the teacher as a resource who facilitates independent efforts to acquire knowledge and self-esteem. Figure 5-1 illustrates the three learner styles depicting the student's need, the teacher's role, and the teacher's behavior.

These authors mention that learning styles vary for different academic subjects, that is, Bob may be a dependent learner when it comes to math, but in social studies he is free and comfortable in a collaborative style. Also, they add that in their own teaching, when they vary the mode of instruction there are less management problems. Curwin and Mendler (1988) list the following modes of instruction:

1. *Lecture.* This mode is most familiar to teachers. The teacher dispenses information to students and is the real focal point of the lesson. All questions and student responses are teacher directed.
2. *Large-Group Discussion.* The teachers and all students participate in a discussion related to a topic. The topic may be defined by the teacher, but all students are invited to share their thoughts and ideas. Effective large-group discussion is directed toward soliciting opinions from the students by asking them to become immersed in the subject itself and to comment on its personal relevance.
3. *Small-Group Discussion.* Groups of two to six students are formed and given a task or a topic to discuss. One student

Learner Style	Need	Teacher Role	Teacher Behavior
Dependent (closed systems suggested)	information approval reinforcement esteem from authority	expert authority	lectures directions assignments criticism rewards
Collaborative (mixed systems suggested)	social acceptance peer exchange varied ideas esteem from peers	co-leader environment setter feedback giver	discussion leader resource provider sharer
Independent (open systems suggested)	ego needs self-esteem	facilitator	resource

Figure 5-1. An illustration of dependent, collaborative, and independent learning styles which shows the relationship between these three styles and the student's needs, the teacher's role, and behavior. From *Discipline with dignity* (p. 165) by R.L. Curwin and A.N. Mendler, 1988, Alexandria: Association for Supervision and Curriculum Development. Copyright 1988 by Association for Supervision and Curriculum Development. Reprinted by permission.

may be selected to summarize the group's discussion for the whole class.

4. *Independent Seat Work.* Following a teacher-directed or group discussion, each student is assigned a project to consider or work to be completed that is related to what proceeded it.

5. *Student Support Teams.* All students are assigned to teams of four to six. Students are heterogeneously grouped so that each team contains dependent, collaborative, and independent learners. The teacher may assign either a group project or individual seat work. If it is a group project, then all students are evaluated according to their group performance. If it is an individual assignment, then students who are having trouble with their work must first solicit the help of team members

before they can ask the teacher for assistance. Only then may a student approach the teacher for help. (p. 167)

Classroom Management for E/BD Children

Although there is much in common between the general literature on classroom management and management practices for children who have emotional or behavioral problems, students with emotional or behavioral disorders, nevertheless, require management approaches which are somewhat different. This is because they are socialization failures who lack many of the behaviors, capabilities, and knowledge learned by most children. Consequently, there are a number of alternative management approaches for working with and educating children who are emotionally or behaviorally disordered. One such classic approach which was originally presented in 1968 and has received a great deal of attention over a long period of time is Hewett's plan for educating E/BD children. Additionally, because his approach is reasonably flexible and emphasizes essential components for managing emotional and behavioral problems, Hewett's management plan is discussed next.

Hewett's Classroom Management Plan

Hewett's management plan is essentially comprised of three components: (a) a developmental sequence of educational goals, (b) a learning triangle, and (c) an engineered classroom. Also, the components are interrelated to emphasize the student's goals and the method for obtaining them (Hewett, 1968; Hewett & Taylor, 1980).

A Developmental Sequence of Educational Goals

Hewett viewed his developmental sequence as both practical and educational. It is practical in that it describes behavior which can be understood and altered and it is educational because each level in the sequence has to do with preparing the child to learn and with how the child can be taught (Hewett, 1968; Hewett & Taylor, 1980). Figure 5-2 depicts Hewett's developmental sequence of educational goals. Following is a description of each educational goal in the developmental sequence.

Hewett's Developmental Sequence of Educational Goals

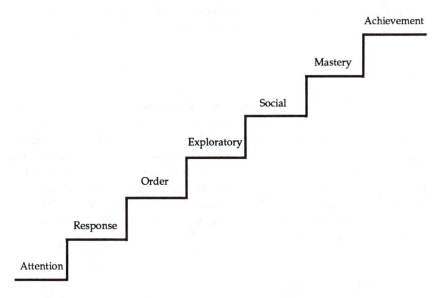

Figure 5-2. An illustration of Hewett's developmental sequence of educational goals. From *The emotionally disturbed child in the classroom: A developmental strategy for educating children with maladaptive behaviors* (p. 43) by F.M. Hewett, 1968, Boston: Allyn and Bacon, Inc. Copyright 1968 by Allyn and Bacon, Inc. Reprinted by permission.

Attention

This is the ability to focus on relevant cues in the environment. Before a student can learn anything, attention must be focused on the learning task and extraneous or irrelevant stimuli must be ignored. Hewett and Taylor (1980) suggest that task characteristics which are useful for getting students to attend include:

1. Removal of distracting stimuli
2. Presentation of small, discrete units of work
3. Heightening the vividness and impact of stimuli
4. Use of concrete, rather than abstract tasks. (p. 176)

Response

Although attention starts the learning process, the student must next make a response. A student could attend to a task all day but unless the student takes some action, learning will not occur. Hewett and Taylor (1980) advise that with regard to response tasks, the teacher should: (a) reduce the criteria for correctness, and (b) guarantee the child some degree of success with learning.

Order

Attending and responding alone does not guarantee learning. Students must develop order to their responding and be able to follow directions. When a student's attending and responding is ordered, learning efficiency increases. Several activities which Hewett and Taylor (1980) suggest for use to help students develop order are: (a) pencil and art activities that do not involve reading, (b) treasure maps that require following arrows to find treasures, (c) toy construction kits which can be used to copy models, and (d) pegboard designs which students can copy also.

Exploratory

The more things a student attends to, the more responding occurs. The more ordered the student becomes in attending and responding, the more learning occurs. Through both concrete types of exploration, for example, petting a dog, and symbolic exploration, for example, reading about pets, students learn to enjoy their world and amass large quantities of information. Hewett and Taylor (1980) emphasize three main elements in exploratory tasks:

1. A wide range of multisensory experiences
2. An emphasis on reality
3. Predictable outcomes. (p. 196)

They believe these elements are particularly evident in science and art activities.

Social

This level of the hierarchy focuses more directly than in lower levels of the sequence on acquiring social approval, which was only a by-product of earlier levels. The desire to please others and to avoid censure is learned in infancy. Social tasks are a part of the learning process, and students test their knowledge and skill in social relationships. Hewett and Taylor (1980) advise that the characteristics of social tasks should emphasize:

1. Communicating with the teacher or one or more peers
2. Maintaining appropriate social behavior
3. Tolerating periods of delay, during which time children must cooperate and "wait their turn." (p. 202)

Mastery

This level relates to mastering basic intellectual and adaptive skills and to acquiring sufficient information to be able to function independently and successfully at a particular skill level. The mastery level for a child who has mild or moderate emotional or behavioral disorders would be quite different than the mastery level for a severely disturbed psychotic child.

Achievement

This level is the highest and involves learning that is self-motivated and highly efficient. Learning is said to be extended in breadth and scope.

Teaching/Learning Triangles

Hewett believes that this developmental sequence of educational goals is an organizational pattern of readiness skill through the first five levels and that prior to school most children arrive at school ready to learn at the mastery and achievement levels. He argues, however, that emotionally disturbed children may have never achieved the various goals of paying attention, responding in learning, ordering their behavior, exploring their environment, and getting along with others (Hewett, 1968; Hewett & Taylor, 1980). In writing about emotionally disturbed children, Hewett (1968) states that as "they are exposed to stress with which they cannot deal and encounter failure and frustration in school, their lack of readiness for learning may seriously increase. The problems of some so called 'drop outs' in secondary school may well be the result of a slow but steady process of being 'pushed out' because the necessary opportunities for getting ready to learn were never provided from the time they entered school" (p. 60). Hewett suggests that the solution to this problem lies in the methodology of getting the child ready for school while he is in school. He believes that if three ingredients in a learning program are provided, there is no emotionally disturbed child who cannot be taught. The three ingredients, namely the structure, the reward, and the task are conceptualized as sides of a triangle with the center being occupied by the student. The learning triangle is illustrated in Figure 5-3.

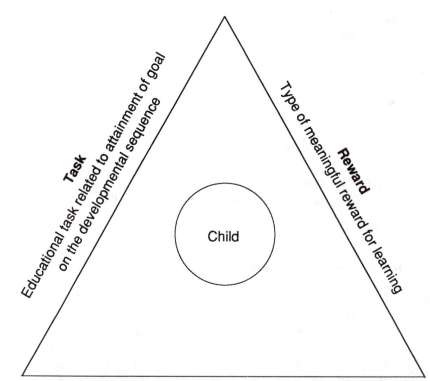

Figure 5-3. An illustration of a learning triangle conceptualized from the point of view of what the child needs. From *The emotionally disturbed child in the classroom: A developmental strategy for educating children with maladaptive behaviors* (p. 62) by F.M. Hewett, 1968, Boston: Allyn and Bacon, Inc. Copyright 1968 by Allyn and Bacon, Inc. Reprinted by permission.

The teacher's job then becomes to: (a) select a task that the student is ready to undertake which is consistent with the educational goal relevant to his problems, (b) provide him with a truly meaningful reward, and (c) establish the degree of structure necessary to ensure efficient learning. Hewett and Taylor (1980) have referred to the task as the curriculum, the reward as consequences, and the structure necessary to assure learning as conditions of learning.

Additionally, the learning triangle is relevant to the teacher, because teaching effectively can occur only when the teacher: (a) understands what task or curriculum is suitable for the student, (b) gets some reward or positive consequence for the teaching, and (c) has a degree of structure or is provided with the necessary conditions in which to teach. Like the student, the teacher occupies a central position in the learning triangle. The teacher's learning triangle is illustrated in Figure 5-4.

The Task

This is defined as any activity, lesson, or assignment which assists the student in mastering one or more goals in the educational hierarchy. Hewett (1968) has seen the need for the teacher to break the goal down into a sequence of instructional objectives, which assures the student of continuous success (content and task analysis). He believes that the teacher needs to be prepared to reduce the complexity of a task at a moment's notice to ensure efficient learning. Additionally, Hewett believes that emphasis should not be placed on complex tasks but instead on discrete tasks, such as seat sitting or hand raising.

Reward

This term is defined as a positive consequence which tends to maintain or increase the strength or frequency of behaviors associated with tasks related to educational goals of the developmental hierarchy. Hewett mentions, however, that it is often difficult to find anything rewarding in school for students who are emotionally or behaviorally disordered, because of their past experiences in schools. When considering consequences it is important to keep in mind that what is one child's reward may be another's punishment (Hewett & Taylor, 1980).

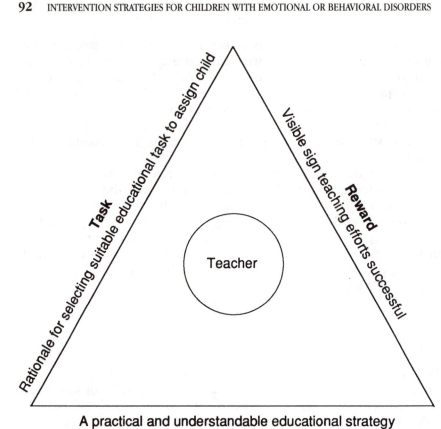

Figure 5-4. An illustration of a learning triangle conceptualized from the point of view of what the teacher needs. From *The emotionally disturbed child in the classroom: A developmental strategy for educating children with maladaptive behaviors* (p. 62) by F.M. Hewett, 1968, Boston: Allyn and Bacon, Inc. Copyright 1968 by Allyn and Bacon, Inc. Reprinted by permission.

Structure

Structure refers to the limits the teacher or school attaches to particular tasks assigned the child which determine whether the child will receive a reward. It refers also to the type of task, the way the task is performed, and how well the task should be performed for the student to receive a reward. Obviously, the decision to select a particular task, reward, and structure is dependent on the student's developmental level. Table 5-1 summarizes the task, reward, and structure provisions at all seven levels of development.

TABLE 5-1. A summary of the task, reward, and structure provisions for seven levels of the developmental sequence of educational goals.

Summary of The Developmental Sequence of Educational Goals

Level	Attention	Response	Order	Exploratory	Social	Mastery	Achievement
Child's Problem	Inattention due to withdrawal or resistance	Lack of involvement and unwillingness to respond in learning	Inability to follow directions	Incomplete or inaccurate knowledge of environment	Failure to value social approval or disapproval	Deficits in basic adaptive and school skills not in keeping with IQ	Lack of self motivation for learning
Educa-tional Task	Get child to pay attention to teacher and task	Get child to respond to tasks he likes and which offer promise of success	Get child to complete tasks with specific starting points and steps leading to a conclusion	Increase child's efficiency as an explorer and get him involved in multisensory exploration of his environment	Get child to work for teacher and peer group approval and to avoid their disapproval	Remedia-tion of basic skill deficien-cies	Development of interest in acquiring knowledge
Learner Reward	Provided by tangible rewards (e.g. food, money tokens)	Provided by gaining social attention	Provided through task completion	Provided by sensory stimulation	Provided by social approval	Provided through task accuracy	Provided through intellectual task success
Teacher Structure	Minimal	Still limited	Emphasized	Emphasized	Based on standards of social appropri-ateness	Based on curriculum assign-ments	Minimal

From *The emotionally disturbed child in the classroom: A developmental strategy for educating children with maladaptive behaviors* (p. 97) by F.M. Hewett, 1968, Boston: Allyn and Bacon, Inc. Copyright 1968 by Allyn and Bacon, Inc. Reprinted by permission.

The Engineered Classroom

Hewett has also designed or engineered a classroom in which the student is assigned tasks he needs to learn, is ready to learn, and with which he can be successful. The tasks are selected to correspond to his deficit in the development sequence and are supported by a classroom designed with a floor plan, facilities, and a program to support the goals of the developmental strategy (Hewett, 1968; Hewett & Taylor, 1980). The floor plan of the engineered classroom is illustrated in Figure 5-5.

Floor Plan

The classroom is arranged so that specific areas correspond to various levels of the developmental sequence which we discussed earlier. As such, the mastery and achievement area includes student desks for assignments in reading, written language, and arithmetic. Also in this area are two study booths or offices for students who, at times, may need a secluded area. Additionally, the teacher's desk is at the front of the mastery and achievement area and adjacent to a blackboard.

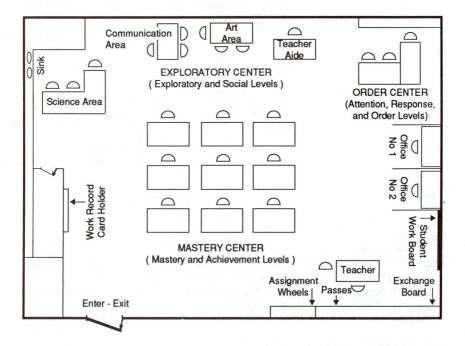

Figure 5-5. An illustration of the floor plan of the engineered classroom. From *The emotionally disturbed child in the classroom: A developmental strategy for educating children with maladaptive behaviors* (p. 243) by F.M. Hewett, 1968, Boston: Allyn and Bacon, Inc. Copyright 1968 by Allyn and Bacon, Inc. Reprinted by permission.

Corresponding to yet different levels of the developmental sequence, the exploratory and social area is set up near a sink and work counter toward the back of the mastery and achievement areas, so that students working at their desks will not be disturbed. In this area, science, art, and communication activities are pursued.

Finally, at the most basic level of the developmental sequence, the attention response and order area is set up in the corner of the room and includes two tables and a storage cabinet. This center provides activities for the student which emphasize active participation, direction following, and task completion (Hewett, 1968; Hewett & Taylor, 1980).

Check-Mark System

The check-mark token system, used in the engineered classroom, is designed to guarantee that even the most disinterested and resistant learner will be rewarded for effort. In the engineered classroom, the day revolves around this system. When entering the classroom in the morning the child picks up a work record card and, during the day, is continuously given check marks which reflect classroom functioning. Cards filled with check marks can later be exchanged for tangible rewards, for example, candy and trinkets. Either the teacher or an aide can give a possible 10 check marks for 15-minute work periods. After each 15-minute work period, the following 5 minutes are devoted to giving the check marks, correcting work just completed, and providing directions for the new assignment for the next 15 minutes (Hewett, 1968).

Additionally, the engineered classroom provides students with 2 check marks for starting work on time, 3 for following through on time, and up to 5 bonus check marks for being a student. Being a student refers to how well the student respected the limits of time, space, activity, and the working rights of others. For students with no problem on the order level, bonus points might be given for functioning in ways critical to learning needs. For some inattentive students, bonus check marks may be given for attending to their work even though no work was undertaken. These marks would be given because the student had tried.

According to Hewett, the structure of the engineered classroom is child centered in that what the student does and when it is done depend on the student's moment by moment functioning level and the student's deficit on the developmental sequence of educational goals.

Hewett's now classic educational plan contains many important ingredients, for example, developmental learning sequence, learning triangle, check-mark reward system, and physical design of classroom. Because many of the elements of Hewett's plan are essential in managing and helping children with emotional or behavioral disorders, teachers may want to consider how to adapt the ingredients in this plan to fit the demands of their particular settings. Although investigators may disagree as to the theoretical rationale for physical structure of the classroom and classroom organization, many understand its importance as an aid in controlling student behavior (Shores, Gunter, & Jack, 1993).

Level Systems

Not unlike Hewett's educational plan, level systems provide a physical structure and a reward system also. Level systems, which originated in restrictive settings, help students develop inner control by progressing systematically from more restrictive environments to less restrictive ones with the acquisition of increasingly more appropriate academic, social, and emotional performance. With this progression, expectations and privileges are increased as the student becomes increasingly capable of self-regulation. Additionally, level systems can be designed to support the objectives of PL 101-476 which encourage education in the least restrictive environment.

Table 5-2 presents an illustration of the expectations and privileges used in some level systems. In this level system students not only evaluated themselves, but also their peers. The evaluations were conducted semiweekly and peers as well as staff determined whether a particular student increased a level, remained on the same level, or decreased a level as a consequence for appropriate or inappropriate behavior (Bauer, Shea, & Keppler, 1986).

Mastropieri, Jenne, and Scruggs (1988) discussed two high school resource room level systems. In both level systems, students stayed at the same level during the first four days of the week. On Thursday, students who had achieved an 85% accuracy criterion on assignments were allowed to request a change to a higher level, which was discussed and put to a majority vote on Friday. Students who had earned a level change negotiated a new contract with the teacher.

Guidelines for Creating a Level System

In discussing level systems, Bauer, Shea, and Keppler (1986) suggest that each system should include a description of each level, the

TABLE 5-2. An illustration of some of the expectations and privileges that were used in the Child's Center of Our Lady of Grace Level System.

Child's Center of Our Lady of Grace Level System			
	Level I	**Level II**	**Level III**	**Level IV**
Sample Expectations	Begin to recognize individual problems Willingness to be responsible Plan treatment with counselor Modify behavior	Become more self-regulating in regard to following rules and accepting responsibilities, to begin to approach staff to discuss problems To begin to exhibit more appropriate social behavior To become more productive and less disruptive	Self-regulating in following rules and accepting responsibilities To exhibit appropriate social behavior To prepare writing contract with counselor Often works up to potential in class	Self-regulation
Privileges	Structure activities accompanied by staff	Soda for lunch Smoking in designated areas Use of weight room with supervision Educational fieldtrips Structured activities accompanied by staff	One free soda per week Soda from machine Smoking in designated areas Off campus lunch at staff discretion Visitor with staff permission Educational fieldtrips Structured activities accompanied by staff	May go out for lunch All previously earned privileges Occasional handling of keys Leave campus with staff permission Tutoring in child unit Fieldtrips designed specifically for this level

From "Level systems: A framework for the individualization of behavior management" by A.M. Bauer, T.M. Shea, and R. Keppler, 1986, *Exceptional children, 12,* 29. Copyright 1986 by Council for Exceptional Children. Reprinted by permission.

criteria for moving from one level to another, and the expectations and privileges for each level. They offer the following guidelines.

> *Step 1.* Determine the usual entry level behaviors of the student population with whom the system is to be applied.

Step 2. Determine the terminal behavior expectations for the students.

Step 3. List at least two but no more than four sets of behavioral expectations which seem to be appropriate steps between those described in Steps 1 and 2.

Step 4. Write the sets of graduated expectations on separate sheets of paper. Label them "Level 1" through "Level 4."

Step 5. Consider using a disciplinary or ground level.

Step 6. Consider using a transition level which would include part time placement in the special program and part time in regular education.

Step 7. Determine the privileges appropriate for students beginning the program (i.e., Level 1).

Step 8. Determine the privileges appropriate for students preparing to terminate the program (i.e., at the highest level).

Step 9. For each level developed in Step 3, list appropriate privileges evenly distributed among the levels.

Step 10. Finally consider:

1. How frequently and in what way will a student's status be reviewed?
2. Will a minimum stay be required at each level?
3. Who will review the student's status?
4. What level of appropriate behavior will be required to remain at the level?
5. What self-monitoring and teacher-monitoring procedures will be needed?

Step 11. Determine the communication system to be used among special education and regular education staff, parents, and students. (pp. 33-4)

The conceptual similarity between Hewett's educational plan and levels systems is great indeed. Both are based on the concept that a hierarchical system can be used to shape self-management, academic, social, and emotional performance. Although Hewett's plan was designed for use in a self-contained classroom, the major elements of the plan can be adapted to fit the demands of a different educational setting. Similarly, level systems can be designed to include transition levels that encourage the integration of special and regular education.

Summary

Experienced regular and special educators view classroom management as a primary concern. Because this issue is so important to both teachers and students, many studies have been conducted regarding general classroom management. The results of these studies have focused attention on characteristics of effective teachers, teacher preparation, the classroom atmosphere, teacher expectations, teaching behaviors, and teaching and learning styles.

Although there is much overlap between the general literature on classroom management and management practices for children who have emotional or behavioral disorders, these students require alternative management approaches which emphasize a physical structure and a reward system to help them progress systematically. Hewett's classic management plan ensures this progression by emphasizing a developmental sequence of educational goals, a learning triangle, and an engineered classroom. Similarly, level systems ensure this progression by providing rewards and privileges as students move from more restrictive environments to less restrictive ones with the acquisition of increasingly appropriate academic, social, and emotional performance. Both management plans for children with emotional or behavioral disorders can be adapted to a variety of educational settings and used to promote the development of increasingly self-regulated behavior.

Review Questions

1. What very obvious teacher characteristics help make a teacher successful at managing behavior?
2. How do Curwin and Mendler suggest that teachers make use of incidents of classroom violation?
3. What does Kounin's research indicate about the cause of management problems?
4. What are some of the characteristics of a healthy classroom environment?
5. How can teachers set appropriate expectations for their students?
6. What do Brophy and Putnam say about how classroom rules should be phrased?
7. What is a collaborative learning style?
8. What are the three major components of Hewett's classroom management plan?
9. How does Hewett's learning triangle satisfy the needs of both the student and the teacher?
10. In what way does Hewett's classroom design support the goals of his developmental strategy?

11. How are bonus points used in the engineered classroom?
12. What is the purpose of Hewett's nine interventions and how do teachers decide when one is appropriate?
13. How are level systems and Hewett's educational plan similar?

Learning Activities

1. Divide into small groups of five to six and develop a lesson plan for each of Hewett's seven educational goals, that is, attention, response order, and so on. Each plan is to include (a) an instructional objective, (b) an input/intervention component, (c) an output/response component, (d) a materials component, and (e) an evaluation component. Each group is to present its lesson plans to the class.

2. Divide into small groups of five to six and design a level system for students who are mild to moderately emotionally or behaviorally disordered. Using the guidelines suggested by Bauer, Shea, and Keppler (1986) include the following in your design: (a) four levels, (b) a ground level, and (c) a transition level which includes part-time placement in regular education. When each group is finished it is to present its level system to the class.

6

Interpersonal Skills Interventions

The interventions discussed in this chapter are derived from the humanistic model and based largely on the early work of Carl Rogers and developed over the years in his counseling work with clients in therapy (Rogers, 1951). Much of his approach has been set forth for teachers in a revision of his classic book *Freedom to Learn* (Rogers, 1980) after having been interpreted and operationalized in *TET-Teacher Effectiveness Training* (Gordon, 1974) and *The Skills of Teaching: Interpersonal Skills.* (Carkhuff, Berenson, & Pierce, 1977). These classroom interventions focus on the relationship between the teacher and student in which the teacher is nonauthoritarian and acts more as a resource and catalyst for learning than as a director of activities. Most importantly, the teacher must (a) learn to be empathetic, (b) be able to provide unconditional positive regard, and (c) become a congruent or authentic person (Rogers, 1980). The first two interpersonal characteristics have been demonstrated repeatedly by Rogers in his writings and through films of his therapy sessions with clients. He suggests that the interpersonal characteristics of empathy and unconditional positive regard are put into practice by the ability to listen and reflect, which he terms "reflection of feeling."

Gordon (1974) has referred to this same interpersonal ability as "active listening" and Carkhuff et al. (1977) have called the demonstration of this skill an "interchangeable statement." Whereas Rogers has never attempted to operationalize his therapeutic responding into a teachable skill, Gordon (1974) and Carkhuff et al. (1977) have. And although their approaches to teaching the interpersonal skill of therapeutic responding differ qualitatively, there is a great deal of similarity between both approaches. With regard to Rogers' third therapeutic characteristic, namely therapeutic congruence, Rogers has described it variously as authenticity, the quality of being a real person, and not having the need to hide behind a facade or having to play a role. Similarly, Gordon (1974), while not discussing the therapeutic quality of congruence directly, has provided teachers with a technique for being congruent when students exhibit behaviors that are truly problematic to teachers. This skill addresses the problem of how teachers can get some of their own needs met without affecting students negatively. Gordon (1974) has called this skill, the skill of "sending I-messages " (p. 151). Finally, he has shown how teachers can put together the skill of active listening and the skill of sending I-messages into the "no-lose method of resolving conflicts" to resolve conflicts in the classroom. Specifically, this chapter discusses how to acquire the major interpersonal characteristics of effective teachers. The interpersonal skills described include: (a) active listening, (b) making interchangeable statements, (c) sending I-messages, and (d) the no-lose method of resolving conflicts.

Establishing Problem Ownership

Before attempting to describe the interpersonal skill of active listening, teachers need to understand when its use is appropriate and inappropriate. According to Gordon (1974), this requires understanding "problem ownership," that is, does the student have a problem or does the teacher have a problem? Gordon uses a rectangle to help teachers decide when student behaviors are interfering with their needs and causing them to feel upset, frustrated, irritated, and so on or whether the student is experiencing a problem in his own life. For example, if a student reveals that she's angry and disappointed in her mother for not letting her spend the night at a friend's house, does the student "own the problem" (have a problem) or does the teacher "own the problem" (have a problem). To decide who owns the problem the teacher must ask whether the student behavior is tangibly and concretely affecting the teacher. If the answer is no, then the student owns the problem and the use of active listening is appropriate. If the answer is yes, then the teacher owns the problem and active listening is not appropriate (Gordon, 1974). Figure 6-1 illustrates the rectangle Gordon uses to help teachers understand the relationship between problem ownership and teaching and how learning follows.

In the upper portion of the rectangle, the student owns the problem and is experiencing difficulties with life which are making

Problem Ownership Rectangle

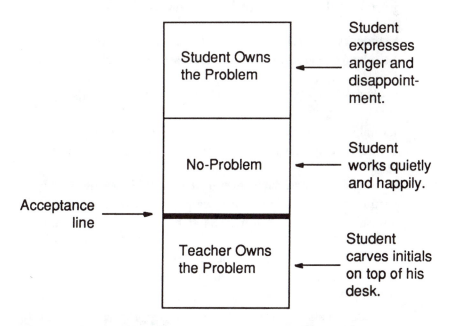

Figure 6-1. An illustration to help teachers understand the relationship between problem ownership and teaching and learning. From *TET: Teacher effectiveness training* (p. 40) by T. Gordon, 1974, New York: Peter H. Wyden Publisher. Copyright 1974, by Peter H. Wyden Publisher. Reprinted by permission.

it difficult to concentrate on classwork. In the bottom portion of the rectangle, the teacher owns the problem because the student's behavior is causing a problem for the teacher that has a tangible and concrete effect. In both the upper and bottom portions of the rectangle, someone has a problem which will interfere with the teaching learning process. In the middle portion of the rectangle no one has a problem and the teaching-learning process is free to occur, that is, if neither the student nor the teacher has a "problem" then there exists a much greater opportunity for something educational to occur. Of course, the central purpose of Gordon's work is to show teachers how they can use therapeutic skills to increase the size of the teaching learning area (Gordon, 1974). Gordon (1974) has listed the following common situations in which the teacher owns the problem and active listening is inappropriate:

> A student is scratching a new desktop.
>
> Several students interrupt your conference with another student.
>
> A student leaves reference books he has used unshelved.
>
> A student repeatedly comes late and disturbs the class.
>
> A student wastes art paper.
>
> A student doesn't check in the lab materials he checked out.
>
> Several students smoke in the darkroom of your photo lab.
>
> A student takes up a lot of your time tattling about other students.
>
> A student uses material from your desk without asking.
>
> A student eats candy and leaves wrappers all over the floor.
>
> Several students argue loudly enough to interrupt you and the rest of the class.
>
> A student is about to spill paint all over a cabinet.
>
> Several students whisper loudly while you are giving directions. (pp. 126-127).

In these situations, active listening is inappropriate, because the teacher owns the problem, that is, each of these student behaviors concretely and tangibly affect the teacher. Gordon (1974) also identifies the following student-owned problems in which active listening is appropriate.

> Bruce can't seem to get his homework done.
>
> Alice thinks she's ugly.

Hal can't decide on a vocation.

Terri hates her parents.

Lawrence is afraid of bigger boys.

Gayle thinks she is pregnant.

Robert is disappointed at being cut from the team.

Margo doesn't have any friends.

Emily hates to take piano lessons.

Ken is angry because he has lost an important tennis match.

Bill is afraid people will laugh at him if he makes a mistake.

Donnie is afraid of the dark.

Karen thinks she is dumb.

Grace is shocked at the behavior of other students.

Phillip is frustrated by long-division problems.

Manuel is afraid of fire.

Molly is afraid to go to kindergarten. (pp. 110-111)

When either the teacher or the student own the problem, the teaching learning process is impeded. To teach effectively, these problems must be managed first. When the student owns the problem, the most effective method for dealing with it in a manner genuinely helpful to students is to use the technique of active listening. The reasons teachers usually fail in helping students with their problems is because they fail to determine problem ownership. Once this mistake is made, teachers tend to exacerbate the situation further by sending messages that communicate to students that their behavior is unacceptable. Teachers generally send these messages because they fail to understand that the student owns the problem (Gordon, 1974).

Roadblocks to Communication

Gordon (1974) has classified the typical unaccepting language of teachers into 12 categories which he calls the "Twelve Roadblocks To Communication." He explains that, when students have problems, these kinds of messages tend to block further communication which is necessary in helping students solve their own problems. Gordon's 12 roadblocks to communication are listed below.

1. Ordering, Commanding, Directing
2. Warning, Threatening

3. Moralizing, Preaching, Giving "Shoulds and Oughts"
4. Advising, Offering Solutions or Suggestions
5. Teaching, Lecturing, Giving Logical Arguments
6. Judging, Criticizing, Disagreeing, Blaming
7. Praising, Agreeing, Giving Positive Evaluations
8. Name-Calling, Stereotyping, Ridiculing
9. Interpreting, Analyzing, Diagnosing
10. Reassuring, Sympathizing, Consoling, Supporting
11. Questioning, Probing, Interrogating, Cross- Examining
12. Withdrawing, Distracting, Being Sarcastic, Humoring, Diverting. (pp. 48-49)

Gordon (1974) explains that the first 5 offer a solution or solutions to the student's problem, which may have the effect of making him feel angry, resentful, guilty, dumb, or hassled. The second 5 communicate judgment, evaluation, put down, or denial of the student's problem, which may have the effect of making him feel lowered self-esteem, defensive, manipulated, angry, exposed, or discontented. Whereas, the last 2 are attempts to make the student's problem go away or to deny the problem, which may have the effect of making the student feel threatened or put down. According to Gordon, the 12 roadblocks "communicate to the troubled person that he must change, had better change and should change" (p. 55).

Active listening is much more helpful because it communicates a genuine acceptance of the student and fosters a relationship in which the student is free to explore his problem and to think about how to grow and change (Gordon 1974).

Active Listening

To understand how active listening works, a diagram is used to illustrate that active listening is essentially a decoding process in which the student sends or encodes feelings or inner experiences by putting them into words. To active listen, it is the teacher or receiver's function to decode these words and to check the accuracy of this decoding by mirroring or feeding back the results of the decoding. This "mirroring" is called active listening (Gordon, 1974). Figure 6-2 illustrates active listening.

The process of active listening also acts as a check on the accuracy of teacher decoding, which is either affirmed or denied by the student. An example of a conversation in which the first decoding

An Active Listening Diagram

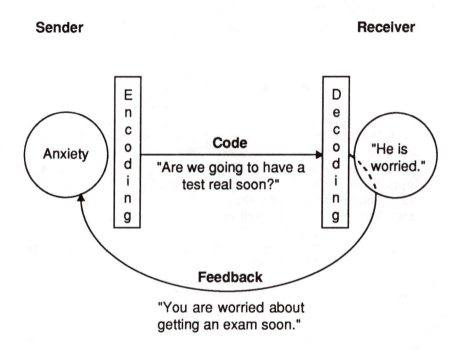

Figure 6-2. An illustration to demonstrate that active listening is essentially a decoding process in which the student sends his feelings by putting them into words which the teacher attempts to decode and mirror back to the student. From *TET: Teacher effectiveness training* (p. 69) by T. Gordon, 1974, New York: Peter H. Wyden Publisher. Copyright 1974, by Peter H. Wyden Publisher. Reprinted by permission.

was inaccurate, but in which active listening served as a check, follows.

Student: Are we going to have our recess period next?
Teacher: You are ready to take a break about now?
Student: No, not really. I'd rather finish my science project.
Teacher: Oh, you'd rather we didn't take our recess next, so you could keep working on the science project.

Student: Yes. I'm behind and want to get it done before it's too late.
Teacher: I see, you need more time to work on it.
Student: Yes, I like science, but I was sick last week and got started late.
Teacher: Well, we have study period next. Recess is after that today.
Student: Great! I'll have time to work on the project.

Additional examples follow.

Example 1
Student: Does somebody get to choose the game today?
Teacher: You want to know whether I'm going to decide which game we play or if a student gets to decide?
Student: No, I want to choose the game.
Teacher: You want to choose the game because you have a favorite?
Student: No, I don't have a favorite.
Teacher: You're saying there are some games you don't want to play.
Student: It's just that everyone else chooses Dodge Ball.
Teacher: You don't like to play Dodge Ball.
Student: I like to play Dodge Ball, but I'm not good at it.
Teacher: You like it but you feel bad because you're not very good.
Student: It's really that nobody wants me on their team and I'm always the last one picked.
Teacher: You feel bad because no one wants you.
Student: Yes.

Example 2
Student: I hate music! It's for sissys.
Teacher: You're angry because of the kinds of kids who are into music.
Student: Yes, some kids are so stuck up.
Teacher: Music is okay. It's just that some kids act like snobs.
Student: Yeah, Mary and Vicky think they're so special, just because they were picked for the chorus.
Teacher: You think Mary and Vicky are acting stuck up because they were picked.
Student: Well, I can sing just as good as Mary and Vicky's voice is lower than mine anyway.
Teacher: You feel disappointed because you're as good as Mary and you didn't get picked.
Student: Yeah, I guess Mary and Vicky are really being Okay. They're so happy and I feel really bad.
Teacher: You're really feeling down because you didn't get picked and you feel kind of left out now.

Student: Yes, well I guess I can try out again next month for the Christmas concert.
Teacher: You're feeling a little better knowing that you've got some more chances to be in the chorus.
Student: Yes, in fact I'm going to start practicing today.

In these examples, it is clear that active listening not only facilitated communication and enhanced the relationship between the teacher and student, but it also facilitated problem solving by helping the student uncover and identify the problem precisely. Gordon (1974) suggests also, that active listening can be used to: (a) facilitate classroom discussions, (b) help dependent students, (c) handle resistance, and (d) help with either parent-teacher or parent-teacher-student conferences.

The Interchangeable Statement

Carkhuff et al. (1977) also teach therapeutic responding. They have used the phrase interchangeable statement to describe the main interpersonal skill they teach. However, prior to teaching interchangeable statements, they devote considerable time to explaining that interpersonal responding skills are dependent on "physically attending to the learner."

Attending Physically

Carkhuff et al. (1980) believe that for teachers to attend maximally they must posture themselves effectively by establishing eye contact, squaring off with the learner, and closing the distance between the learner and the teacher. By physically attending, teachers are better able to pick up the details of the learner's appearance and behavior, focus with intensity on the learner's characteristics, and pick up cues which will be helpful in responding (Carkhuff, 1980).

Responding to Feelings

The second step in the training program is to teach how to "respond to feelings." To become good at this, the teacher must observe the learner's behavior, facial expression, tone of voice, and words while suspending judgments. Sometimes the teacher is so interested in responding that he fails to really hear the learner's words. Carkhuff et al. (1977) suggest that teachers start learning to respond to feelings by simply trying to repeat the learner's expression verbatim. In training materials, teachers either practice this exercise with a friend or by reading a written "learner expressions" (a lengthy statement made by a student) and covering it and then trying to repeat or write it verbatim. Once able to repeat the exact words of a two- or three-line expression verbatim, teachers are ready for the third step which is formulating a response to the learner's expression that captures feelings. Carkhuff et al. (1977) suggest that teachers practicing this should take time to think about an appropriate feeling word. The goal is to find a word that is interchangeable with the feeling and the intensity of the feeling in the student's statement. This is facilitated by providing a learner expression and a list of feeling words. For example, for the category of sad, an individual may feel unhappy, which is categorized as weak in intensity or as depressed, which would indicate a strong level of intensity. After considering the learner expression, for example, "I've tried and tried to make friends since coming here, but still nobody likes me" and inspecting the list of feeling words, the task is to select the appropriate word. The feeling words are categorized into types of feeling and intensity of feelings (Carkhuff et al., 1977). The learner expression and an accompanying category of feeling words is illustrated in Figures 6-3 and 6-4, respectively.

Responding to Feelings

Learner Expression:
"I've tried and tried to make friends since coming here, but still nobody likes me."

Response Format:
"You feel ＿＿＿＿＿＿ ."

Response:
"You feel upset."

Figure 6-3. An illustration of a learner expression, and a response format for helping the teacher find a word that is interchangeable with the feeling and intensity of the feeling in the student statement. An appropriate response is also provided. From *The Skills of teaching: Interpersonal skills* (p. 97) by R.R. Carkhuff, D.H. Berenson, and R.M. Pierce, 1977, Amherst: Human Resource Development Press. Copyright 1977 by Human Resource Development Press. Adapted by permission.

Feeling Words

Feeling Category: Sad

Levels of Intensity

Strong	burdened crushed dejected despairing despondent depressed	distressed downtrodden grave grieved hopeless miserable	morose mournful remorseful sorrowful terrible unloved unwanted
Mild	blue disappointed disturbed downcast downhearted feeling unwanted	forlorn gloomy heavyhearted hurt lonely low	melancholy moody pitiful plaintive self-pitying upset woeful
Weak	angry apathetic bad defeated disenchanted down drab unpleasant dreary	embarrassed emotional glum hateful lost low spirits mistrustful	painful sober sorry turned off uneasy unhappy

Figure 6-4. A list of feeling words which may help teachers to identify the appropriate feeling word that is interchangeable with the feeling and the intensity of the feeling in the student statement. From *The skills of teaching: Interpersonal skills* (p. 101) by R.R. Carkhuff, D.H. Berenson, and R.M. Pierce, 1977, Amherst: Human Resource Development Press. Copyright 1977 by Human Resource Development Press. Adapted by permission.

Carkhuff et al. (1977) believe that after sufficient practice, with time allotted to think about the appropriate feeling word, teachers are able to respond more quickly and naturally. Also, expanding the list of the feeling words provided with additional feeling words that fit the slang or expressions of particular learners is recommended. In the example in Figure 6-3, the teacher might respond by filling in the feeling word "upset," for example, "You feel upset."

Complementing Feeling With Meaning

The third step of "complementing feeling with meaning" is to teach how to respond to the meaning of the learner's expression. Carkhuff et al. (1977) say that to demonstrate a complete understanding of what the learner is saying, teachers must capture and express the learner's personal reason for the feeling, for example, "you feel sad because the teacher didn't pick you" or "you feel happy because the teacher made you captain of the team." Again teachers are provided with a learner expression, a list of feeling words, and a response format. Figure 6-5 is an example of a learner expression and a possible therapeutic response.

For Carkhuff et al. (1977) these interchangeable responses are termed "minimally effective" (p. 116) because, while the response accurately communicates an understanding of the learner and facilitates an exploration of the problem, they do not involve the learner directly in the expression by making him or her responsible for the feeling and meaning expressed. This level of interpersonal responding is acceptable to Rogers (1969) and Gordon (1974) as the final level of interpersonal teacher response necessary. This is because of the belief that students will eventually take responsibility for these personal expressions and ultimately solve their own problems. Therefore, they would continue to respond at this level to help students acquire insight and solve their problems. Carkhuff et al. agree with Rogers and Gordon to the extent that they believe this level of interchangeable statement should be used for an extended period of time, for example, during several separate conversations with the student. However, they believe this level should be used only in the beginning of the dialogue to ensure a good relationship with the learner.

Complementing Feeling with Meaning

Learner Expression:
"This math is too hard."

Response Format:
"You feel _____

because _____. "

Response:
"You feel frustrated because the math is too difficult."

Figure 6-5. An illustration of a learner expression and a response format that helps the teacher demonstrate that he has captured the learner's personal reason for the feeling. An appropriate response is also provided. From *The skills of teaching: Interpersonal skills* (p. 115) by R.R. Carkhuff, D.H. Berenson, and R.M. Pierce, 1977, Amherst: Human Resource Development Press. Copyright 1977 by Human Resource Development Press. Adapted by permission.

Personalizing the Meaning

After laying a base of the interchangeable statements described above, the teacher should "personalize the meaning" so that learners become accountable for their part in the experience. Once again teachers are provided with a learner expression, a list of feeling words, and a response format (Carkhuff et al., 1977). This fourth step is achieved by following the format illustrated in Figure 6-6.

In this example, the teacher has responded in terms of the implications of the experience for the learner by thinking about what it means to the learner personally to say math was too hard. It means the learner does not understand it. This step is sometimes difficult for the student because it starts to make him own the problem. The phrase "because you" makes it difficult for the student to project the problem away from himself, thereby avoiding his responsibility to provide a solution to the problem. This is why a base of previous interchangeable statements, which captured feeling and meaning only, are necessary first. If the teacher moves too quickly to personalize the meaning, the student will be unlikely to accept it, and open communication will likely cease (Carkhuff, et al.).

Personalizing the Problem

The fifth step is to "personalize the problem" by getting learners to state the problem from their point of view, that is, what does the learner believe the deficit is. What is it that the learner feels he cannot do? This is achieved by following the format illustrated in Figure 6-7.

Personalizing the Meaning

Learner Expression:
    "This math is too hard."

Response Format:
    "You feel _____ because you _____ . "

Response:
    "You feel frustrated because you don't understand your math."

Figure 6-6. An illustration of a learner expression, a response format, and a response for helping a student assume responsibility for the problem. From *The skills of teaching: Interpersonal skills* (p. 136) by R.R. Carkhuff, D.H. Berenson, and R.M. Pierce, 1977, Amherst: Human Resource Development Press. Copyright 1977 by Human Resource Development Press. Adapted by permission.

Personalizing the Problem

Learner Expression:
"This math is too hard."

Response Format:
"You feel _____ because you cannot _____ ."

Response:
"You feel frustrated because you are unable to do your math problems."

Figure 6-7. An illustration of a learner expression, the response format, and a response for helping the student "own" the problem by stating what he cannot do. From *The skills of teaching: Interpersonal skills* (p. 137) by R.R. Carkhuff, D.H. Berenson, and R.M. Pierce, 1977, Amherst: Human Resource Development Press. Copyright 1977 by Human Resource Development Press. Adapted by permission.

Like "personalizing the meaning," Carkhuff et al. believe that "personalizing the problem" represents a big step and that it must be accomplished with care. In this step teachers, are clearly completing what was started in the step of "personalizing the meaning." When the student accepts this step, he or she has completely "owned" the problem. Like the step of "personalizing the meaning" the step of "personalizing the problem" may require many of the previous types of interchangeable statements before the learner will accept an interchangeable statement at this new level.

Personalizing the Feelings

The sixth step in Carkhuff's training program is "personalizing the feelings." In this step, teachers are taught to personalize the feeling after having considered the implications of the personalized meaning and the problem. To personalize feelings, a reconsideration of what the student is feeling at this point in the exploration of the problem is required. Figure 6-8 illustrates this step.

It should be clear from the illustration in Figure 6-8 that the strategy of personalizing takes the learner more deeply and more accurately into understanding his or her problem. Whether this deeper understanding will occur naturally as it appears to for Rogers (1969) and Gordon (1974) is a matter of debate.

Personalizing the Feeling

Learner Expression:
    "This math is too hard."

Response Format:
    "You feel ＿＿＿＿＿＿ because you cannot ＿＿＿＿＿＿ ."

Response:
    "You feel discouraged because you are unable to do your math problems."

Figure 6-8. An illustration of a learner expression, a response format, and a response for interpreting what the student is now feeling after having completely owned the problem. From *The skills of teaching: Interpersonal skills* (p. 137) by R.R. Carkhuff, D.H. Berenson, and R.M. Pierce, 1977, Amherst: Human Resource Development Press. Copyright 1977 by Human Resource Development Press. Adapted by permission.

Initiating Responding

Carkhuff et al. (1977) explain that once the problem has been identified it is relatively easy to initiate responding by establishing a goal for the learner. This is the beginning of formulating initiative responses. Figure 6-9 illustrates this seventh step.

    Carkhuff et al. (1977) have explained that the goal is the "flip side" of the problem, for example, the flip side of "I can't handle these

Initiating Responding
Stating a Goal in General Terms

Learner Expression:
    "This math is too hard."

Response Format:
    "You feel ＿＿＿＿＿＿ because you cannot ＿＿＿＿＿＿ and

    you want to ＿＿＿＿＿＿ ."

Response:
    "You feel down because you don't know how to do your math problems and you want very much to be able to."

Figure 6-9. An illustration of a learner expression, a response format, and a response for establishing a goal for the learner. From *The skills of teaching: Interpersonal skills* (p. 140) by R.R. Carkhuff, D.H. Berenson, and R.M. Pierce, 1977, Amherst: Human Resource Development Press. Copyright 1977 by Human Resource Development Press. Adapted by permission.

math problems" is "I want to be able to do these math problems." At this point it is the task of the teacher to define the goal in terms that are operational and to develop a step-by-step program to help the learner achieve his goal. This is of course the same skill that teachers consistently perform when they individualize instruction and design educational plans.

Sending I-Messages

Remember that Rogers had defined therapeutic congruence as the quality of being authentic or real and as not having to hide behind a facade. "I-messages" are messages that help teachers be congruent. These messages help the teacher communicate real feelings to students when they are exhibiting behaviors that are annoying and tangibly and concretely affect teachers (Gordon, 1974). Examples of these annoying student behaviors were provided in the section Establishing Problem Ownership. When teachers experience feelings of frustration, annoyance, irritation, or resentment, they are receiving clues that tell them they have a problem, or as Gordon would say, that they "own" a problem. To be authentic, teachers cannot afford to hide feelings and pretend everything is okay. Gordon believes that teachers have a legitimate right to confront students whose behaviors are interfering with the teacher's needs. Inappropriate student behaviors that have a tangible and concrete negative effect on teachers cannot be handled by using active listening or by making interchangeable statements. Something must be done about these aversive student behaviors. To be truly authentic or congruent, teachers have to tell the student that their behavior is causing the teacher to have a problem. The challenge, however, is how to do this in a way that increases the likelihood that the student's behavior will change, while not harming the teacher-student relationship. Gordon's solution is to send an I-message instead of the "you-messages" which most teachers tend to send. You-messages contain a negative evaluation of the student and put ownership for the problem on the student when in fact the problem is happening inside the teacher. What follows in Figure 6-10 is one of Gordon's illustrations of the different encoding and decoding processes which occur in both you-messages and I-messages. Notice that the encoding is inaccurate in the you-message.

The accurate match between this teacher's inner experience and the code is contained in the I-message, not the you-message. This is because when teachers send a you-message they are failing to take

I-Messages Vs. You-Messages

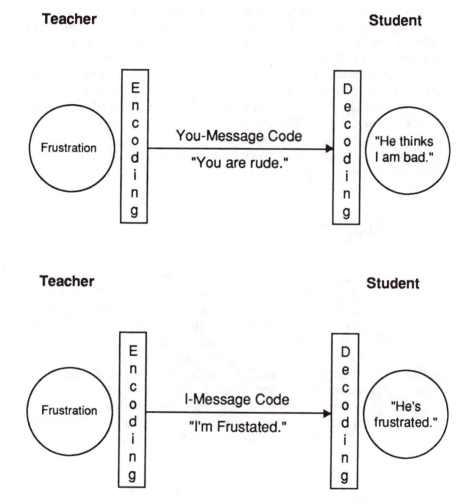

Teacher   **Student**

Frustration | Encoding | You-Message Code "You are rude." | Decoding | "He thinks I am bad."

Teacher   **Student**

Frustration | Encoding | I-Message Code "I'm Frustated." | Decoding | "He's frustrated."

Figure 6-10. A comparison between I-Messages and You-Messages designed to illustrate that the I-Message contains a more accurate match between the teacher's inner experience and the code contained in the I-Message. From *TET: Teacher effectiveness training* (p. 139) by T. Gordon, 1974, New York: Peter H. Wyden Publisher. Copyright 1974, by Peter H. Wyden Publisher. Reprinted by permission.

responsibility for their own inner condition. Teachers are also not being authentic when they fail to share openly their assessment of what is going on inside of them. By contrast, when they send I-messages, not only do they openly share what is going on inside of them but they also avoid the counterresistance which you-messages tend to create. Gordon (1974) reports the experience of one teacher who was reluctant to try I-messages, but who finally decided to send one to a group of kids who were making a mess with water paints. She said, "When you mix paints and spill them all over the sink and table, I have to scrub up later or get yelled at by the custodian. I'm sick of cleaning up after you and I feel helpless to prevent it from happening" (p. 140). She went on to say that she fully expected them to laugh at her, but instead they looked at her as if amazed and then just proceeded to clean up the mess. While I-messages may not be a panacea, they will help teachers expose their real feelings and make them more transparent and real to their students. This will, of course, foster intimacy.

Constructing I-Messages

Gordon explains that putting an I-message together is relatively simple. It is comprised of three parts. The first part is a nonjudgemental description of what it is that is creating the problem for the teacher, for example, "When I see students returning late from recess everyday..." The second part identifies the tangible or concrete effect on the teacher of the behavior described in the first part, for example, "I can't get the lesson started on time." And the third part states the feelings generated in the teacher, for example,"I feel frustrated and upset." According to Gordon (1974), I-messages will fail to have impact unless the students can see from their perspective that the claim has tangible or concrete effects and is real for the teacher. An illustration of the above situation and the accompanying response format is depicted in Figure 6-11.

The "I-Message"

Problem Situation	When I see students returning late from recess every day
Tangible Effect	I can't get the lesson started on time
Teacher Feelings	I feel frustrated and upset

Figure 6-11. An illustration of the components of an "I-Message." From *TET: Teacher effectiveness training* (pp. 142-145) by T. Gordon, 1974, New York: Peter H. Wyden. Adapted by permission.

Shifting From I-Messages to Active Listening

Although I-messages will produce less counter-resistance then you-messages, resistance and counterattack may still occur. When it does, Gordon suggests that the teacher try "shifting from I-messages to active listening" to help the student assimilate the message. Shifting to active listening will help the student deal with the newly created problem. A conversation between a teacher and student is provided to demonstrate how to shift between I-messages and active listening when confronting a student with an I-message.

Teacher: When you talk to Phil while I'm giving directions, I have to repeat them later to you personally and I'm tired of doing that.

Student: Well, Phil and I are working on the map project together and we're trying to get it completed on time. That's why we're talking.

Teacher: I see. You and Phil need more time to discuss the map project.

Student: Yeah, Phil was absent when you explained what we were supposed to do. So I'm trying to make sure he understands it so we finish it on time.

Teacher: You're really just trying to make sure you get the map project done on time, and to do that you and Phil need to talk.

Student: Yeah.

Teacher: Well, I don't want to keep repeating directions and you need to talk to Phil. I guess we've got a problem.

Student: Yeah. But I don't think you should have to repeat the directions either. Maybe Phil and I could have some time alone just until the project is done.

Teacher: Okay, let's see. You are saying that if you and Phil could have class time to discuss the map project then you'd be able to listen to the directions I give, and I wouldn't have to repeat them.

Student: Yeah.

Teacher: Okay, that sounds good. In fact, other students need to discuss their projects too. What if I give 10 minutes at the beginning of each class period for discussion until the project is due. Would you be willing to listen to me for the rest of the time?

Student: Yeah, sure. I really don't want to miss anything.

The No-Lose Method of Resolving Conflicts

Two types of situations have been discussed in which either the student or the teacher owned a problem. The accompanying skills for dealing with each situation have been discussed also. In the first situation, the student had a problem and the teacher had the option of applying either the skill of active listening (Gordon, 1974) or the skill of making an interchangeable statement (Carkhuff et al., 1977). In the second situation the teacher had a problem and was to apply the skill of sending an I-message (Gordon, 1974). Shifting from sending I-messages to active listening was described also. There is a third type of situation which Gordon (1974) calls conflict. In "conflict situations" the teacher needs to be able to use the skill of shifting from sending I-messages to active listening. Gordon describes conflict as a situation in which both the student and the teacher are not getting their needs met and in which both own the problem. Gordon believes that conflicts between students and teachers are typically resolved through a "win-lose method," that is, either the teacher uses her authority and wins or acts permissively and loses in the power struggle that ensues. Most teachers try to win, whereas some adopt a permissive attitude believing that it is their job to put up with unacceptable behavior, allowing students the freedom to vent their emotions. In general, the results of the teacher's "win" leave the student resentful, whereas teachers who act permissively and let students win feel resentful also. Illustrations of these two types of exchanges follow. In the first exchange the authoritarian method is used, and in the second exchange the permissive method is used.

Authoritarian

Mrs. Smith: When you don't bring your textbook to my class you don't have the application activities at the back of each chapter, and I have to take my time to write them on the board just for you. I feel tired of doing that.

Janice: Well, I forgot to bring it because the only time I get to see Steve (boyfriend) is after math class and the walk to my locker takes too much time. That's why I don't bring it.

Mrs. Smith: I know you like to see Steve and it's a long walk, but social studies is important too. You won't be able to graduate without passing it.

Janice: Look, I'm getting a satisfactory grade aren't I? I don't see why I should have to run all the way to my locker when it only takes a little of your time to write a few activities on the board. It might help other students who forget their books too.

Mrs. Smith: Listen Janice, I didn't mind doing this at first, but I'll be darned if I'm going to take my valuable time writing activities on the board so that you can flirt with your boyfriend. From now on if you don't have a book, don't bother coming. Just go to the principal's office!

Janice: But . . . .

Mrs. Smith: No buts. If you want to pass social studies bring your book. Now sit down!

Janice: Okay!!!

Permissive

Mrs. Smith: When you don't bring your textbook to my class you don't have the application activities at the back of each chapter, and I have to take my time to write them on the board just for you. I feel tired of doing that.

Janice: Well, I forget to bring it because the only time I get to see Steve (boyfriend) is after math class and the walk to my locker takes too much time.

Mrs. Smith: I know you like to see Steve and it's a long walk, but social studies is important too. You won't be able to graduate without passing it.

Janice: Look, I'm getting a satisfactory grade aren't I? I'll talk to the principal (Janice's uncle) and tell him you're giving me a hard time for forgetting my textbook occasionally, and then I'll drop this course and take it from Ms. Jones next term. She won't give me all the trouble.

Mrs. Smith: Listen Janice. I'm not being difficult to get along with, and I don't want you to drop the course.

Janice: Well, I'm going to have to do something. You are always on my case and I don't always forget the book either.

Mrs. Smith: Janice, all I'm saying is at least try. If you forget the book, you forget it.

In the first example, the teacher had decided she was going to win. When Janice didn't accept her solution she resorted to her power by telling her she would risk failing the course. In the second example, Janice resorted to her power by threatening to tell her uncle, the principal, and drop the course. In both cases a battle was won, but someone had to lose and accept a solution that was unacceptable to her. Gordon (1974) has reported many of the conclusions of the research which has been conducted on the use of power or the resolution of conflict by using either the permissive or authoritarian method and, in general, the most positive findings are that the authoritarian method may be necessary for situations requiring emergency action and that the permissive method may foster creativity. By comparison, the pitfalls of using either method are numerous. The major limitations of the authoritarian method are that (a) the teacher will run out of power as the student gets older and (b) power is destructive to students because they will learn to evaluate themselves negatively and develop defensive coping mechanisms such as rebellion and conformity (Gordon, 1974).

Gordon (1974) suggests that limitations for the permissive method are similar in that the teacher will "develop defensive coping mechanisms" such as retaliating by "springing pop quizzes," "escaping through heavy drinking and compulsive eating, and so on" (p. 212).

According to Gordon (1974), the alternative to these power oriented approaches is for both the teacher and the student to join together in a search for a solution that is acceptable to both. In this way no one loses and both win. This approach has been used successfully to resolve conflicts in almost every other relationship, for example, marriages, partnerships, labor-management relationships, and so on, where no power differential exists. The following is an example of how to use the no-lose method for resolving conflicts.

No-Lose Method

Mrs. Denst: John, I can't finish my sentences or answer other questions when you talk out. I feel frustrated.

John: But, I've got to ask questions or I won't understand what to do.

Mrs. Denst: Oh, I see. Your feel that in order to understand the assignment, you need to ask questions.

John: Yes, I never feel like I've quite got it, unless I ask a question or two.

Mrs. Denst: It sounds to me like you're afraid you're going to miss something important unless you interrupt me to ask a question and yet I feel like I need to complete my sentences and give the others time to ask their questions too. Sounds like we have a problem here.

John: Yeah?

Mrs. Denst: Do you have any ideas how we could solve the problem so we'd both be happy?

John: Well maybe when I have questions, I should raise my hand, but I'm afraid you'd forget me.

Mrs. Denst: I see, you'd feel okay raising your hand if you were sure I'd call on you.

John: Yeah.

Mrs. Denst: Okay, how would it be if I called the names of everyone who raised their hand, so you'd know I'd get to you, for example, I'd say, "Okay, John has a question, Fred has a question," and so on.

John: Then I'd know you saw me and I'd get to ask my question before you started talking about something else.

Mrs. Denst: That's right. Then you wouldn't be afraid I might miss you and I'd get to complete my sentences and everyone would have time to ask questions.

John: I'd like that.

In this example, the teacher needed to use the skill of active listening and sending I-messages to make sure her situation was understood but also to find out what the student's needs were. When the needs of both were known, it was not difficult to find a solution that was satisfactory to both. Here is an additional example.

Mrs. Smith: When you don't bring your textbook to my class, you don't have the application activities at the back of each chapter, and I have to take my time to write them on the board just for you. I feel tired of doing that.

Janice: Well, I forget to bring it because the only time I get to see Steve (boyfriend) is after math class and the walk to my locker takes too much time. That's why I don't bring it.

Mrs. Smith: I understand, you feel that you really need to see Steve and you can't see him and get the book from your locker in the time between classes.

Janice: Yes, well I know this class is important and I want to get to class on time, but Steve is my first real boyfriend. You know?

Mrs. Smith: You really would like to be here on time, but seeing Steve is more important for you right now because you haven't had a boyfriend before.

Janice: Yes.

Mrs. Smith: Okay Janice, I can understand why you're late, but that's not really my problem. What's bothering me is having to write the application activities on the board. When you're late, I have to stop what I'm doing and give you the assignment. I don't want to do that anymore. Do you have any idea how we might solve this problem?

Janice: Well, what if I brought my book into your class before math class. I always go by my locker then and that way I wouldn't have to go all the way back there and I could see Steve.

Mrs. Smith: I don't see anything wrong with that. If you bring the book to me before math class, I'll take the responsibility of holding it for you until you get here. It will be on the right-hand corner of my desk.

Janice: I'll come in quietly, get it, and sit down.

Mrs. Smith: Okay, it's a deal. See you tomorrow.

In this case the student came up with the solution. Gordon (1974) explains that it does not matter who provides the solution, just that the solution is acceptable to both. Again, Gordon (1974) emphasizes the need to shift between sending I-messages and active listening and lists the following six well tested scientific problem-solving steps that lead to the resolution of conflict.

1. Defining the problem
2. Generating possible solutions
3. Evaluating the solutions
4. Deciding which solution is best
5. Determining how to implement the decision
6. Assessing how well the solution solved the problem. (p. 228)

Additionally, before teachers can use this method successfully in class they must somehow communicate to their students that they are trying a new method and that they will not use their power. Finally the no-lose method for resolving conflicts can be used with (a) individual students to resolve conflicts, (b) several students to resolve conflicts between students, and (c) the class as a whole to establish classroom rules and policies (Gordon, 1974).

Summary

Effective teachers possess interpersonal skills. These skills have been largely derived from the humanistic conceptual model and have been developed by counselors in their counseling work with clients in therapy. Several of the most important interpersonal skills have been interpreted and operationalized for teachers for use in the classroom. These skills show teachers how to be empathetic, demonstrate positive regard, and remain authentic or congruent. The interpersonal characteristics of empathy and positive regard can be operationalized and put into practice by learning how to either reflective listen or active listen or make interchangeable statements. Each of these skills involves listening and mirroring or feeding back the content of what students feel and mean. One way for teachers to operationalize the interpersonal characteristic of congruence or authenticity is to send I-messages when students are exhibiting behaviors that are problematic to teachers. To do this, the teacher must communicate accurately in a nonthreatening way exactly which student behaviors are annoying and have tangible and concrete impact. Using the skills of active listening and sending I-messsages in combination can resolve conflicts in the classroom.

Review Questions

1. On what conceptual model are interpersonal skills interventions based?
2. What two very similar interpersonal skills do Gordon and Carkhuff teach?
3. What technique has Gordon proposed that seems to ensure that teachers are congruent when they have problems?
4. How can you contrast Gordon's active listening with Carkhuff's interchangeable statement?
5. Why does Gordon believe it is important to determine problem ownership?
6. What does Gordon believe the second five roadblocks to communication communicate to students?
7. How would you describe the process of active listening?
8. Why does Carkhuff believe you should complement feeling with meaning in the interchangeable statement?
9. What are the three components of an I-message?
10. What does the student have to understand for I-messages to be effective?
11. Why is it sometimes necessary to shift from I-messages to active listening?
12. Why is it inappropriate to use authoritarian methods to resolve conflict?

13. How does Gordon suggest teachers resolve conflict?

14. What are some additional uses for the no-lose method?

Learning Activities

1. Divide into groups of either 8 or 10 and generate 10 feeling words for the categories of happy, sad, angry, scared and confused. The feeling words are to be arranged in order of intensity. Each group is to present its feeling words to the class so that the other groups can add to their list any feeling words they do not have.

2. Divide your small group into dyads. One student is to role-play the student, while the other role-plays the teacher. Students are to select either to active listen (Gordon, 1974) or to complement feeling with meaning (Carkhuff et al., 1977). Each dyad is to rotate every 10 minutes. The first rotation is to be between role playing the teacher and the student. The second rotation is to be between active listening and complementing feeling with meaning. Each student is to have an opportunity to role-play both the teacher and the student and to practice using both listening techniques.

3. Divide into groups of 8 or 10 and generate 20 problem situations which would clearly represent teacher-owned problems, for example, a student mumbles obscenities under his breath during seat work activity. Present these situations to the class so that other groups can add to their list situations they do not have.

4. Number each of the above problem situations so that all groups can identify each situation by number. Divide your small group into dyads. Each dyad is to jointly write an I-Message (Gordon, 1974) for each problem situation. All dyads present their I-Message for each situation to the class, one situation at a time, that is, all dyads present their I-Message for problem situation number one before going on to problem situation number two. The class is to comment and/or discuss each dyad's I-Message. Consensus is sought regarding the most effective I-Messsage.

7
Behavioral Interventions

T he behavioral interventions discussed in this chapter are based largely on (a) the work of B. F. Skinner, (b) I. Pavlov, and (c) J. Wolpe. As well known behaviorists, Skinner, Pavlov, and Wolpe established principles and methodologies that have been transferred to many applied situations, including the classroom. Although Skinner, Pavlov, and Wolpe are all behaviorists, the principles and methods of Pavlov and Wolpe are based on the paradigm of respondent conditioning, whereas the methodologies of Skinner are based on the paradigm of operant conditioning. This chapter, therefore, begins with a discussion of the two major paradigms of operant and respondent conditioning. Next, the major behavioral approaches to defining and measuring behavior are described. Third, the methods of recording and displaying data are outlined. Finally, numerous operant and respondent strategies are described.

Respondent Conditioning Paradigm

The well known and now prototypic respondent conditioning experiment, of conditioning a dog to salivate upon the presentation of a ringing bell, was conducted by Ivan Pavlov. After repeatedly pairing the bell (the neutral stimulus) with meat powder (the uncon-ditioned stimulus), the dog learned to salivate (conditioned response) when the bell (the newly conditioned stimulus) was presented alone. Pavlov called this stimulus pairing procedure respondent or classical conditioning. Figure 7-1 illustrates this prototypic experiment.

Earlier in 1920 Watson and Raynor conducted a similar experiment with an 11-month-old infant named Albert to demonstrate empirically that some fears could be learned conditioned responses. Prior to the beginning of the experiment, these investigators established that Albert was not particularly afraid of anything except two events which would reliably make him afraid. These were the loss of support and loud noises. Because loud noises would frighten Albert, Watson and Raynor designed their experiment so that a stimulus pairing was made to occur between a loud noise and a white rat. After several stimulus pairings, Albert learned to be afraid. Figure 7-2 illustrates this experiment.

Behaviorists who view learning as the result of respondent con-ditioning believe that children with emotional or behavioral disorders acquire many of their fears and anxieties through the same mechanisms of learning by which Pavlov's dog learned to salivate upon the presentation of the bell and Albert learned to be fearful when presented with a white rat. For example, behaviorists believe that some children who have school phobia learn to fear school because the school environment, initially a neutral stimulus, got paired

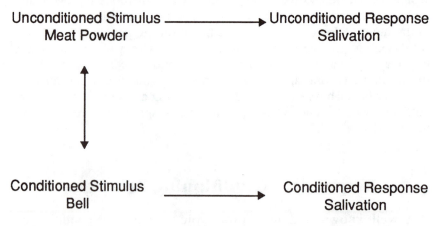

Figure 7-1. An illustration of Pavlov's prototypic classical conditioning experiment.

Unconditioned Stimulus   Unconditioned Response

Loud Noise   Fear

Conditioned Stimulus   Conditioned Response

Furry Rat   Fear

Figure 7-2. Watson and Raynor's classic experiment. An illustration of a respondently conditioned fear.

with an aversive unconditioned stimulus such as a severe reprimand or paddling. Eventually, the school itself causes fear. Figure 7-3 illustrates how respondent conditioning may result in a school phobia.

Operant Conditioning Paradigm

Behaviorists who support the operant conditioning point of view explain that responses that have received reinforcement increase in

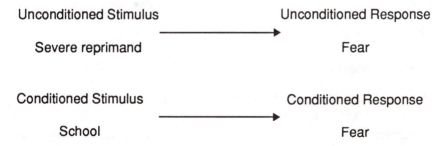

Unconditioned Stimulus   Unconditioned Response

Severe reprimand   Fear

Conditioned Stimulus   Conditioned Response

School   Fear

Figure 7-3. An illustration of how a school phobia may be acquired through respondent conditioning.

frequency and strength. B. F. Skinner conducted an operant conditioning experiment with pigeons to demonstrate that behaviors can
become conditioned quite accidentally. In this experiment, a pigeon
was placed in an experimental chamber and delivered grain at the
end of every 15-second interval independently of whatever response
occurred. The pigeon learned to emit responses, which immediately
preceded the delivery of reinforcement. Skinner demonstrated that
contingencies of reinforcement produce behaviors which have not
been consciously designed. Figure 7-4 illustrates Skinner's experiment.

Behaviorists who view learning as the result of operant
conditioning believe that children with emotional problems acquire
certain responses through the same mechanisms of learning as those
by which the pigeon's responses were accidently learned. For
example, a child who is afraid of falling and who appears uncoordi-
nated may have acquired these two overlapping deficiencies because
of past episodes of falling, which became inadvertently reinforced by
the attention of those around him. Figure 7-5 illustrates how operant
conditioning may result in a falling phobia.

Definition and Measurement

After outlining the two principal behavioral paradigms of learning
which support a wide variety of behavioral interventions, the major
behavioral approaches to measurement which underlie these
interventions are described below.

Defining Behavior

Behaviorists are concerned with defining behavior accurately. To
avoid confusion, behaviorists insist on objective descriptions of be-

Pigeon Response   Accidental Reinforcement
                    ——————————————————▶
Head Tossing   Grain

Figure 7-4. An illustration of Skinner's accidental conditioning experiment.

Response   Accidental Reinforcement
                    ——————————————————▶
Falling   Solicitous Attention

Figure 7-5. An illustration of how accidental reinforcement may condition falling.

havior and the avoidance of general labels, for example, "anxiety," when the objective for the student is to change a behavior so that it will occur more or less often. In this way teacher attention can be directed toward a behavior which is objective and measurable, and goals can be established based on the attainment of specific targets or terminal behaviors. An example of a behavioral definition might read as follows.

> Anxiety is operationally defined as hand wringing in which both of the hands come into contact with one another so that at least one of the hands clasps, grabs, squeezes, or twists the other. The hands must be in contact for at least 2 seconds. Such contact is mutually exclusive with clapping and/or praying, such that these behaviors are not to be included in this definition.

Characteristics of Behavior

In writing definitions of behavior, it is helpful to be aware of certain characteristics of behavior which may be useful in formulating the behavioral definition. Common characteristics include: (a) frequency, (b) duration, (c) latency, (d) magnitude, and (e) topography. Following is a brief definition and description of each of these characteristics.

Frequency

The frequency of an event refers to the number of times the event occurs per unit of time. For example, you might be interested in how frequently a student talked out every hour. If a student talks out 15 times every hour, you would know not only this, but also that his talk out rate assumed the ratio of 1 to 4 or 25%.

Duration

The duration of an event refers to either (a) the length of time the event lasted, (b) the length of time the event must last for it to be counted as a behavior, or (c) the length of time which must exist between responses to begin counting the next response as a new and discrete one. An example of the length of time the event lasted might be how long a student looks at his reading material before getting distracted and looking away from his assignment. An example of how long an event must last for it to be counted as a behavior might be defining a task as having to occur for at least 20 seconds. Finally, an example of the use of duration for determining the length of time which must exist between responses, might be to count "hand flapping" (a response often emitted by autistic children in which the hands move back and forth very rapidly) as a separate response only if it followed a prior response by at least 3 seconds.

Latency

Latency refers to either (a) the time between a stimulus and a completed response, for example, when a teacher asks her class to get their workbooks out, latency would be the time between the instruction and the student compliance or (b) the time that must pass to satisfy a behavioral definition before the behavior can occur, for example, when a student is asked to remember lines from a play, he may initially practice, after reading several lines, by waiting at least 1 minute before trying to recall his lines.

Magnitude

Magnitude refers to the intensity of a response. Noise levels in classrooms have been defined in terms of magnitude and recorded electrically by mechanical devices which are activated according to noise levels and measured in decibels. Also, biofeedback interventions define responses in terms of magnitude when attempting to control hypertension, galvanic skin response, finger temperature, muscle tension, and brain-wave frequencies.

Topography

The topography of a behavior refers to the physical components of a behavior or to the movements of the behavior in relation to the surrounding space. For example, eating from a fork requires a different topography than eating with one's hands. Most definitions of behavior include topography either implicitly or explicitly.

Categories of Measurement

Behavioral measurement can be classified as measurements of either (a) a permanent product which has been generated by a machine or

(b) a permanent product which has been generated by either a teacher or a student. In both categories these products are permanent; however, in the first category the product is automatically generated by machine, whereas in the second category the products are generated by humans and are not automatic.

Permanent Product Generated by a Machine

In certain situations, it is possible to use mechanical devices to measure behavior. Some schools have installed clocks in lunch rooms on which the hands are automatically set forward to reduce the recess period when volume levels as measured in decibels reach high levels. Some toilet training programs have relied on mechanical devices to sound alarm systems which signal trainers when urination occurs. In any case, mechanical devices provide the permanent records as products that can be used to provide important and useful data.

Permanent Product Generated by Humans

In most situations, permanent products are generated by humans. Sometimes, students leave things behind which they have generated that can be counted by at a later time. Examples of this include completed puzzles, number of correctly written spelling words, beads strung, and so on. These are considered as student permanent products because students leave records of their behavior. Sometimes students do things which leave no record of the behavior unless teachers make the record. Examples include talk outs, out of seats, correctly articulated "s" sounds, and so on. These are considered as teacher permanent products because teachers record student behavior into a permanent product.

How to Express Data

All data are expressed in some unit of measurement. For example, length is expressed in inches, feet, yards, and so on. These are some of the units of measurement in which length is expressed. All of the units in which a measurement is expressed are referred to as datum, and the specific numeral used in the expression is the data. For example, in the expression "the length is 5 yards," "5" is the data and "yards" is the datum. Similarly, behaviorists have units of measurement or datum in which to express data, the most common datum used by behaviorists are count, rate, and percent.

Count

Count is the simplest datum and refers to how many responses were made, or how long each response lasted or the time between responses. It is considered the simplest datum because nothing is done to alter the data to make it more useful, that is, the data are simply counted.

Rate or Frequency

Rate or frequency refers to how many responses were made per some unit of time, that is, when data are altered by expressing them in relation to time, the data are said to be expressed in rate or frequency datum.

Percent

The behaviorist unit of measurement of percent has the same meaning that it would have for nonbehaviorists. It is simply a summary of the relation of one event to another, for example, Johnny spent 50% of recess period playing.

Recording Data

The selection of a method for recording data is dependent on: (a) the behavioral characteristic being measured, (b) the precision of the measurement required and (c) the practicality of using a particular method. Some methods of recording data require that the observation be continuous so there is no break in recording during the times that are established for recording. Other methods do not require continuous observation, that is, they are discontinuous because these methods mandate that observations occur at certain predetermined times. The continuous methods of recording are: (a) frequency recording, (b) duration, and (c) interval recording. The discontinuous methods of recording are: (a) time sampling and (b) task sampling.

Frequency Recording

Frequency recording simply requires measuring the amount of time when recording begins and ends and tallying or marking each occurrence of responding, for example, the number of talk outs, hits, hand raises, out of seats, and so on. The responses recorded are usually discrete or of short duration and are often referred to as events.

Duration Recording

Duration recording requires measuring how long a response lasts, for example, out of seat, on task, a tantrum, and so on. The responses recorded are usually of variable duration.

Interval Recording

Interval recording requires dividing a session into a number of small intervals and recording the presence or absence of responding in each interval. In interval recording the intervals in which responding occurred are recorded, for example, the teacher determines in how many intervals tantruming occurred. In the case of interval recording, intervals are recorded and not responses, for example, the teacher might divide a 50-minute session into ten 5-minute intervals and count tantruming as having occurred in 8 out of 10 intervals. There are two variations of interval recording: (a) partial interval recording and (b) whole interval recording. In partial interval recording the teacher counts the interval regardless of whether a response occurs many times within the interval or just once. In whole interval recording, the teacher only counts the interval when a response has lasted for at least the duration of the interval. Obviously, more intervals will be counted using the partial interval method of interval recording. In general, the partial interval method is used to measure inappropriate behavior, whereas the whole interval method is used to measure appropriate behavior.

Time Sampling

Time sampling is much like interval recording in that sessions are divided into intervals. The difference, however, is that each interval is sampled at predetermined times, for example, the teacher might divide a 50-minute session into ten 5-minute intervals and check for responding during the last 30 seconds of the interval. If responding occurs during this last 30-second sampling period, the interval is counted. In time sampling, there is a trade off between accuracy and freeing up the teacher to do other things. Obviously, the advantage of time sampling over interval recording is that constant observation is not required. The disadvantage of time sampling is that the periods of nonobservation will distort the data somewhat.

Task Sampling

Task sampling requires that the teacher either: (a) determine whether a student can complete a task correctly or not or (b) collect data on the performance of a task that is comprised of graduated steps. The first type of task sampling is helpful in assessing the progress of students in mastering various tasks. The second type of task sampling is useful in assessing how well students are able to master subcomponents or subskills of a task. This latter type of task analysis is also helpful in determining the degree to which tasks have been appropriately fractioned down. It can be used to make decisions about which subcomponents of the task need to be further fractioned into subskills.

Displaying Data

After recording data, it is necessary to display it so that it can be interpreted readily. Baseline trends and clinical teaching designs facilitate the interpretation of data.

Baselines and Trend Projections

Baselines are a record of the operant or pre-treatment levels of a behavior. Prior to intervention, it is helpful to record several sessions of baseline data to determine whether the student's behavior shows movement which is therapeutic, countertherapeutic, or stable. This can be accomplished by doing a trend projection. Behavioral trends are determined by looking at the six most recent data points and placing a plus sign at the second highest point for the first three sessions and also at the second highest point for the second three sessions. A straight line is connected between these marks and extended to show the predicted level of behavior over subsequent sessions (Haring, Liberty, & White, 1980). A baseline trend is said to be stable if it meets some criterion of stability over a specified period of time, for example, a baseline trend of behavior may be deemed stable if for any 6 days it does not vary from the mean of behavior for those 6 days by more that 15%. A baseline trend is viewed as therapeutic if either: (a) the trend is ascending when the purpose of intervention is to increase the frequency of the behavior or (b) the trend is descending when the purpose of intervention is to decrease the frequency of the behavior. Conversely, a baseline trend is said to be countertherapeutic if either: (a) the trend is ascending when the purpose of intervention is to decrease the frequency of the behavior or (b) the trend is descending when the purpose of intervention is to increase the frequency of the behavior. Figure 7-6 illustrates a trend projection which indicates that behavior is changing in a therapeutic direction.

In Figure 7-6, Tim's behavior is changing in a therapeutic direction. By extending the trend line, the teacher is able to predict that Tim should be getting 9 out of 10 words correct and functioning in spelling at a 90% performance criterion by about the 12th day.

Clinical Teaching Design

Although many behaviorists recommend that classroom teachers use single-subject experimental designs, an evaluation design referred to as an A-B design or a clinical teaching design is more practical. Baseline and intervention data are collected and displayed in two phases: (a) a baseline phase and (b) an intervention phase. The data for both phases are evaluated visually to determine whether the treatment phase has been therapeutic. A graph displaying baseline and intervention data in a clinical teaching design is illustrated in Figure 7-7. By using this design, teachers are able to monitor the student's behavior continuously and to make intervention modification accordingly. The graph for this data should include a label for both the horizontal and vertical axes, a dashed line separating the baseline and intervention phases, and data points with a connecting line. The connecting lines should not be drawn across the dashed line separating phases.

A Therapeutic Trend Projection

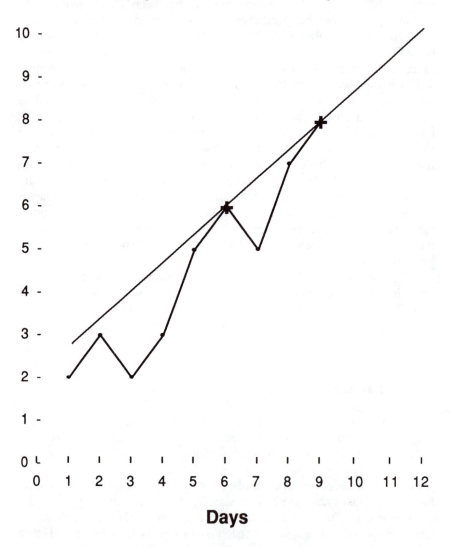

Days

A baseline record of Tim's daily spelling performance

Figure 7-6. An illustration of the use of baseline data to conduct a trend projection.

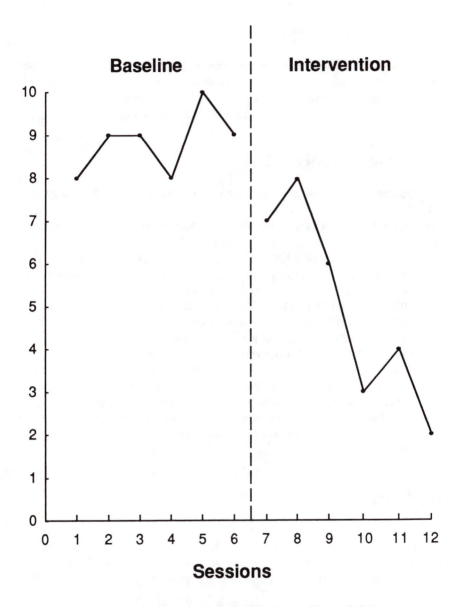

Sessions

An illustration of a Clinical Teaching design showing baseline and intervention

Figure 7-7. Clinical teaching design. An illustration of a clinical teaching design including baseline and intervention phases.

Respondent Strategies

There are several respondent strategies which have been shown to be effective in working with children who have emotional or behavioral problems such as anxiety or fear. They are: (a) respondent extinction, (b) graduated extinction, and (c) counterconditioning.

Respondent Extinction

Respondent extinction requires that children who exhibit negative emotional responses, for example, fear and anxiety, be exposed repeatedly to the specific negatively conditioned stimulus (the fear situation or stimulus), which evokes the fear. This should be continued until the stimulus gradually loses its capability to evoke the conditioned negative emotional response (the fear). In theory, a sufficiently lengthy exposure to the feared situation should diminish its potency to such an extent that the fear would virtually disappear. For example, a child with an irrational fear of cats should theoretically lose this fear after being sufficiently exposed to cats, because the response of fear would undergo extinction. Because reinforcement would be intentionally withheld from the fear response at a time when the fear was being deliberately made to occur by the presence of the cat, the fear response should decrease in frequency and strength. Eventually the presence of a cat would no longer be able to produce the fear reaction it once had. Figure 7-8 illustrates respondent extinction.

Graduated Extinction

In practice, because of the maximization of fear which would occur as the result of forcing a phobic child to remain in the presence of a negatively conditioned stimulus, an alternative procedure called graduated extinction is used instead. In applying this procedure, the

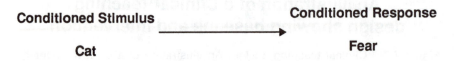

Conditioned Stimulus ———————▶ **Conditioned Response**

Cat   **Fear**

Figure 7-8. An illustration of presenting a conditioned stimulus repeatedly until its conditioned response undergoes extinction.

conditioned stimulus is attenuated by either: (a) modifying the distance of the conditioned stimulus to the negative emotional response or by (b) modifying the features of the conditioned stimulus in a graduated sequence.

Modifying the Distance From the Conditioned Stimulus

In the example in which a child experienced a cat phobia, the child might be presented with a view of the cat, and the two would be separated by quite a distance. At first, through a graduated sequence of steps, the child would be encouraged to move closer to the cat. With each adjustment the discomfort to the child must be relatively minor, and all discomfort must subside before graduating to the next step in the hierarchical sequence of distance. Figure 7-9 illustrates a hierarchy in which the distance from the conditioned stimulus is gradually changed.

1. **Looking at a picture of a cat in a magazine**

2. **Looking a cats play on television**

3. **Looking at cats fight on television**

4. **Looking at neighbor's cat play behind the fence in their yard**

5. **Looking at cats play in my yard**

6. **Looking at a cat being held by a friend**

7. **Petting a cat being held by a friend**

8. **Playing with a cat with a friend**

9. **Playing with a cat alone**

Figure 7-9. An illustration of a hierarchy for use in graduated extinction in which the distance from the conditioned stimulus is modified gradually.

Modifying the Features of the Conditioned Stimulus

For this example, public speaking anxiety is used as the negatively conditioned emotional response problem. To use graduated extinction, the features of the conditioned stimulus must be modified. To do this, the teacher might initially ask the anxious student to speak in an empty classroom. A typical modification of the conditioned stimulus that might follow would include: (a) the presence of the teacher, (b) the teacher and a friend, (c) the teacher and several friends, and finally (d) the original conditioned stimulus of speaking in front of the entire class. In this example, the graduated set of requirements diminish the fear of speaking in public by removing most of the features of the fear-evoking stimulus in the beginning and then by gradually adding these back sequentially upon observing a reduction in the fear response. Again, as with the modification of distance, the teacher would ensure with each modification that the discomfort to the child was relatively minor and would make certain that all discomfort subsided before adding another feature of the conditioned stimulus. Figure 7-10 is an illustration of a hierarchy in which features of the conditioned stimulus are gradually modified.

Counterconditioning

Counterconditioning requires that a child who is experiencing anxiety learn how to exhibit an anxiety antagonistic response, such as relaxation, during times when the feared or anxiety-evoking stimulus is present. For example, a student might use a relaxation technique, such as picturing a pleasant scene while speaking in public. However, for counterconditioning to occur, the teacher must make certain that the relaxation response is stronger than the anxiety response.

Like graduated extinction, this intervention is most effective when exposure to the anxiety eliciting stimulus occurs gradually through either: (a) modifying the distance of the eliciting stimulus to the child or (b) modifying the features of the stimulus presented. In this way, the student is able to become fully relaxed before graduating to the next step in the hierarchy. The principal difference, however, between graduated extinction and counterconditioning, is that in counterconditioning, the child is first taught how to exhibit an appropriate anxiety antagonistic response such as relaxation. Training the child to do this often takes several separate sessions. Also, it is helpful to train the child how to be able to produce the anxiety antagonistic response rapidly, so that during future training sessions,

1. **Preparing notes to speak in front of the entire class**

2. **Using notes to speak in an empty room**

3. **Using notes to speak in a room with a close friend as the audience**

4. **Using notes to speak in a room with three friends as an audience**

5. **Using notes and standing behind a podium to speak to five friends**

6. **Using notes and standing behind a podium to speak to five strangers**

7. **Using notes and standing behind a podium to speak to ten strangers**

8. **Using notes and speaking to a room full of friends**

9. **Speaking without notes to a room of friends and strangers**

Figure 7-10. An illustration of a hierarchy for use in graduated extinction in which the features of a conditioned stimulus are modified gradually.

the focus can be on counterconditioning. When relaxation has been use as the anxiety antagonistic response, several techniques have been shown to have promise. These include the use of breathing exercises, listening to audio cassette tapes that emphasize relaxation, the visualization of pleasant imagery, and progressive relaxation exercises that emphasize tightening and relaxing certain muscles. Table 7-1 illustrates a relaxation narrative which can be used prior to counterconditioning to help teach the child how to relax and feel calm.

TABLE 7-1. An Illustration of a Narrative Used in Relaxation Training.

Begin by lying in a very comfortable position. Take a deep breath which will help you relax your body. Then let your breath out again. You will notice that your body is beginning to relax and letting go of tension. Now focus your vision on some place in the room that's nice to look at. And as your body is comfortable and your eyes are focused, continue to focus your eyes, concentrating on the place that you have chosen in the room. Now as you continue to concentrate by focusing on a place in the room, your body will continue to relax more, and eventually your vision will begin to blur. As you feel the need to blink, allow yourself to blink long and slowly. Keep your eyes as comfortable as possible until your eyelids begin to press closed, on their own, in a very natural way. As you continue to concentrate, while keeping your mind from wandering to other thoughts and feelings, your thoughts will begin slowing down, letting your mind relax and narrowing your focus and allowing your vision to blur, so that a sense of sleepiness, drifting, and drowsiness can be felt. This will help your body continue to relax and soon you will notice that your eyelids begin to feel heavy and you may have a tendency to blink more. While you allow yourself to blink long and slowly, your eyelids will grow heavier and heavier. As you continue to concentrate by putting all your attention, as you relax now, into watching the place in the room, you'll develop a mental image, a picture in your mind, of the place that you're watching. The image will be so clear so that even when your eyes grow closed you'll still be able to imagine the place in the room in your mind. It will help you focus and continue to go into a deeper relaxed state of mind. This relaxed state of mind will help you listen and learn as your body becomes more and more relaxed. Notice the warm feeling of relaxation. You will find it more difficult to keep your eyes open as your vision begins to blur and your eyes grow heavier. Your eyelids will want to close and shut out the light, as you continue to relax. Your eyelids feel heavy, so very heavy. You may find it difficult now to hold them open, so let them go closed when they are ready. Your eyelids are getting heavier and heavier. You may feel a sense of listlessness now, a drowsy listless feeling. It's a very pleasant feeling. You feel so listless and drowsy, and so sleepy. Let yourself relax still more, so that a feeling of well-being can gradually come over you, as you continue to allow yourself to fall into a deep relaxed state of mind. You will let go of all everyday thoughts and all everyday feelings. Notice the feeling of relaxation throughout your body. You are just so very relaxed now, and it's okay to feel very relaxed. It can be so pleasant, just letting yourself go, drifting deeper and deeper into a more relaxed state of mind. You're going deeper with every breath, getting more and more relaxed . . . deeper and still deeper into an extremely relaxed deep state of mind. Because you are so relaxed, so deeply relaxed, you can begin to concentrate without effort. A creative part of your mind in some way takes over the task of concentration. You need pay attention only to my voice, and if your mind wanders now it doesn't matter, for your creative mind continues to listen, continues to think, and continues to learn. Now nothing

(continued)

TABLE 7-1. *(continued)*

else need matter to your mind. Nothing else will disturb you, as long as there is no need to be disturbed. In the event that it is necessary for you to be alert, your mind will respond. So let yourself relax completely now. Every muscle in your body is so limp and loose that you will notice a growing feeling of heaviness in your arms, in your legs, and perhaps over your entire body. You may also notice a tingling feeling here and there. Perhaps, you're experiencing a quiet pleasant bodily numbness and noticing that your breathing may be getting slower and more easy. Your breathing changes, slowly and easily, giving way to the drowsy feeling of sleep, relaxation, and of letting go completely. You're becoming more and more relaxed now. You are relaxed completely. Your entire body is letting go from the top of your head all the way down to your feet and toes. You are totally relaxed now, letting yourself drift into a completely relaxed and comfortable state of well being. You are relaxed completely now, both physically and emotionally. Notice how good if feels to relax. You are more relaxed now than you have been in a very long time. Now let your mind drift and as you let your mind drift easily and comfortably, explore your body and experience the feeling of relaxation. Just lie there and feel very relaxed and calm. I want you to stay this way for a little while longer and then I am going to count to five. When I reach five, you may open your eyes, feeling very calm and clear and refreshed. Just be comfortable and relaxed for a while, I'll begin counting very slowly. One . . . feeling very relaxed, two . . . very calm, three . . . very clear, four . . . very refreshed . . . and five . . . you may open your eyes and awaken.

Regardless of the anxiety antagonistic response selected, the task of the teacher must be to ensure that exposure to the fear-evoking stimulus occurs only during those times when the student is exhibiting a very strong anxiety antagonistic response. The most common counterconditioning intervention is called systematic desensitization, and the graduated sequence used to modify either the distance of the eliciting stimulus to the child or the features of the stimulus presented has been referred to as a desensitization hierarchy (Wolpe, 1973). The counterconditioning intervention can often be as effective imaginally as when employed in vivo. Sometime the intervention is begun imaginally and culminated in vivo. In any case, the teacher and the student should develop the hierarchy together, and the teacher must make certain that the student is not exposed to higher levels of the hierarchy until complete relaxation is evident in the presence of the conditioned stimulus at the current level of the hierarchy. When the intervention is conducted imaginally a self-reporting system must be used which enables the student to report to the teacher the degree to which he or she is relaxed. It is important that the reporting system not disrupt the specific procedure used for creating the anxiety antagonistic response. The usual reporting procedure is to ask the student to raise the appropriate number of fingers for the level of anxiety experienced, for example, zero fingers for no anxiety, one finger for mild, two fingers for moderate, and three fingers for maximum anxiety. A desensitization hierarchy for test anxiety that might be used either imaginally or in vivo is illustrated in Figure 7-11.

You are attending a regular class session.
You hear about someone else who has a test.
You are studying at home. You are reading a normal assignment.
You are in class. The teacher announces a major exam in two weeks.
You are home studying. You are beginning to review and study for a test that is a week away.
You are at home studying, and you are studying for the important test. It is not Tuesday and three days before the test on Friday.
It's Thursday night, the night before the exam on Friday. You are talking with another student about the exam tomorrow.
It's the night before the exam, and you are home studying for it.
It's the day of the exam, and you have one hour left to study.
It's the day of the exam. You have been studying. You are now walking on your way to the test.
You are standing outside the test room talking with other students about the upcoming test.
You are sitting in the testing room waiting for the test to be passed out.
You are leaving the exam room, and you are talking with other students about the test. Many of their answers do not agree with yours.
You are sitting in the classroom waiting for the graded test to be passed back by the teacher.
It's right before the test, and you hear a student ask a possible test question which you cannot answer.
You are taking the important test. While trying to think of an answer, you notice everyone around you writing rapidly.
While taking the test, you come to a question you are unable to answer. You draw a blank.
You are in the important exam. The teacher announces 30 minutes remaining but you have an hour's work left.
You are in the important exam. The teacher announces 15 minutes remaining but you have an hour's work left.

Figure 7-11. A desensitization hierarchy for text anxiety. From "Systematic desensitization of test anxiety in junior high students" by J.L. Deffenbacher and C.C. Kemper, 1974, *The School Counselor, 21,* 216-222. Copyright 1974 by American School Counselor Association. Reprinted by permission.

Group Counterconditioning

This intervention is similar to individual counterconditioning except the various stages are adapted for a group of approximately five to eight children who have the same fear. Hierarchy construction is conducted by the group, and the group decides which items are acceptable. Desensitization proper is geared to the group member who is slowest to progress through the imagined scenes. For example, if one child is experiencing anxiety over a specific imagined scene, the others in the group are told to continue relaxation or to imagine neutral scenes. While the rest of the group do this, the teacher goes through repeated presentation of the troublesome scene or returns to previously passed scenes until the child who is stuck can get through the problematic scene. Several studies have shown success in the use of this approach for treating school related problems, for example, text anxiety, speech anxiety and reading difficulties (Morris & Kratochwill, 1983).

Operant Strategies

Although behaviorists are generally concerned with stimulus events that occur both before and after responses, operant approaches to interventions more often focus on the manipulation of stimuli which follow or consequate responding. Because there are many operant strategies which rely on these stimulus consequences, the discussion of operant strategies begins by considering the stimuli that occur subsequent to responding and the procedures that make use of these stimulus consequences.

Primary Reinforcers

Some stimulus consequences are automatically reinforcing and do not depend on previous conditioning. These stimulus consequences are referred to as unconditional or primary reinforcers. For example, food and water are primary reinforcers because they automatically satisfy certain biological needs.

Secondary Reinforcers

Secondary reinforcers are not automatically reinforcing. Instead their reinforcing power is acquired by being paired with primary reinforcers. These reinforcers are also referred to as conditional reinforcers. Among the many secondary reinforcers available to teachers are attention, approval, and the opportunity to engage in desired behaviors.

Token Systems

A token system is based on the concept of secondary reinforcement. A token can be anything, for example, a chip, marble, or check mark that is earned for a desired behavior, saved, and then exchanged for a desired object or activity at a later time. The token becomes valuable because it becomes paired with other reinforcers. Token systems are excellent systems for handling most of the problems faced in a special education classroom. The token system provides a sort of psychological structure to classroom events by establishing uniform expectations which can help students develop a sense of purpose and responsibility.

Reinforcement

Reinforcement refers to a procedure in which a response produces a stimulus change that increases the probability that the response will occur more frequently. There are two types of reinforcement procedures, that is, positive reinforcement and negative reinforcement.

Positive Reinforcement

Positive reinforcement is defined as a procedure in which a response adds a stimulus consequence that increases the probability that the response will occur more frequently. For example, a hungry dog will learn to do a trick if each time it does the trick it is given a bite of food. In this example, the response is the trick and the added stimulus consequence which the trick or response produces is the bite of food.

Stimulus consequences or positive reinforcers that increase the frequency of behavior for some persons may have little or no effect on the behavior of other persons. A teacher may see that Janice works harder if told "You're doing great," whereas the same statement may cause Joe to quit working. The only way to tell whether a consequence is reinforcing for a particular individual is to try it out and observe its effect on the behavior it follows.

Negative Reinforcement

Negative reinforcement is defined as a procedure in which a response subtracts a stimulus consequence and as such increases the probability that the response will occur more frequently. For example teachers who have noisy students often inadvertently learn to raise their voices or shout if it stops the noise momentarily. In this example, the teacher's behavior is being inadvertently manipulated by students. The teacher response is shouting and the stimulus consequence which the shouting removes or subtracts is the noise. In the case of negative reinforcement, as in the case of positive reinforcement, the procedure increases the frequency of the behavior. However, in negative reinforcement, this increase is brought about by removing or subtracting a noxious or aversive stimulus. To identify additional examples of this procedure, think about situations in which a behavior subtracts or removes an aversive stimulus and increases its probable frequency. For example, people who are hot often remove the aversive heat by turning on the air conditioner or taking off clothing; because these actions subtract or remove the aversive condition of being hot, the probability of acting in these ways in the future, when it is hot, is increased.

Punishment

Punishment refers to a procedure in which a response produces a stimulus change that decreases the probability that the response will occur.

Positive Punishment

Positive punishment is a procedure in which a response adds a stimulus consequence that decreases the probability that the response will occur. For example, if a dog were swatted with a newspaper whenever it barked, it would learn to bark less frequently. In this example, barking is the response and the added stimulus consequence which the response produces is the newspaper swat.

Negative Punishment

Negative punishment is defined as a procedure in which a response subtracts a stimulus consequence that decreases the probability that the response will occur. For example, if Rodney lost 5 minutes of recess time whenever he talked out without requesting permission, he would probably learn to talk out less frequently. In this example, talking out is the response and the subtracted stimulus consequence which the response removes is recess.

In thinking about punishment some authors, for example, B. F. Skinner, contend that punishment is not simply the inverse of reinforcement. They argue that punishment depresses other behaviors in addition to the punished behavior and results in emotional or adjunctive responses. Others believe that both punishment and reinforcement operate on a continuum, that is, strong punishment (electric shock, spanking, and ridicule) as well as strong or very powerful reinforcement (winning a $6,000,000 lottery) result in similar emotional responses, for example, screaming, flushing, shedding tears, waving hands, increased heart rate, respiration, and so on. In any case, stimulus consequences which decrease responding in one person may have little or no effect on the behavior of other persons. As with reinforcement, the only way to tell whether a consequence is punishing for a particular individual is to try it out and observe its effect on the behavior it follows.

In addition, there is a great deal of evidence that teachers, in attempting to use positive punishment, fall into what Patterson (1980) has called the negative reinforcement trap. For example, a teacher who tries to use shouts and threats as punishers when her class is too noisy will get an immediate and very short-term suppression of the behavior at the time of punishment. This often will lead her to believe that her yells and threats were effective. However, when the noisy behavior returns shortly at higher levels, the same teacher will again respond by threatening and yelling, albeit with more intensity. Studies have shown that through this reciprocally interactive pattern, the teacher's behavior of yelling and threatening becomes negatively reinforced and increases in frequency, that is, the teacher's yelling behavior is negatively reinforced and increases in frequency because of the immediate, short lived, cessation of student noise. Because of this and the strong emotional responses associated with positive punishment, teachers must consider other approaches to eliminate inappropriate behaviors.

Operant Extinction

Operant extinction refers to the procedure of withholding the reinforcement from a previously reinforced response until the behavior rate decreases. For example, if every time Jimmy talks out without permission, and the teacher responds by answering his questions and by providing him with attention, the attention is probably the reinforcer. If the teacher decides at a later date to withhold this attention until Jimmy's talk outs decrease, and in fact they do decrease, the talk-out behavior has probably been decreased through operant extinction. In this situation, attention is the reinforcer and the teacher was able to withhold it from following the response until a response decrement was obtained. However, there are many situations in which teacher attention is not the reinforcer that's maintaining the inappropriate behavior. Many teachers confuse ignoring with extinction and simply ignore behavior, believing that they are using an extinction procedure. Many inappropriate behaviors, however, are maintained physiologically or by other aspects of the environment such as by student attention. To confuse ignoring with extinction in these situations can result in a serious error in which students are denied treatment under the misguided impression that a behavioral intervention is being provided.

Shaping

Shaping, or the method of successive approximations, is a method of teaching a behavior that has never been exhibited and that the individual cannot now exhibit. The method accomplishes this in an orderly manner starting with a behavior the individual can perform presently, which resembles the target behavior, then links, through a series of subsequent behaviors, the starting behavior with the target behavior. After the starting behavior is made to occur frequently, reinforcement is withheld from it and delivered to the next behavior in the link only, until this behavior occurs frequently. Once this behavior occurs frequently, reinforcement is withheld from it and delivered to the following behavior in the chain. This process continues until the target behavior occurs. For example, in teaching a child to print, the first approximation of the letter S is accepted and reinforced. Gradually as the student practices, he is required to make strokes which look much more like an "S" for the teacher to provide reinforcement. The reinforcement of the initial response, the reinforcement of each small step or approximation, and the continuing change in what is required for reinforcement to be provided are the principal elements that comprise the method of successive approximations or shaping.

Modeling

Modeling, or observational learning, is acquiring a response as the result of vicarious experience or observation. In modeling, the model does something and we copy it. For example, a young child hears language and learns to speak by copying it. Consequences delivered to the model or the absence of consequences will affect the observer's behavior, for example, models whose behavior is reinforced will be more likely to be imitated than models whose behavior is not reinforced. Bandura and Walters (1963) and Bandura (1977) have researched characteristics of the model and concluded that models are more likely to be imitated when:

1. They are of the same sex as the observer.
2. There is a similarity between the age of the model and the observer.
3. They are personable.
4. They receive positive reinforcment.
5. They are competent and have social status.
6. They have characteristics with which the observer can identify.

Schedules of Reinforcement

Schedules of reinforcement refer to the exact manner in which reinforcement is delivered according to the number of responses, time between responses, or both.

Continuous Reinforcement

Continuous reinforcement refers to a reinforcement schedule in which every desired response is reinforced, that is, every time a student emits the desired behavior she is reinforced. For example, every time Sharon raises her hand without talking out, she is reinforced by the teacher acknowledging her and answering or attending to her remarks. This is the best schedule to use to support the acquisition of new behaviors. It is the fastest way to establish new behaviors and the most effective schedule to use for shaping. In addition, a continuous schedule is always used in a punishment procedure.

Intermittent Reinforcement

Intermittent reinforcement implies that only certain responses are reinforced. It is the most effective schedule to use in maintaining behavior once sufficiently high rates have been established. Intermittent schedules are more resistant to extinction so that once reinforcement stops the behavior will persist longer than if it had been reinforced on a continuous schedule. There are numerous intermittent schedules of reinforcement of which four are the most basic.

Fixed Ratio (FR). A fixed ratio schedule which has been abbreviated as FR-2, indicates that reinforcement is delivered after every 2nd reponse. Other fixed ratio schedules might include an FR-10, FR-50, or an FR-100 which indicates that reinforcement is delivered after the 10th, 50th, and 100th response. FR schedules result in high rates of responding, with a pause after the delivery of reinforcement. For example, when a teacher asks a student to write the definition of five dictionary words and then provides reinforcement immediately after the five words are defined, the teacher is placing definition writing behavior on an FR-5. Under this schedule, the student will work rapidly and steadily until the 5 words are produced, consume his reinforcer, take a break, and then start on the next 5 words. Employers who require their workers to do piecework automatically produce worker behavior which typifies fixed ratio responding. Figure 7-12 is a cumulative record of FR responding.

Variable Ratio (VR). A variable ratio schedule which has been abbreviated VR-5, indicates that reinforcement is delivered on the average after every five responses, but that the actual number of responses required to produce reinforcement will vary each time. Other variable ratio schedules might include a VR-10, VR-50, or a VR-100 which indicate that on the average every 10th, 50th, or 100th response respectively will produce reinforcement. VR schedules result in high and steady rates of responding with no postreinforcement pause. For example, when a teacher asks a student to complete an intricate jigsaw puzzle and provides reinforcement on the average after every five pieces are placed correctly, the teacher is putting his behavior on a VR-5. Under this schedule, the student will work rapidly and steadily. This schedule is very resistant to extinction and as such is a good maintenance schedule. Figure 7-13 is a cumulative record of VR responding.

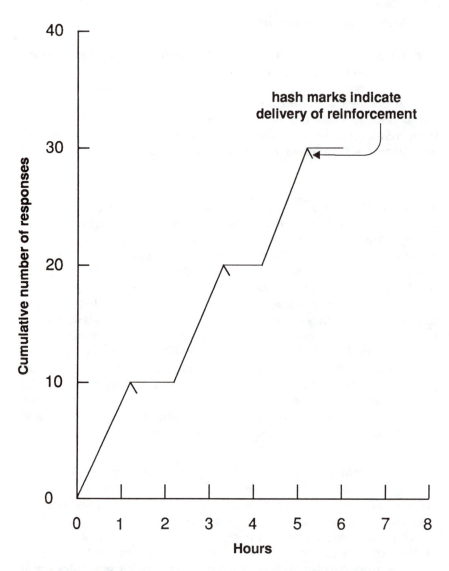

Figure 7-12. A cumulative record of fixed ratio responding.

Fixed Interval (FI). A fixed interval schedule which has been abbreviated FI-5 min. indicates that reinforcement will occur on the first response after 5 minutes have transpired. In this schedule, for a response to receive reinforcement, 5 minutes must first pass, after which the first response will get reinforced. Responses occurring prior to the end of the 5-minute interval will receive no reinforce-

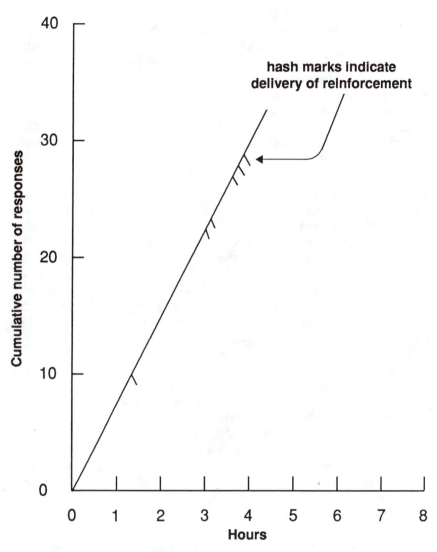

Figure 7-13. A cumulative record of variable ratio responding.

ment. Other fixed interval schedules might include a FI-10, FI-50, or an FI-100 which indicates that reinforcement will be forthcoming on the first response after 10, 50, or 100 minutes, respectively. FI schedules typically show scallop patterns, that is, after reinforcement there is an initially slow rate of responding which increases to a very high rate immediately prior to the end of the interval. For example, when a teacher assigns a term paper and allows students 8 weeks to complete it, the teacher is putting their behavior on an FI-8. Under this schedule, the student is likely to view the deadline as far away and will spend little time initially working on the term paper. Finally, as the due date approaches, the student will increase efforts until during the last few days, the student is frantically quadrupling output in order to produce a term paper worthy of a high grade. After the assignment due date has transpired and a new project is assigned, the behavior will all but cease and once again increase slowly in a scallop pattern as the next assigned due date arrives. Figure 7-14 is a cumulative record of FI responding.

Variable Interval (VI). A variable interval schedule which has been abbreviated VI-15 sec. indicates that reinforcement will occur on the first response after an average of 15 seconds have transpired. In this schedule, for a response to receive reinforcement, an average of 15 seconds must first pass, after which the first response will receive reinforcement. Other variable interval schedules might include a VI-10 sec, VI-50 min, or a VI-100 hrs, which indicate that reinforcement will be forthcoming on the first response after an average of 10 seconds, 50 minutes, or 100 hours, respectively. Variable interval schedules result in sustained responding at low rates. For example, when a teacher asks a student to keep his eyes on his reader and reinforces this every 15 seconds on the average, the teacher has placed looking behavior on a VI-15 sec. Under this schedule, the student will continue to look at the page in order to receive the reinforcement. The variable interval schedule is very resistant to extinction and as such is a good maintenance schedule. Figure 7-15 is a cumulative record of VI responding. In scheduling, it is best to start with a continuous schedule to establish a new behavior and to end with an intermittent schedule to maintain the behavior. Similarly, to achieve a high terminal ratio, it is important to raise the ratio gradually by starting with a low ratio and progressively introducing higher ones. **Straining the ratio** refers to the procedural error of making the ratio too high too quickly so that the responses extinguish. Shifting from a continuous to an intermittent schedule should be gradual, for example, a continuous schedule might be appropriately stretched to an FR-3, then to an FR-6, FR-10, FR-12, VR-5, VR-8, VR-10, and VR-15. When the ratio is accidently strained, simply shift back to a lower ratio and begin again.

Discrimination Training

Mona had been taught well. At dinner she would watch the dog food being poured into her bowl without moving toward it. In fact, once a

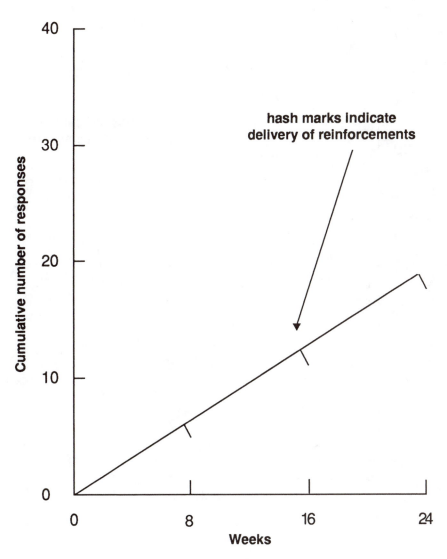

Figure 7-14. A cumulative record of fixed interval responding.

small child from across the street was given the responsibility of feeding her. The bowl was being filled with food and the food package returned to the cupboard. The process was taking so long that saliva was starting to form around Mona's mouth. Finally, the command "go" was given, but Mona remained motionless. The child looked at Mona's master. "Why doesn't she eat?" he asked. "You have to give the correct command" was the answer. Mona was all but

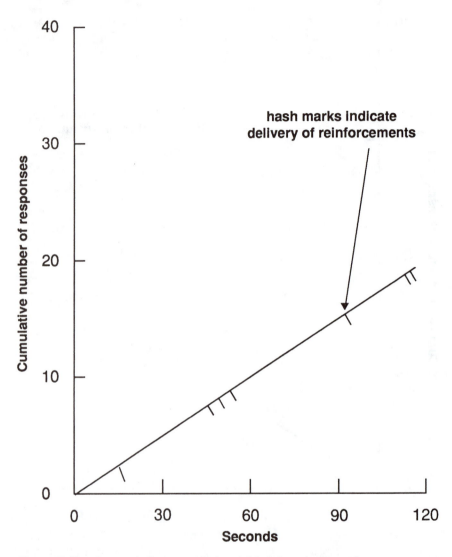

Figure 7-15. A cumulative record of variable interval responding.

salivating on the floor when she heard the word "Okay." This time Mona reacted immediately and consumed her dinner very quickly.

In the example above, Mona had learned to eat her dinner only on hearing the command "Okay." The behavior which Mona exhibited was brought about by a procedure referred to as the discrimination training procedure. This procedure consists of conditioning a response in the presence of one stimulus and extinguishing it in the presence of another stimulus. In the case of Mona, the procedure consisted of reinforcing Mona with food every time she sat still and waited for the command "Okay." When she moved toward the dish of food at any other time, she was purposely not reinforced with food, so that these approach responses would soon be extinguished. In the discrimination training procedure the stimulus with which reinforcement is associated is called the discriminative stimulus, for example, the word "Okay." The stimulus with which reinforcement is not associated is called a nondiscriminative stimulus, for example, any other word or action. The abbreviations for the discriminative stimulus and the nondiscriminative stimulus are S^D and $S^\triangle$ (pronounced ess delta) respectively. In many of the teaching techniques teachers use, the discrimination training procedure is implicit. For example, when teaching new vocabulary words, and expecting the student to be able to recognize the word and say it, the written vocabulary word is an S^D for the correctly spoken vocabulary word. Similarly, in teaching letters of the alphabet, numbers or the addition of numbers, and so on, what is set forth in writing becomes an S^D for the correct response.

Fading

Fading is a useful procedure in which the teacher attempts to increase the probability of success by using additional antecedent stimuli or cues to help students master a task. Fading refers to the gradual removal of these additional stimuli, for example, the teacher might decide to fade out such cues as directions, prompts, physical guidance, or any other S^Ds which have served their purpose. This author used fading to help a student with her basic addition facts.

Maria was placed in the author's charge because she had learned only six or seven of her addition facts. At the end of the year she would be entering junior high school, and it was generally agreed that an all-out effort should be made before she left for junior high. In the fading procedure used, numbers one through nine were given dots which occupied certain positions on each number. A chalkboard was supplied with all of the addition facts and Maria was asked to add these facts each session. Additionally, she was instructed to count the dots as the means for adding each problem. But as time progressed over sessions, the author faded the dots so that they became increasingly more difficult to make out. However, they also appeared to be less necessary because Maria became increasingly able to either solve the problem without the dots or seemed able to imagine where they had been placed and to add the imagined dots. Eventually she was able to solve each problem immediately. The dots were faded over approximately nine sessions, at the end of which Maria was able to complete 90 randomly presented basic addition facts in less than 5 minutes. Also, the author recorded that the total teaching time was less than 3½ hours. In the first phases of the intervention, the numbers were adorned with big obvious countable dots. During the middle phases the dots were not so apparent, and during the final phases the dots were completely gone. Figure 7-16 illustrates how the dots looked as they were gradually faded.

Fading is a useful technique that can be used in a variety of situations to help students acquire skills that would otherwise be too difficult for them.

Chaining

Chaining consists of linking steps or combining behaviors with other behaviors in a proper sequence. For example, in shoe tieing there are a number of steps that must be taught and placed in the proper sequence. Sometimes the chain is taught in a forward manner, for example, social skills, or in a backward manner, for example, dressing. When the chain is taught in a backward manner with the last step being taught first, the procedure is referred to as backward chaining. Feeding oneself is generally taught through backward chaining. To do chaining, the teacher must first sketch out the components of the chain. These are usually comprised of S^Ds and responses. For example, a stimulus response chain for shoe tieing may consist of the following:

S^D untied shoe

R wrap string *a* around string *b*

S^D string *a* wrapped around string *b*

R form string *a* into loop

S^D string *a* looped

R wrap string *b* around string *a*

S^D string *b* wrapped around sting *a* held in loop

R pull string *b* through hole under string *a*

S^D shoe tied

Each chain consists of a sequence of discriminative stimuli (S^Ds) and responses, and each response changes the environment. This changed

$$+\frac{2}{3} \quad +\frac{2}{3} \quad +\frac{2}{3} \quad +\frac{2}{3} \quad +\frac{2}{3} \quad +\frac{2}{3} \quad +\frac{2}{3} \quad +\frac{2}{3} \quad +\frac{2}{3}$$

Number one through nine were given dots which occupied certain positions on each number. The student did all of her basic addition facts during each session. The dots were faded over approximately nine sessions.

Figure 7-16. An illustration of the use of fading to teach addition facts.

environment then becomes an S^D for subsequent responses. Some investigators believe that the S^{D}s also become conditioned reinforcers for the responses that precede them. In any case, the chain terminates in some kind of reinforcement. The reinforcer may be artificial, for example, candy, or natural, for example, the satisfaction derived from completing the task. One of the advantages of chaining is that the teacher can use as many steps in a stimulus response chain as are necessary to teach the skill and can modify the chain at any point during the intervention. A second advantage is that the teacher can condition the terminal responses in the chain first and then the response that precedes it and so forth until the initial response is conditioned. For example, in teaching shoe tieing, the teacher could start with the shoe almost all tied and ask the student to complete the last component first by pulling string *b* through hole *a*. Once the student had mastered this terminal response, by repeating it several times, the teacher could then go backward in the chain and help her master the second-to-the-last step of wrapping string *b* around *a*. Each time the student completed this response, the teacher would also have her complete the terminal response. The teacher would proceed backward in this way until reaching the initial response and finally complete the entire chain. This backward chaining approach is successful in teaching many behaviors because conditioning the terminal response first makes the reinforcer at the end of the chain, for example, "Good, you tied your shoe," immediately available during the initial training phase of the intervention.

Combination Interventions

A number of interventions designed to eliminate inappropriate behavior have emerged as a result of combining many of the basic principles of behavior discribed. Center (1989) has organized and discussed the following interventions (pp. 85-88).

Differential Reinforcement of Other Behavior (DRO)

There are three types of DRO interventions which increase appropriate behavior so that there will be less inappropriate behavior.

Differential Reinforcement of Other Behavior—Incompatible (DRO-I).

DRO-I means differential reinforcement of an appropriate behavior incompatible with the deviant behavior, for example, keeping your hands on the desk and waving your hands in the air randomly cannot be engaged in at the same time. The teacher selects the incompatible behavior and, by increasing its frequency, correspondingly decreases the deviant behavior.

Differential Reinforcement of Other Behavior—Alternative (DRO-A).

DRO-A means differential reinforcement of an alternative and appropriate behavior, for example, raising your hand instead of talking out. In this intervention it is possible to engage in both of these behaviors simultaneously.

Differential Reinforcement of Other Behavior—Omission (DRO-O).

DRO-O reduces inappropriate behavior by reinforcing the omission or absence of inappropriate behavior. To begin, the teacher provides reinforcement for short periods of time in which the inappropriate behavior has not occurred and gradually lengthens the interval until the student can go for a long time without exhibiting the inappropriate behavior.

Differential Reinforcement of Low Rates of Behavior (DRL)

There are three types of DRL procedures in which the basic idea is to reinforce lower levels of the behavior.

Differential Reinforcement of Low Rates of Behaviors—Full (DRL-F).

DRL-F means setting an interval for a full session, such as a class period, and placing a ceiling on the behavior. If the behavior stays below the interval for the full session, the teacher reinforces the behavior. At the end of the session, the behavior either receives reinforcement or not, and the next session begins. For example, if the teacher wants fidgeting to stay below a certain level during a class session and it does, the student is reinforced at the end of the interval.

Differential Reinforcement of Low Rates of Behavior—(DRL-I). DRL-I means DRL using variable intervals. For this procedure the teacher sets an interval and sets a ceiling on a behavior, for example, the interval may be 20-minutes and the ceiling might be that the student cannot get out of his seat more than twice. If the student does not get out of his seat more than twice during the 20 minute period, reinforcement is provided and the interval starts over. If, however, the students gets out more than twice, no reinforcement is forthcoming and the interval starts over immediately after the level of behavior exceeded the ceiling. Intervals yielding reinforcement will all be equal and will be the length of the established interval. Intervals not yielding reinforcement will vary in length because a new interval will begin whenever the level of the behavior exceeds the ceiling.

Differential Reinforcement of Low Rates of Behavior—(DRL-S). DRL-S is DRL using spaced responding. This procedure is conducted by setting an interval for the length of time the teacher would like to see separate occurrences of the response. Responses separated by, for example, 5 minutes, get reinforced. For example, if a student asked too many questions, the teacher might respond to those questions which are spaced by at least 5 minutes from the last question and avoid responding to questions which are spaced by less than 5 minutes.

Overcorrection (OC)

There are three overcorrection procedures. These procedures have both an educational or corrective component as well as a punitive dimension.

Overcorrection Through Positive Practice—(OC-P). OC-P is accomplished by having a student practice repeatedly the correct rather than the incorrect way of doing something. For example, if a student always bumps into others when coming to sit in a reading circle, the teacher would have the student practice sitting in the reading circle appropriately 30 times for 2 seconds each for each occurrence of the inappropriate behavior.

Overcorrection Through Restitution—(OC-R). OC-R is accomplished by having a student overcorrect the effect produced by his inappropriate behavior. For example, if a student paints graffiti on a garbage can, the teacher might make him scrape off his graffiti as well as any other graffiti on the can.

Overcorrection Through the Full Use of Both Methods—(OC-F). OC-F is conducted by combining both OC-P and OC-R. For example, if a student uses another student's data disk and destroys some of the data while placing the diskette into the drive, the teacher may have the careless student type back all the missing data and practice 30 times the correct placement of data diskettes into drives.

Response Cost

There are three response cost procedures which decrease inappropriate behavior by taking away reinforcement when a student exhibits inappropriate misbehavior.

Response Cost Using Bonus Reinforcers (RC-B). RCB is accomplished by giving the student a certain number of reinforcers, usually in the form of tokens, free. The teacher then takes away a specified amount of reinforcers each time an inappropriate behavior occurs. When the day is over, the student can spend the remaining reinforcers or tokens.

Response Cost Combined with Earned Reinforcement (RC-C). This is essentially the same procedure as RC-B, except that in RC-C the reinforcers the teacher takes away on instances of inappropriate behavior were earned by the student usually for academic work or good conduct.

Response Cost Using a Transfer of Reinforcers (RC-T). RC-T can be used with either RC-B or RC-C because it does not matter whether the reinforcers were earned or given to the student. In RC-T, a specific number of reinforcers are transferred from a student who is behaving inappropriately to one who is behaving appropriately, on the occurrence of inappropriate behavior. Occasionally the student who loses his reinforcers will act aggressively toward the student to whom the reinforcers are transferred. Therefore, the teacher must consider carefully the potential effects of this procedure on the particular students involved.

Time-Out From Reinforcement (TO)

There are three ways to do TO procedures which are based on removing the opportunity to receive reinforcement.

Time Out From Earning Reinforcement (TO-E).   TO-E is accomplished by suspending the opportunity to earn reinforcement immediately following a misbehavior. For example, on the occurrence of an inappropriate behavior such as "talking to friends" the student would not be eligible to receive reinforcement for the next 10 minutes.

Time Out by Suspension of Spending or Consumption (TO-S).   TO-S is conducted by telling the student immediately following an inappropriate behavior that he or she cannot use the reinforcers for a specified period of time. If tokens are used and there are specified times for exchanging tokens for reinforcers, the suspension would be effective during the next exchange period.

Time Out by Isolation from Reinforcement (TO-I).   TO-I is accomplished by isolating the student from all sources of reinforcement for a brief time immediately after engaging in the inappropriate behavior. This procedure is usually associated with a time-out room. Isolation periods should be brief, for example, 5 to 10 minutes, and the student should not be removed from time out until calm.

Summary

The paradigms of respondent and operant conditioning have produced many principles and interventions. Many respondent conditioning strategies are based on the work of I. Pavlov and J. Wolpe, whereas many operant conditioning strategies are based on the work of B. F. Skinner. Many behavioral approaches to defining and measuring behavior underlie these interventions. Behavior is usually defined in terms of characteristics of behavior and recorded as a machine permanent product or a human permanent product. Data is expressed in count, rate, and percent datum and recorded either as continuous or discontinuous data. Data is displayed in baseline trends and clinical teaching designs so that it can be readily interpreted. Respondent strategies are helpful in working with children who have anxieties and fears. The most effective and useful respondent procedures are graduated extinction and counterconditioning. Operant strategies which make use of primary and secondary reinforcers and token systems rely on reinforcement, extinction, punishment, shaping, modeling, schedules of reinforcement, discrimination training, fading, and chaining. By combining elements of these strategies, combination interventions have been developed to eliminate inappropriate behavior.

These interventions include differential reinforcement of other behavior, differential reinforcement of low rates of behavior, over-correction, response cost, and time out.

Review Questions

1. How do proponents of respondent conditioning believe learning occurs?
2. How do proponents of operant conditioning believe learning occurs?
3. How does a neutral stimulus become conditioned?
4. How might fear be operantly learned?
5. Why do behaviorists operationally define behavior?
6. What is the frequency, duration, latency, magnitude, and topography of a behavior?
7. How can you differentiate between datum and data?
8. What are five methods of recording data?
9. What is the purpose of a clinical teaching design?
10. Why is graduated extinction generally preferred over respondent extinction?
11. How would you modify the features of the conditioned stimuli associated with test anxiety?
12. How can you distinguish between graduated extinction and counterconditioning?
13. How are secondary reinforcers acquired?
14. How can you differentiate between operant and respondent extinction?
15. What is shaping?
16. What kind of student behavior would a fixed ratio schedule produce?
17. What should you do if you accidently strain the ratio?
18. Why did Mona not eat her food on the command "go"?
19. What is the major advantage of the fading technique?
20. Why is backward chaining sometimes preferable to forward chaining?
21. What combination procedures would use interventions for increasing appropriate behavior to decrease inappropriate behavior?

Learning Activities

1. Divide into small groups of five to six and select three be-haviors to define, for example, talking out. Each definition is to

include observable properties of the behavior as well as examples of what is to be included and excluded so that little is left to judgment. Each group writes its three definitions on the blackboard for the class to discuss and refine.

2. Betty was observed by her teacher over a 7-day period during which she talked out the following number of times: 3, 4, 3, 2, 5, 6, and 9. The teacher then began an intervention. During this period talk outs were recorded as 3, 2, 2, 1, 1, and 1.

Individually test your understanding by completing the following activities:

    a. Graph the data points.
    b. Label the horizontal and vertical axes.
    c. Separate the data points into a baseline and intervention phase.
    d. Decide whether a talk out was defined?
    e. Decide what specific characteristic of behavior is emphasized in the description.
    f. Decide what kind of datum is most appropriate for the expression of the data.
    g. Select the specific method of recording for the behavior.
    h. Do a trend projection of the baseline phase and decide whether this trend is stable, therapeutic, or counter-therapeutic.
    i. Select three potentially appropriate specific interventions for Betty's problem behavior and describe in detail the components of the intervention. Include a rationale for the selection of the reinforcers or punisher to be used.

3. Divide into groups of five to six and select a phobia. Develop a hierarchy for the phobia that could be used with either the graduated extinction or counterconditioning intervention. Depending on the phobia selected, either modify the temporal, physical distance, or the number of stimulus features of the conditioned stimulus. Each group is to present its heirarchy to the class.

4. Divide into groups of five to six and decide on an academic or social behavior that you want to teach to a child. Design a shaping procedure for teaching this behavior. The procedure is to include: (a) a target behavior and (b) an initial behavior which resembles the target behavior and the "links" or intermediate behaviors which connect the initial behavior with the target behavior. Each group is to present its design to the class.

5. Divide into groups of five to six and decide on an academic or social behavior that you want to teach to a child. Design a discrim-

ination training procedure for teaching this behavior. Include a description of how the procedure will be undertaken as well as an explanation of the discriminative and nondiscriminative stimuli and the responses with which these are to be associated. Each group is to present its design to the class.

6. Divide into groups of five to six and decide on an academic or social behavior that you want to teach to a child. Design a fading procedure for teaching this behavior. Include a description of how the procedure will be conducted as well as an explanation of the stimuli or cues which will be added and later faded to help the student master the skill. Each group is to present its design to the class.

7. Divide into groups of five to six and decide on an academic or social behavior that you want to teach to a child. Design a chaining procedure for teaching this skill. Identify the linking stimuli and responses that make up the chain and provide a rationale for selecting to teach the behavior either through forward or backward chaining. Each group is to present its design to the class.

8

Cognitive Learning Interventions

In this chapter, the major concepts associated with cognitive learning approaches are identified first. Second, the major cognitive learning interventions, generally referred to as cognitive-behavior modification, which grew out of attempts to consolidate cognitive and behavioral psychology are discussed. Finally, the chapter culminates by discussing in detail Rational Emotive Therapy, an effective and practical cognitive learning intervention, which is based on the work of Ellis (1962, 1971, 1974, 1977, 1992).

Major Concepts

The three major concepts associated with all cognitive learning approaches are: (a) cognition influences emotions, behavior, physiology, or all three; (b) faulty cognition or errors in thinking can be identified; and (c) treatment can be directed to correct thinking errors and as such improve academic, psychological, and social functioning. Although it would seem obvious to the lay person that cognition is important to the acquisition of certain skills, research associated with respondent and operant conditioning (Kazdin, 1978; Murray & Jacobson, 1978) as well as with cognition in learning and psychological adjustment had to be conducted to establish how cognition affected skill acquisition. These investigations established that cognitive appraisals, self-talk, or verbal mediation influenced learning, psychological adjustment (Lazarus, 1966; Murray 1964), and autonomic functioning (Schacter, 1966). Once practitioners had begun to examine the relationship between: (a) cognition and emotions; (b) cognition and behavior; and (c) cognition, emotions, and behavior, only then were they able to identify cognitive or thinking errors that impeded learning and ultimately lead to direct treatment toward the modification of these errors. Although some of the treatment approaches which will be discussed differ historically, each intervention is designed to help children use verbal mediation to improve either their internal emotionality, their external behavioral repertoire, or both. Also, each approach lends itself to being used jointly with several of the others, so that the potential exists for the development of combination approaches.

Cognitive Social Problem Solving

The goal of social problem solving is to teach children a cognitive process that will help them think correctly about their interpersonal social behavior so that they are able to solve interpersonal social problems when they arise. In some of the interventions that have been conducted, the emphasis of the training has been placed on generating alternative solutions to interpersonal problems and recognizing good versus poor solutions (Spivak & Shure, 1974).

In a training program developed by Weissberg and Gesten (1982), teachers identify children's problems by using interpersonal skills such as "reflection of feelings" and then ask the children to generate alternative solutions and consequences. In the Spivak and Shure (1974) training program, the teacher may ask an alternate solution question such as "That's a good idea. Can anyone think of another idea?" or an alternate consequences question such as "Who can name some different things that might happen next?" "That's one, who can think of something else?" or they may ask paired solution/consequence questions such as "What might happen next?" after the child has already provided a particular solution. In some programs, teachers model interpersonal problem solving by using their own problems and sometimes they use role play to help children see the functionality of a plan. The following example was used in role play:

Sharon: (to herself) I have a problem. I'm upset because Jenny has been riding the bike for a long time. My goal is to get a turn. I could push her off the bike and grab it, but she might get hurt. I could tell on her, but she'd say I was a tattletale . . . maybe she'd let me have a turn if I asked her nicely. "Jenny, can I please ride the bike?"

Jenny: "No, I'm using it."

Sharon: (to herself) I have another solution that might work. "Jenny, I've been waiting a long time. Let me ride the bike for 10 minutes and then you can ride it again."

Jenny: "Okay." (Weissberg & Gesten, 1982, p. 59)

Weissberg and Gesten (1982) teach children to apply the following six steps to the solution of a social problem:

Problem definition	1. Say (how you feel and) exactly what the problem is.
Goal statement	2. Decide on your goal.
Impulse delay	3. Stop and think before you act.
Generation of Alternatives	4. Think of as many solutions as you can.
Consideration of Consequences	5. Think ahead to what might happen next
Implementation	6. When you have a really good solution, try it! (p. 59)

Recent studies that have relied on cognitive problem solving using similar internal verbal strategies have been quite promising (Ager & Cole, 1991; Etscheidt, 1991; Harris & Pressley, 1991).

Other investigators have taught problem solving skills by showing short videotapes of youngsters dealing with common problems, for example, peer pressure to take a dare, followed by group discussion guided by the teacher (Elias, 1983).

The cognitively based social problem-solving approach is attractive to teachers because teaching strategies are conventional and because deviant behavior is viewed as a failure to learn (Carpenter & Apter, 1988).

Cognitive Self-Monitoring

The purpose of self-monitoring is to get the student to attend to specific behaviors in a systematic way. Self-monitoring has been used as a standard observational procedure in many applied behavioral analysis programs. Generally, self-monitoring is viewed as one technique among many of which all are components of a larger intervention. Self-monitoring has been used to increase study behavior, keep hyperactive kids on task, and with other strategies to teach cognitive skills (Camp & Bash, 1981; Hogan & Prater, 1993; McCarl, Svobodny, & Beare, 1991; Prater, Hogan, & Miller, 1992).

In a typical procedure, the teacher might set several timers to sound at different times or record tones on a tape recorder which would be played at random intervals. On hearing a sound, the student would ask herself "Was I working?" and indicate on a check list whether she was on task. Although students require some training prior to implementing the procedure, highly motivated students have modified their behavior simply by monitoring it.

On the basis of recent research, Kauffman (1993) makes the following concluding statements:

> Self-monitoring of on task behavior has resulted in increased on task behavior in most cases.
>
> Self-monitoring of on task behavior has also tended to result in increases in productivity.
>
> Improvement in behavior and performance has been found to last for at least two-and-a half months after the procedure was discontinued.
>
> The beneficial effects of self-monitoring have been achieved without the use of back-up reinforcers; extrinsic rewards, such as tokens or treats for improved behavior, have not been necessary.
>
> Cues (tones) are a necessary element of the initial training procedure, although students can be weaned from them after initial training.
>
> Students' self-recording responses—marking the answers to their self-questions—are a necessary element of the initial training, but can be discontinued after students learn the full procedure.
>
> Self-recording appears to be more effective when the student assesses his or her own attentional behavior than when the teacher assesses it.

Accuracy in self-monitoring is not critically important; some students are in close agreement with the teacher's assessment of their on task behavior, but others are not.

The cuing tones and other aspects of the procedure are minimally disruptive to other students in the class. (pp. 304-305)

Cognitive Self-Instruction

The purpose of this intervention is to get children who exhibit inappropriate behavior to use verbal self instruction to improve their behavior. If the teacher can help the child link internal self-instruction to appropriate behavior, then it is assumed that inappropriate behavior can be decreased, while appropriate behavior is increased. This intervention has been used primarily to teach impulsive, nonreflective children to slow down and deliberately develop a problem-solving plan. Usually, training procedures include a number of steps which are first modeled by the teacher, then imitated by the student, and finally used independently by the student.

Meichenbaum (1977) has suggested that the steps involved in teaching self-instruction include: (a) problem definition, (b) focusing attention and response guidance, (c) self-reinforcement, and (4) self-evaluative coping skills and error correcting options. Kendall (1981) has adapted Meichenbaum's content and identified, in addition, what he views as the steps the teacher must use in teaching self-instruction. This is set forth in Table 8-1.

Although self-instruction has been used primarily with impulsive children, it has also been used as a component of more complex interventions to teach self-control. Robin, Schneider, and Dolnick (1976) used it to teach children, on being threatened, to withdraw to a "turtle position" and begin a relaxation and problem-solving procedure, and Larson and Gerber (1987) used it to teach delinquent youth to stop and think before responding to social situations which might get them in trouble or put them in danger.

Cognitive Social Skills Training

The goal of this intervention is to teach children social skills or social competence, that is, to teach children to exhibit behaviors that are reinforced and to avoid exhibiting behaviors that are placed under

TABLE 8-1. Content and Sequence of Self-Instructional Procedures with Impulsive Children.

CONTENT OF SELF-INSTRUCTION	SEQUENCE OF SELF-INSTRUCTION
Problem definition: "Let's see, what am I supposed to do?"	The therapist models task performance and talks out loud while the child observes.
Problem approach: "Well, I should look this over and try to figure out how to get to the center of the maze."	The child performs the task instructing himself out loud.
Focusing on attention: "I'd better look ahead so I don't get trapped."	The therapist models task performance while whispering the self-instruction, followed by the child's performing the task, whispering himself;
Coping statements: "Oh, that path isn't right. If I go that way, I'll get stuck. I'll just go back here and try another way."	The therapist performs the task using overt self-instructions, with pauses and behavioral signs of thinking (e.g., stroking beard or chin, raising eyes toward the ceiling);
Self-reinforcement: "Hey, not bad. I really did a good job."	The child performs the task using covert self-instructions.

Source: From Developing nonimpulsive behavior in children: Cognitive-behavioral strategies for self-control (p. 57) by P.C. Kendall and A.J. Finch, 1979, In P.C. Kendall and S.D. Hollen (Eds.), *Cognitive-behavioral interventions: Theory, research and procedures.* New York: Academic Press. Copyright 1979 by Academic Press. Reprinted by permission.

extinction or punished by others (Libet & Lewinsohn, 1973). Cognitive social skills training programs have been based on the work of Bandura (1977) and generally teach new social skills by using self-instruction techniques, modeling, cognitive and behavioral rehearsal, prompting, and feedback. Generally, attempts are made to encourage generalization and maintenance.

Some of the social skills training programs are primarily behavioral (Goldstein et al., 1980), whereas others emphasize the cognitive aspect of training such as covert verbalization. In Skill-streaming the Adolescent, a mostly behavioral training program, Goldstein et al. have identified 50 prosocial skills, many of which they believe are deficient in behaviorally disordered adolescents. They teach these through the instructional steps of: (a) modeling the skill, (b) asking the students to role play the skill, and (c) providing feedback following each role play. The Skillstreaming the Adolescent program begins with an opening session which is used to stimulate the trainee's interest in what skill training is all about and to orient them to the training procedure. Next a modeling phase occurs in which all the steps of the skill to be taught are modeled in the correct sequence. After the modeling phase, the trainer solicits comments on how the steps in the skill might be useful in real life and then gets the students to role play or act out the behavioral steps that have been modeled. All trainees get to role play the skill. Finally, feedback is provided by the other students first and next by the teacher who also provides social reinforcement such as praise, approval and encouragement. A list of the 50 prosocial skills contained in the Skill-streaming the Adolescent program follows in Table 8-2.

More recently, Goldstein and his associates developed an aggression replacement training (ART) program designed to improve the social competence of youth with aggressive tendencies (Goldstein & Glick, 1987). However, some researchers have found only limited cognitive gains and questioned the link between cognition and actual behavior in disturbed populations (Coleman, Pfeiffer, & Oakland, 1992).

In other cognitive social skills training programs, the role of covert verbalization is assessed for determining the degree to which maladaptive self-statements may be influencing social behavior. Halford (1983) uses a thought-listing method to help youngsters identify their positive and negative self-statements. For example, if the youngster is having problems responding to failure, it would be helpful to know if he's telling himself "I'm dumb" or "I guess I made a mistake, let's see, what can I do to improve." The purpose of this assessment is to teach the student to use positive self-controlling statements which enhance the probability that the more overt behavioral strategies of modeling, role play, and feedback will be effective.

Yet other cognitive social skills training programs, such as the self-control curriculum of Fagen, Long, and Stevens (1979) use a less structured approach to teach cognitive and social skills. This approach, which is somewhat representative of the psychoeducational approach to behavioral problems, emphasizes feelings, insight and introspection. Their curriculum includes eight skill clusters:

Selection: ability to perceive incoming information accurately

Storage: ability to retain the information received

Sequence and ordering: ability to organize actions on the basis of a planned order

Anticipating consequences: ability to relate actions to expected outcomes

Appreciating feelings: ability to identify and constructively use affective experience

Managing frustration: ability to cope with external obstacles that produce stress

TABLE 8-2. The 50 Prosocial Skills in the Adolescent Skillstreaming Program.

Group I.   Beginning Social Skills
      1. Listening
      2. Starting a Conversation
      3. Having a Conversation
      4. Asking a Question
      5. Saying Thank You
      6. Introducing Yourself
      7. Introducing Other People
      8. Giving a compliment

Group II.   Advanced Social Skills
      9. Asking for Help
      10. Joining In
      11. Giving Instructions
      12. Following Instructions
      13. Apologizing
      14. Convincing Others

Group III.   Skills for Dealing with Feelings
      15. Knowing Your Feelings
      16. Expressing Your Feelings
      17. Understanding the Feelings of Others
      18. Dealing with Someone Else's Anger
      19. Expressing Affection
      20. Dealing with Fear
      21. Rewarding Yourself

Group IV.   Skill Alternatives to Aggression
      22. Asking Permission
      23. Sharing Something
      24. Helping Others
      25. Negotiating
      26. Using Self-control
      27. Standing up for Your Rights
      28. Responding to Teasing
      29. Avoiding Trouble with Others
      30. Keeping out of Fights

Group V.   Skills for Dealing with Stress
      31. Making a Complaint
      32. Answering a Complaint
      33. Sportsmanship After the Game
      34. Dealing with Embarrassment
      35. Dealing with Being Left Out
      36. Standing Up for a Friend
      37. Responding to Persuasion
      38. Responding to Failure
      39. Dealing with Contradictory Messages
      40. Dealing with an Accusation
      41. Getting Ready for a Difficult Conversation
      42. Dealing with Group pressure

(continued)

TABLE 8-2. *(continued)*

Group VI. Planning Skills
   43. Deciding on Something to Do
   44. Deciding What Caused a Problem
   45. Setting a Goal
   46. Deciding on Your Abilities
   47. Gathering Information
   48. Arranging Problems by Importance
   49. Making a Decision
   50. Concentrating on a Task

Source: From *Skillstreaming the adolescent: A structured learning approach* (pp. 84-85) by A. Goldstein, R.P. Sprafkin, N.J. Gershaw, and P. Klein, 1980, Chicago, Research Press Company. Copyright 1980 by Research Press Company. Reprinted by permission.

Inhibition and delay: ability to postpone or restrain action tendencies

Relaxation: ability to reduce internal tension (p. 70)

Although each of the approaches presented here is representative of somewhat different theoretical threads, that is, behavioral, cognitive, and psychoeducational, they are presented under the category of cognitive social skill training because they all possess cognitive components, share characteristics of the other strategies, and attempt to teach social skills.

Stress Inoculation

The goal of stress inoculation is to provide an individual with a system for coping with situations and events which previously prompted debilitating emotional reactions such as anxiety and fear. Stress inoculation was developed by Meichenbaum and Cameron (1973, cited in Bernard & Joyce, 1984) to help individuals cope with anxiety. The training session begins with an educational phase in which rapport is established between the trainer and trainee and the trainee is taught how maladaptive thoughts can lead to emotional reactions. In this phase, diaries or logs are used to help identify dysfunctional emotional reaction patterns. According to Meichenbaum and Turk (1975, cited in Bernard & Joyce, 1984), in the next phase, the rehearsal or skill acquisition phase, the trainee is taught to monitor her self-defeating thoughts and to use these as cues for new adaptive self-statements. The trainee learns in this phase how to: (a) prepare for a stressor, for example, "Don't worry; just think of a plan,"

(b) confront and handle the stressor, for example, "Just relax; I can do it," (c) cope with the feeling of being overwhelmed, for example,"It's okay, I'm almost through it," and (d) make reinforcing self-statements, for example, "Alright, it worked!" In the final phase, application training, the trainee practices the newly acquired skills in either role play with the trainer or in contrived stress situations. Cartledge and Milburn (1980) outline how stress inoculation may be used for children who overreact to critical teacher feedback as follows:

Preparing for provocation

> If the teacher marks something wrong I can handle it.
> I know what to do if I get upset.
> Making a mistake is not so bad.

Impact on confrontation

> Keep calm.
> Think about the ones you got correct.
> It's silly to get angry about one problem.
> The teacher is really right to show me what I did wrong.
> Being corrected helps me learn.

Coping with arousal

> I'm beginning to breathe hard, relax.
> Stop and think about all the good work you did today.
> Try to keep cool.

Reflection on provocation

> a. When conflict is unresolved
> It partly worked.
> I can do better next time.
> This is hard to do, but I'll keep trying.
> b. When conflict is resolved or coping is successful.
> I did a good job that time. I even smiled at the teacher.
> I can be a good student. The teacher likes me. (pp. 81-82)

In most stress inoculation training programs, self-instruction is used to help children cope and solve problems. The following is an example of a coping self-instructional sequence which might be useful to a child who has test anxiety:

> "Okay, just relax and read the instructions carefully. Now don't panic. A little excitement is fine. I feel myself getting tense. I'll just practice my breathing. And remember to relax. I know I can do this."

The self-instructional component of stress inoculation differs somewhat from the cognitive self-instructional intervention discussed earlier because of its direct tie to the individual's internal psychological functioning. As such, stress inoculation is directed toward altering emotions first and affecting behavior second.

Finally, stress inoculation programs appear to be easily adapted to suite a variety of emotional and behavioral problems and can be integrated with other interventions.

Rational-Emotive Therapy

Of all the cognitive approaches which attempt to influence emotions, Ellis's (1973) approach of Rational-Emotive Therapy (RET) is probably one of the most attractive for teachers of students with emotional and behavioral problems. This is because there are two components of RET, known as Rational-Emotive Education (REE) and Rational-Emotive Group Counseling (REGC), which have been applied successfully in the classroom and for which there exists a large body of literature and materials.

Theory of Rational-Emotive Therapy

According to Ellis (1973), the reason that individuals become emotionally disturbed is because of the irrational ideas people have about how the world should be and because of the self-defeating statements they make to themselves which are comprised largely of errors in logic. Ellis gives credit for this central idea to Epictetus, the Roman Stoic philosopher who wrote that "Humans are disturbed not by things but by the view they take of them." After numerous years of work as a clinical psychotherapist using RET, Ellis has come to believe that individuals have: (a) a biological and hereditary tendency to think irrationally and that (b) errors in thinking interact reciprocally with an individual's belief system or underlying value system. Therefore, RET adopts and values the scientific method as the means for knowing and thinking. According to Walen, DiGuiseppe, and Wessler (1980) RET endorses the premise that all humans value survival, satisfaction with living, a positive affiliation with others, intimacy with some, and becoming absorbed in a fulfilling endeavor.

The ABCs of Rational Emotive Therapy

Because faulty thinking can lead to emotional and behavioral problems, one of the main tasks of RET is to get the disturbed individual to identify beliefs or thinking mistakes. To explain how this is accomplished, Ellis has developed an ABC theory of personality and emotional disturbance. When attempting to help someone, the therapist typically begins with C, the Consequence or disturbing emotional experience, for example, anxiety, panic, depression, or anger and then traces this back to A, the Activating event, for example, failing a test or being shunned or rejected. Generally the client believes that A (failing the test) has caused C (the depression and anxiety). What is wrongly believed and often said out loud is, for example, "I failed the test and that made me depressed." What the client fails to see and often has to be helped to see is that A cannot possibly cause C, that is, that an event in the outside world cannot possibly cause or create a feeling. If this were so, then everyone who failed a test would become depressed and this is certainly not the case. Instead, C has to be primarily caused by B, the individual's Belief System, that is, the client must have said something covertly immediately after A at B. In fact at B, the client must have said something irrational, for example, "I must be stupid and I deserve to feel bad; isn't it awful that I failed the test?" This kind of belief would almost certainly lead to a negative emotional consequence, or C. If, conversely, the client had held a rational belief and at B said to himself, for example, "Isn't it unfortunate that I failed the test. I'll have to study more for the next test," then the feelings at C would be feelings of disappointment, regret, and perhaps frustration and would be quite appropriate to the Activating Event because they would motivate the client to alter study behavior so that success would be more likely on the next test. In fact this rational belief would ultimately increase the student's satisfaction with living.

Because proponents of RET believe that irrational beliefs are uncritically held, that is, the client never really examines them to determine their rationality, it is the therapist's role to show the client not only that A cannot cause C, but also that B is comprised of at least one, or more often, several irrational beliefs. The therapist does this, at point D, by disputing the client's irrational beliefs. The therapist will often ask the client: (a)"Why is it awful to fail a test?" (b) "How are you stupid because you failed a test?" (c) "Where is the evidence that you deserve to feel bad?" Once the therapist has succeeded in showing the client these errors of logic, the therapist must then teach the client to recognize his own irrational thinking and self-challenge and self-dispute irrational thoughts when they occur.

Rational-Emotive Therapy Intervention

Although the main technique of RET is that of disputation (D), RET is considered a "comprehensive approach to therapy" in that clients are taught how to dispute their irrational thoughts by using not only cognitive, but also emotive and behavioral techniques. According to Bard (1980), disputation is any technique which shows clients that their thinking is faulty. Because disputation is the most central aspect of the RET intervention, the major disputational approaches are reviewed next.

Cognitive Disputation

For the practitioner to dispute irrational statements, it is helpful to be able to identify some of the common ones and understand why they are irrational. There are four types of problematic statements: should, awful, need, and worth statements.

Should statements are irrational because they suggest that things must be a certain way. Clients who "should" on themselves, as Ellis often says, seem to believe that the world revolves around them. When clients fully realize how infinitely tiny they really are in a cosmos comprised of many galaxies, then it becomes easier for them to understand the irrationality of should statements. If a client said, for example, "The world should be fair," the RET therapist, by asking the client, for example, "Who says the world should be fair"? would teach the client to locate his own needless redundancies. This is not to imply that people cannot show a preference for a fair and just world.

Awful statements suggest that things are unbearable. When people use awful statements, they are also said to be catastrophizing. These statements tend to increase the negativity of a situation to catastrophic proportions. The irrationality of these statements is usually disputed by showing clients that what they are really intending to say by using the word awful is that something is more than 100% awful and that in fact they believe they can't stand it any longer. The RET therapist would dispute this by asking how could, for example, "being told to make my bed," when my friends are around be more than 100 % awful, when, a tornado which wipes out the entire town could be only 95% to 100% awful. This kind of comparison will often help clients reduce their estimate of awfulness considerably (Bernard & Joyce, 1984). Additionally, the therapist will dispute the client's belief that he cannot stand something by asking him to prove it. Such a proof is very difficult to make.

Need statements suggest that things are absolutely necessary to survive. These are irrational because we really need very few things to survive, that is, food, water, clothing, and shelter. When people are asked what they mean, they usually define the word "need" to mean want or desire. Most of the things we seek are wants, for example, we want to be loved, to be good at something, to have a car, and so on. The therapist, among other things, helps the client, through dispute, to distinguish wants from needs.

Worth statements indicate that a person's intrinsic worth can be objectively determined. When we say "She's a good person," we imply that we have some kind of objective means for the assessment of "good" and that in fact we are able to empirically support our claim by showing proof that "She has never been bad." This claim would be almost impossible to verify.

At the same time the practitioner is listening for should, awful, need, and worth statements, she is also attending to the client to detect common irrational beliefs. Waters (1982, cited in Center, 1989) has identified irrational beliefs in children and in adolescents. These are listed below.

Common irrational beliefs found in children

1. It's awful if others don't like me.
2. I'm bad if I make a mistake
3. Everything should go my way
4. I should always get what I want.
5. Things should come easy to me.
6. The world should be fair.
7. Bad people must be punished.
8. I shouldn't show my feelings.
9. Adults should be perfect.
10. There's only one right answer.
11. I must win.
12. I shouldn't have to wait for anything.

Common irrational beliefs found in adolescents

1. It would be awful if peers didn't like me.
2. It would be awful to be a social loser.
3. I shouldn't make mistakes, especially social mistakes
4. It's my parents' fault that I'm so miserable.

5. I can't help it, that's just the way I am.
6. I guess I'll always be this way.
7. The world should be fair and just.
8. It's awful when things don't go my way.
9. It's better to avoid challenges than to risk failure.
10. I must conform to my peers.
11. I can't stand to be criticized.
12. Others should always be responsible.

Other cognitive tactics that have been used include: (a) getting the client to read RET literature which is directed to giving up irrational beliefs, (b) cognitive modeling in which the therapist verbally models the self-statements the client should employ, and (c) the use of mini-lectures, parables, and humorous exaggeration.

Emotional Disputation

The purpose of emotional disputation is to connect the client's emotions with newly acquired rational cognition. This is often necessary because although the client's cognition may have begun to change significantly, emotional reactions may lag behind. If a link can be made between the client's emotion and cognition, then she should be better able to dispute the specific thoughts that trigger high levels of negative emotion. Also, emotive strategies are used sometimes just to show the client that she can tolerate a particular situation or learn to cope with a negative emotional reaction. The principal technique of emotional disputation is Rational-Emotive Imagery (REI). In using this technique, the clients are asked to imagine themselves in the problem situation. When positive imagery is used, clients are told to imagine themselves acting more appropriately and feeling better. Usually when clients are taught to do this, they report that they used rational self-statements to create the positive imagery that helped them act and feel better. Sometimes clients are taught to make use of negative imagery. This technique usually begins by asking clients to imagine themselves in a problem situation, feeling and acting emotionally upset. Once this is accomplished they are asked to pro- gressively shift their emotions to more positive ones. After they be- come able to make this change, their self-talk is analyzed to determine what statements they had used to produce this positive change.

Other emotive techniques that have been used include: (a) teaching the client to make passionate self-statements, in which rational self-statements are repeated in an intense and emotional manner, (b) having clients who are afraid of failure and ridicule do ridiculous things to desensitize them to their fears, (c) using modeling to demonstrate the basic concepts of RET, and (d) using role-playing exercises to enhance performance and reduce the anxiety associated with a situation (Bernard & Joyce, 1984).

Behavioral Disputation

The purpose of behavioral disputation is to give clients the in vivo training they need to enable them to face and cope with their problem situation. The principal strategies involve the use of role play and homework assignments which are designed to get the client, by performing, to refute his irrational beliefs. This technique is based primarily on the behavioral technique of respondent or graduated respondent extinction discussed in Chapter 7 in which the client is exposed to situations or stimuli that elicit fear and anxiety until the negative emotions diminish.

Rational-Emotive Education

Rational-Emotive Education (REE) has a preventative and educational aim, the goal of which is primarily to teach children the principles of rational-emotive thinking. Teachers show children that thoughts cause feelings and that it is possible to change the irrational thoughts that cause negative feelings. REE teaches children how to accept themselves as imperfect; to eliminate should, awful, need, and worth statements from their language; and to avoid confusing wants with needs.

Developmental Guidelines

Teachers who use REE with their students need to understand that the objectives they set for their students and the corresponding activities they employ in their lessons must be tied to their student's present level of cognitive development. Based primarily on the work of Piaget, Bernard and Joyce (1984) have established the following guidelines.

Preoperational Children—Less Than 7 Years. Teachers who work with children who are developmentally in Piaget's preoperational stage of cognitive development need to realize that these children have difficulty understanding things from another's point of view and cannot easily consider two important things at the same time. With preoperational children, teachers should rely mainly on activities that make use of concrete and simple material, for example, pictures, illustrations, and stories, so that these children can use their imaginal and pictorial abilities to benefit from instruction. Additionally, learning should be the result of doing as much as seeing and of using a variety of methods that will help maintain the younger child's interest. The principal objectives for preoperational children should be to teach them to acquire and spontaneously communicate rational self-statements. A sample lesson is illustrated in Figure 8-1.

Concrete Operational Children—7-11 Years. Teachers who work with children who are developmentally in Piaget's concrete operational stage of cognitive development must understand that

Notes for the Leader

In this session the children are given practice in paying attention to ways in which people express feelings. They also practice expressing feelings to the group, and identify the subjective quality of the feelings.

Objectives

For each child

1. to identify feelings expresed by other children.
2. to mime expressions of feelings to the group.
3. to identify feelings as pleasant or unpleasant.

WHAT AM I FEELING?

(Materials: red stickers with pluses on them, for pleasant feelings; blue stickers with minuses on them, for unpleasant feelings.)

Each child may choose two feelings to mime. The group tries to guess what the feeling is. When they have guessed, the mimer is asked whether the feeling was pleasant or unpleasant ("A feeling you like to have?" or "A feeling you don't like to have?"). If it is pleasant he puts a red sticker beside the feeling word on the classroom wall chart. . . . If it is unpleasant he puts a blue sticker beside the word. The leader may mime some of the words also; the group continues to take turns untill all words are mimed and labeled.

Figure 8-1. An example of a lesson that makes use of concrete and simple material to help maintain the interest of preoperational children. From *Rational emotive therapy with children and adolescents: Theory, treatment strategies, preventative methods* (p. 383) by M.E. Bernard and M.R. Joyce, 1984, New York: John Wiley & Sons, Inc. Copyright 1984 by John Wiley & Sons, Inc. Adapted by permission.

these children view their world concretely in terms of specific situations. This implies that children in this stage can learn concepts, but that the concepts they learn are connected to specific situations that are within the child's experience. With these children, as with children in the preoperational stage of development, the teacher should employ very concrete examples and use many teaching illustrations. The primary objective for these children is to teach them general attitudes and beliefs by getting them to discuss and analyze specific situations and internalize and apply rational self-statements to these as well as novel, but similar, life situations. A sample handout assignment which would help children who are in the concrete operational stage analyze specific situations is illustrated in Figure 8-2.

Formal Operational Children—11 Years and Older. Teachers who work with these children will be able to do in-depth RET work with them. Students who have reached the formal operational cognitive stage should be able to apply abstract reasoning to the process of disputing irrational beliefs. Because they are able to engage and think through hypothetical situations, they should be able to learn self-analysis, effectively examine their own values and beliefs, develop different beliefs, and apply them to similar as well as quite different situations. Because the principal objective for these children is to teach them to dispute irrational beliefs, lessons may be developed around core irrational attitudes that many adolescents appear to have accepted, for example, that others are to blame for what happens to them (Vernon, 1989). A sample lesson is illustrated in Figure 8-3.

Rational-Emotive Group Counseling

Although almost everything said about REE would also apply to Rational-Emotive Group Counseling (REGC), it's important to note that REE is preventative, whereas REGC has specific therapeutic aims directed toward group member needs. For example, in REE a lesson would be designed to anticipate problems which the children in the group may encounter in the future, whereas in REGC the approach would be to target problems already evident in group members, for example, to reduce anxiety or anger.

Teacher/Therapist Characteristics

According to Bernard and Joyce (1984) and Rossi (1977) the group leader should be enthusiastic, use positive reinforcement and physical

Happening	Thought	Behavior	Feeling
1. Getting up in class and discussing an item reported in the news.			
2. You have just been told you will be having a very important math test.			
3. Your mother or father has just yelled at you for breaking an expensive vase (you didn't do it on purpose).			
4. A schoolmate has just told you that he has lost your favorite pen.			

Figure 8-2. A work sheet. A pencil and paper assignment that concrete operational children could use to help them analyze specific situations. From *Rational emotive therapy with children and adolescents: Theory, treatment strategies, preventative methods* (p. 404) by M.E. Bernard and M.R. Joyce, 1984, New York: John Wiley & Sons, Inc. Copyright 1984 by John Wiley & Sons, Inc. Adapted by permission.

contact, and communicate the ideas of rational thinking through managing difficulties that arise during the session authentically. The teacher should reinforce (a) learning the concepts and skills of RET,

COPPING OUT

Objective
To recognize avoidance or cop-out behaviors

Materials
Paper and pencils as needed

Procedure
1. Explain that a cop-out is when you refuse to take responsibility for yourself and blame others for what happens. Examples might include blaming your coach because you didn't get to start on the team, your parents for grounding you if you got home late, or your friend for ruining your day. Cop-outs represent irrational thoughts because you usually want to change the other person rather than take personal responsibility.

2. Avoidance behaviors can involve procrastination, in which you put off doing something because you feel uncomfortable about it or may not want the hassle of doing it.
   Avoidance may also include behaviors such as ignoring certain people because you don't want to face them, drinking too much to avoid facing painful or tough situations, overeating or undereating, etc.

3. Invite students to brainstorm personal examples of avoidance or cop-out behaviors.

4. Share examples in small groups (4-5 participants).

Discussion
Content Questions
1. Was it difficult to think of examples of avoidance or cop-out behaviors?
2. Do you think avoidance or cop-out behaviors are healthy or unhealthy?

Personalize Questions
1. How can you recognize cop-out or avoidance behaviors in your own life?
2. What would you like to do about these kinds of behaviors?
3. Do you know persons who exercise lots of cop-out or avoidance behaviors? How do you see this affecting their lives? Do you think these behaviors are good?

To the Leader
Help students take personal responsibility for their own behaviors and recognize the unhealthy pattern and effects of avoidance.

Figure 8-3. A lesson designed for adolescents who have reached the stage of formal operations. From *Thinking, feeling and behaving: An emotional education curriculum for fdolescents* (p. 121) by A. Vernon, 1989, Champaign, IL: Research Press. Copyright 1989 by Research Press. Reprinted by permission.

(b) following the rules of the group, (c) listening to one another, and (d) helping others understand rational concepts. The leader should be nonjudgmental and create a climate of acceptance by not criticizing and by gently persuading the student to think about the new ideas presented. Additionally, Bernard and Joyce have found that it is helpful to relate new rational-emotive abilities to youngsters by saying such things as "You got that quickly" and by listening carefully. They believe that when teachers listen carefully, often they will be able to remind students in later sessions, who are having difficulty connecting RET material with their own experience, of what these students had been saying previously to themselves. For example a student may have been saying something like "I just can't do that." If the children are especially anxious, and appear to need time before they feel comfortable discussing their own problems, the teacher may want to present the problem as if it belonged to another child. Among other suggestions, Bernard and Joyce advise teachers to be sensitive to body language and to help children who fail to attribute their successes to themselves to do so by making comments such as "You did a really great job because you really put out the effort this time," and so on.

Group Characteristics

Because group instruction is the most probable approach in most educational settings, the teacher needs to consider (a) how to select the group, (b) group size, and (c) group composition.

Most groups are selected informally without the use of self-report or rating-scale procedures because teachers generally have a good idea of the kinds of problems their students have. Nevertheless, formal scales are available, for example, the Revised Behavior Problem Checklist (RBPC) (Quay & Peterson, 1987), which provide a means for collecting systematic information.

With regard to group size, four to six children will most often be suitable, unless the group is composed of primarily aggressive children. In this case, it is good to make the group smaller. If the group is composed of primarily withdrawn children, the group can be somewhat larger.

Some authors believe the group should be heterogeneous with regard to the type of behavioral characteristics the children exhibit (Muro & Dinkmeyer, 1977); however, the composition of the group is also dependent on the particular goals the teacher is trying to achieve for her class. In any case, group members should be relatively homogeneous in age, with an age difference no greater than 2 years (Bernard & Joyce, 1984).

Stages of Rational-Emotive Group Counseling

Although there is considerable overlap between the stages of REGC and although the stages that occur in practice do not always follow a particular order, most teachers are best advised to: (a) build rapport, (b) identify the problem, and (c) explore and dispute irrational beliefs.

Building Rapport. Whereas Ellis (1973) and other practitioners have maintained that it is acceptable to begin disputing a new client's irrational ideas during the first session (Wessler & Wessler, 1980), more recent writings suggest that a good rapport is an essential element in getting clients to change (Walen et al., 1980). Further, many practitioner believe that the ingredients necessary for a good rapport are the ones that were discussed in Chapter 6, that is, empathy, unconditional positive regard, and congruence or authenticity (Bernard & Joyce, 1984; Carkhuff et al., 1977; Gordon, 1974; Rogers, 1980). In fact, Bernard and Joyce (1984) have modified Carkhuff's last step of communicating empathy to reflect not only the student's feelings and wants, but also the student's thoughts. Figure 8-4 compares the Carkhuff et al. response format to the Bernard and Joyce modification.

With regard to young clients in individual therapy sessions, Bernard and Joyce (1984) make the following suggestions, which could easily be adapted by teachers for use in REGC.

1. Tell them your name.
2. Find out what they like to be called (Tom, Tommy, or Thomas).
3. Show interest in their real life context—family, friends, hobbies, pet.
4. Find ways to set the relationship apart from other adult-child relationships. Sit beside the child or adolescent, never behind a desk, or, for early sessions with very young children, choose a relaxed setting such as bean bags or the floor or the garden swings.
5. Guide the child as to what you expect. State the rules for the relationship. "This is not like other places. You can say anything you like. You can say just what you think and what you feel."

Feeling and Want Response Format

"You feel _____ because you cannot _____
and you want to _____ . "

Thinking and Want Response Format

"You feel _____ because you are thinking _____
and you want _____ . "

Figure 8-4. A comparison of the Carkhuff step of initiating responding with the Bernard and Joyce modification designed to reflect the student's thoughts. From *Rational emotive therapy with children and adolescents: Theory, treatment strategies, preventative methods* (p. 184) by M.E. Bernard and M.R. Joyce, 1984, New York: John Wiley & Sons, Inc. Copyright 1984 by John Wiley & Sons, Inc. Adapted by permission.

6. Early disclosure of feelings is helped by first suggesting to the child a general statement about children: "Children sometimes feel afraid about someone new" (or . . . "cross at having to do something"). "Do you think children feel this way?" "Maybe you feel this way right now?"
7. For the inhibited youngster, the practitioner may "read" the body language and tentatively put the feeling into words for the child. This can give the child confidence that the practitioner knows how he or she feels inside.
8. Show that you are a person who listens by not continuously interrupting, and by responding to what they have said. (p. 189)

Problem Identification. Because problem identification and self-analysis are so interrelated, it is difficult to separate them. However, helping students to understand, define, and own the problem is necessary before a thorough analysis can occur. In this phase, many teachers can help students do this by having them describe when and where the problem occurs and what situations seem to elicit the problem. The student is also ask to describe his feelings and to rate their intensity. Students who have difficulty in either finding a label for their feelings or in owning their problems can be helped to do this through participating in group REE exercises. The exercise in Figure 8-5 is designed to help students identify the words used to describe feelings (Gerald & Eyman, 1981, p. 49). The handout in Figure 8-6 is useful in helping students own their emotions (Vernon, 1989, p. 190).

What About Feelings?

We have looked at facts and opinions, conditions and contexts, causes and effects. We have a better idea of what we can be sure of and what is open to interpretation. We have learned ... that the way we feel about something or someone is not the only view we can take. So what about feelings (which are also called emotions)? Aren't we "supposed" to have them? "I'm *feeling* some way almost all the time," one student said after working through the first lessons in this course. "And now I'm confused. I can't help the way I feel, can I?"

Yes, everyone has feelings. And, yes, you can help the way you feel. That's what this course is about -- to help people learn how to train their emotions. People can learn how not to get angry, how not to make themselves feel worthless, how to get what they want some of the time and not to make themselves unhappy when they don't get everything they want. Later units will show how to gain these and similar skills, but the first step is to learn what words and signals express feelings.

Figure 8-5. An exercise to help students identify emotions with words. From *Thinking straight and talking sense: An emotional education program* (pp. 48-50) by M. Gerald and W. Eyman, 1981, New York: Institute for Rational-Emotive Therapy. Copyright 1981 by the Institute for Rational-Emotive Therapy.

192

W HAT words do you use when you want to describe a feeling? List as many as you can individually on a separate sheet of paper and then put your list together with others to make a master list for the whole class.

Here is one list. Use it as an example.

down	flying	together
tense	angry	groovy
all right	weird	hopeful
crazy	turned on	trusting
ashamed	turned off	bad
hanging in	terrific	embarrassed
happy	excited	afraid
scared	thrilled	mellow
disappointed	hot	hostile
frustrated	sorry	great
in the pits	nervous	silly
fascinated	O.K.	blue
confused	depressed	concerned
messed up	sad	worried
guilty	upset	confident
low	curious	lonely
freaked out	relaxed	high
annoyed	anxious	naughty
in love	faded out	distraught
dynamite	cool	apathetic
wiped out	zonked	in a buzz
arrogant	uptight	funny
cheerful	determined	envious

Here are some projects that can help us look at the variety of feelings people have.

Make a list of some synonyms or near-synonyms for feelings. (Some examples are emotions, moods, sentiments.)

Write down all the different "I feel _____" or "I'm in a _____ mood" statements that you hear others make in one day.

Have someone in your group make a card file of "I feel ____" statements. Have everyone practice going through the cards and acting out each statement. (This will included facial expressions and body motions with out talk)

Have one person go through the file and wordlessly act out each "I feel" statement in front of the rest of the group. See if the group can guess what feeling that person is expressing. (Your guesses can't be right or wrong - that's why they are called guesses. There's not one way to express the same feeling.)

(continued)

193

Figure 8-5. *(continued)*

Now take the same "I feel" expressions and show them first only with eyes. Then only with the hands. Next only with the shoulders. Now only with the lips. Next only with the head. And, finally, only with the index finger.

Choose five "I feel" statements and express them only by using a nonsense sound like "Ba, ba, ba." This will show how much feeling you can convey just by the tone of your voice.

Make a wall chart of all the "I feel ____" statements you have collected. Keep adding to it.

Start a diary of "I feel" or "I felt" statements. At first just write the statements. Don't put down any "becauses."

After you have kept your diary for a day, begin to add clauses that tell when you feel a certain way. Leave the "becauses" out. As an example, you might write, "I felt silly when I started writing this diary."

Choose one "I feel" statement (like "I feel happy") and take snapshots of everyone in the group expressing that feeling. Make a wall chart headed I FEEL ____ and attach all of the snapshots to it.

Cut pictures of people out of old magazines and newspapers and paste them onto cards or cardboard. Don't label them. Ask several people to describe what they think they themselves would be feeling if they looked like the people in the pictures. They could say, "This is my picture and I feel ____."

Notes for Students

• •

Remember –
• The same "I feel" statement can be shown and said in many different ways.
• The same "I feel" expression on different people's faces may mean different things.

• •

You all look sad.

No, I am just tired.

Yeah, I am.

Nope. I feel great. I'm just thinking something deep.

Owning Your Emotions Worksheet

Directions: Decide who owns the problem in the situations described below.

1. You get a bad grade on a paper and blame the teacher because you feel upset about it. Who owns the problem?
2. You turn down a date and later hear that the person went out and got drunk and was really depressed. Who owns the problem?
3. Your parents won't let you stay out until 3:00 a.m. like some of the other kids. You're upset about it. Who owns the problem?
4. Your friend encourages you to take a few drinks and you do. When you get home, you are grounded. Now you're angry. Who owns the problem?
5. Someone in your class asks if you'll give her the answers for a midterm test. You don't, and the person yells at you. Who owns the problem?
6. You've been dating someone pretty steadily but want to end the relationship. You do. The next day, you hear that the person committed suicide. Who owns the problem?
7. Write your own!

Figure 8-6. An example of a handout exercise which could be used to help children take responsibility for their emotions. From *Thinking, feeling and behaving: An emotional education curriculum for adolescents* (p. 190) by A. Vernon, 1989, Champaign, IL: Research Press. Copyright 1989 by Research Press. Reprinted by permission.

Although Waters (1982, cited in Bernard & Joyce, 1984) believes that it is sometimes necessary to teach students additional concepts, for example, whether the problem is of a kind that causes internal feelings or not, at this point the teacher should have a tentative idea of the activating events (A) and the emotional and behavioral consequences (C) which they appear to cause. Once this identification is complete, the teacher is ready to move on to the phase of exploring and disputing irrational beliefs.

Exploration and Disputation of Beliefs. During the exploration phase, the teacher must identify the thoughts presented and ask herself whether they are rational or irrational. Grieger and Boyd (1983) suggest that practitioners try to isolate (a) errors of inference in which the student makes predictions or draws conclusions that are not based on evidence or (b) errors of evaluation in which the student is distorting reality, for example, "Everyone hates me." Bernard and Joyce (1984) use prompt questions to help students verbalize and discover their self-talk, for example, "What were you thinking when _____ happened?" "What sorts of things were you saying to yourself when _____ ?" or "Tell me the first things which come into your mind when you think about _____." (p. 195). With very young children, however, learning activities such as some of the REE games may be necessary because they have not had sufficient practice with introspection and have yet to acquire the necessary language to discuss their thoughts and emotions. In any case, teachers must be patient and try as many different techniques as possible to enable students to uncover their beliefs (B).

Once these beliefs have been exposed, the teacher must finally focus on the disputation of these beliefs as discussed previously. One approach is to ask for a confirmation of the ABC analysis prior to beginning the disputation. Also, as discussed earlier, older children can be taught to dispute or challenge their irrational beliefs. Finally, Waters (1982, as cited in Bernard & Joyce, 1984) teaches children to dispute their irrational beliefs by having them ask and answer the following questions:

1. Is this belief based on fact, opinion, inference or assumption? Where is the evidence that this is really so?
2. Is it really awful? Is it true I couldn't stand it? Is it the worst that it could be?
3. Is this belief getting me what I want?
4. Why shouldn't it be so? Do I always have to get what I want?
5. Where is the evidence that this makes me worthless? How can this make me worthless or less than human? (p. 576)

Summary

In attempting to consolidate cognitive and behavioral strategies, a number of interventions have developed which have been referred to as cognitive behavior modification. These include cognitive social problem solving, cognitive self-monitoring, cognitive self-instruction, cognitive social skills training, and stress inoculation. Similarly, Rational-Emotive Therapy, which is based primarily on the work of Albert Ellis, combines cognitive and behavioral components. While the cognitive behavior modification interventions and Rational-Emotive Therapy differ historically, each single intervention is designed to help children use verbal mediation to improve either their internal emotionality, their behavorial repertoire, or both. Cognitive behavior modification strategies teach children to cognitvely solve problems, monitor their behavior, instruct themselves, practice social skills, and anticipate stressful events. Rational-Emotive Therapy strategies teach children to engage in rational thinking and to dispute irrational thoughts. Rational-Emotive Therapy has an educational component which is referred to as Rational-Emotive Education.

Review Questions

1. What three major concepts are associated with all cognitive learning interventions?
2. In applying the intervention of cognitive problem solving, how might the teacher get students to generate alternate solutions and consequences?
3. What are some of the uses of cognitive self-monitoring? How might a typical self-monitoring procedure be designed?
4. How might cognitive self-instruction be used to help students learn self-control?
5. What is the role of covert verbalization in some cognitive social skills training programs?
6. What is the role of modeling in some cognitive social skills training programs?
7. In what major way is stress inoculation similar to Rational-Emotive Therapy?
8. What makes Rational-Emotive Therapy attractive to teachers?
9. In Rational-Emotive Therapy, why doesn't the activating event cause the consequence?
10. What are some cognitive disputations that a teacher might use in helping his students to identify faulty thinking?
11. What is the major purpose of emotional disputation?
12. How is negative imagery used?
13. What are some principal strategies in behavioral disputation?
14. What is the aim of Rational-Emotive Education?
15. What is the principal objective in the use of Rational Emotive Education for preoperational children?
16. What is the principal objective in the use of Rational-Emotive Education for concert operational children?
17. What teacher characteristics are helpful for use in Rational-Emotive Group Counseling?
18. What group characteristics are appropriate for Rational-Emotive Group Counseling?
19. What are the stages of Rational-Emotive Group Counseling?

Learning Activities

1. Divide into groups of five to six members and as a group select one of the following major cognitive learning interventions: (a) Cognitive Social Problem Solving, (b) Cognitive Self-Monitoring, (c) Cognitive Self-Instruction, (d) Cognitive Social Skill Training, or (e) Stress Inoculation. Each group is to select a different intervention. After selecting an intervention, describe a hypothetical student problem and develop a lesson plan for remediating the problem. The lesson plan is to include a modeling phase and a role play phase. The evaluation phase of the lesson plan is to include a means for monitoring and evaluating the use of the skill in real life situations. Each group is to present its lesson plan to the class.

2. Divide into small groups of five to six and develop a REE lesson plan that would help preoperational children understand their feelings. Include an input/intervention phase and an output/response phase which describe respectively the specific activities of the teacher and the students. Each group is to present its lesson plan to the class.

3. Divide into small groups of five to six and develop a REE pencil and paper assignment that would be helpful to concrete operational children. Each group is to put its activity on the blackboard.

4. Divide into small groups of five to six and ask for a volunteer who is able to discuss a disturbing emotion. If no one is willing to do this, ask for a volunteer who is able to role play the experience of having a disturbing emotion. Next, ask for a volunteer who is willing to role play the teacher or leader. The teacher's role will be to conduct a REGC session in which the class attempts to identify the irrational thoughts that are causing the dysfunctional emotion. Under the teacher's leadership, the class then disputes these irrational thoughts.

9
Integrating Interventions

I n this chapter, some of the pieces are put together. First, the need to integrate interventions is discussed. Next, the major elements of the engineered classroom and the level system, which provide physical and psychological structure, are identified. Third, the principal purposes and underlying assumptions behind the interventions discussed in Chapters 6, 7, and 8 are identified. Next, the scientific method is examined as a meta-paradigm for problem solving. Finally, the use of the scientific method as a tool for applying and integrating interventions is discussed.

The Need to Integrate Interventions

In the past, arguments have abounded over which model of intervention was the most helpful in solving the problems of children with emotional and behavioral problems. Generally, three positions have been taken with regard to the selection of an intervention. One position was to adopt a single intervention model as the framework or theme against which all research and hypotheses should be evaluated. The second position was to adopt a nonjudgemental attitude and view all models of intervention as equally worthy of respect. The third was to select only those models of intervention which could be empirically supported with strategies that could be replicated (Kauffman, 1993).

Although the third position is generally favored over the first two, many practicioners report that they have effectively employed interventions that are difficult to support empirically. Chapter 6 is replete with interventions that are supported by anecdote frequently because of the difficulty involved in trying to operationalize the interpersonal process. Chapter 7 describes behavioral interventions that can be supported by replicable and empirical data. Chapter 8, which has been introduced in part to demonstrate the connection between thoughts, feelings, and behavior, contains many interventions which can be replicated, while describing interventions designed to alter internal events, for example, thoughts and feelings, which are very difficult to verify empirically. In addition, many authorities have voiced the need to integrate interventions. Kauffman et al. (1991) have argued that it is past time that scientists representing different interventions come together to consider integrating their efforts about how to help children with emotional and behavioral problems. In his book, *The education and treatment of socioemotionally disturbed children and youth,* Morse (1985) discusses the need for multifaceted interventions, while more recently Jones (1992) mentions the need to supplement behavioral methods with cognitive-behavioral, social-cognitive, and insight-oriented methods, of which the latter is relatively lacking in educational writing and teacher-training programs. Finally, at the 1993 International Convention of the Council for Exceptional Children, Shores (1993) quipped that although he was a behavior analyst, some his most recent data appeared to indicate that something very much like Unconditional Positive Regard (high density noncontingent reinforcement) was at work in reducing the number of aggressive episodes of severe behavior disordered students. Consequently, for today's special education teacher to be able to help emotionally or behaviorally disordered children understand their perceptual world and alter both their internal and external behavior, teachers need to become more sophisticated in their abilities to apply and integrate interpersonal skills, behavioral, and cognitive-learning interventions.

Physical and Psychological Structure

When Brophy and Putnam (1979) consider the qualitatively phrased classroom rules, when Hewett and Taylor (1980), review the engineered classroom, and when Bauer et al. (1986) discuss level systems, they all appear to emphasize the need for structure. For Brophy and Putnam, classroom rules provided the student with a structure that is found in teacher expectations. For Hewett, structure was provided in the engineered classroom which had a particular physical design, a reward system, and was designed to assure a match between teacher expectations and moment to moment student functioning. For Bauer et al., the criteria for moving from one level to another, as well as the expectations and privileges associated with each level, provided structure.

Consequently, to implement an effective intervention with emotionally and behaviorally disordered children, the teacher must establish the necessary structure to ensure learning. This means that academic, social, and emotional tasks should become tied to the student's developmental level. This was discussed also in Chapters 2 and 3 in which the IEP and individualized curricula were designed to match student ability, that is, the IEP provided the broad match by describing the student's general level of performance, while the individualized curricula continued the process more specifically and precisely. Also as Kirk (1972) has suggested, expectations for students should be neither too high nor too low. Teachers working in self-contained classroom settings can be helped to accomplish this match by arranging the classroom as Hewett has suggested, so that specific areas correspond to various levels of development. The activities which become associated with each classroom area are thereby made to correspond to the developmental functioning of students assigned there. Once the academic, social, and emotional curricula have been task analyzed and each student's capabilities have been measured against this curricula, teachers will be able to place each student in a specific classroom area and select an appropriate activity. Also, if teachers are expected to either assist regular classroom teachers, serve as a resource teacher, or work in a capacity which facilitates the transition from more restrictive to less restrictive environments, they will want to design a level system. Special education and the regular classroom teachers as well as other professionals with whom they work, should reach consensus on the criteria for moving from one level to another and the expectations and privileges associated with each level.

The Interventions

In Chapters 6, 7, and 8, the interpersonal skills, behavioral, and cognitive-learning interventions were discussed. These interventions were selected because of the need to show teachers how to (a) use facilitative interpersonal skills, (b) institute behavioral interventions, and (c) help students examine the relationship between their thinking, emotions, and behavior. Additionally, these interventions are practically compatible with one another in that they can be combined or integrated to provide solutions to the problems of children with emotional and behavioral disorders. However, before examining the problem solving process, some of the major underlying assumptions or purposes behind each of the selected interventions are summarized. As depicted in Figure 9-1, the interpersonal skills approach attempts to help the student understand himself and develop insight into the nature of his problem. Insight, it is believed, facilitates cognitive and affective change which lead to behavior change. For example, often students identify their problems incorrectly. For both teacher and student to grasp the true nature of the problem, the teacher will have to use effective interpersonal listening skills. Alternatively, the behavioral approach focuses on the behavior itself and attempts through a variety of techniques to directly alter behavior. For example, for a child who hits others, the technique of Differential Reinforcement of Other Behavior-Omission (DRO-O) may be used to reinforce the omission or absence of inappropriate hitting behavior. By comparison the cognitive learning approaches focus on either (a) changing cognition which produces behavioral change or (b) changing cognition which affects emotional change first and as a result produces behavioral change. An example of the first type of cognitive-learning approach, is cognitive self-monitoring. In cognitive self-monitoring, when students regularly ask themselves whether they are paying attention, this regular pattern of cognition is expected to increase the time they spend attending. Alternatively, Rational-Emotive Therapy (RET) is an example of the second type of cognitive-learning approach. When students learn in RET that the statements they make to themselves make them feel bad and produce dysfunctional behavior, the technique of disputing irrational statements produces a new pattern of cognition which will lead to more positive emotional consequences and improved behavior.

How to Solve Problems

For too long, teacher educators have attempted to provide teachers with ready-made techniques that are presumed to provide the answers to different educational problems. Such techniques become more or

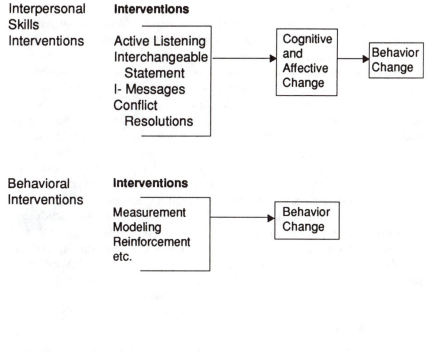

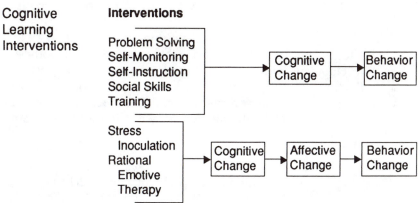

Figure 9-1. A diagrammatic illustration of the Interpersonal Skills, Behavioral, and Cognitive-Learning Interventions.

less in vogue for several years and then diminish in importance as teachers find that these techniques do not provide the solutions that were promised. Additionally, after trying techniques that appear not to work, teachers become disenchanted and begin to believe that either they are failures as teachers or that their students are simply too disturbed or too incapable to learn. As a result, many teachers often either quit teaching or continue to teach halfheartedly without expecting very much in the way of student improvement.

Teacher failures can be avoided when teachers are taught how to solve problems. John Dewey, the great American pragmatist educator and philosopher, pointed out that education was not the application of specific ready made ideas to the solution of problems, but instead the formation of the right mental attitude to use in attacking problems. Additionally, in his book, *How we think,* Dewey (1933) demonstrated how ideas can be used as tools in providing the solutions to real problems. The problem-solving stages he outlined approximate the steps in the scientific method, which are the steps that scientists use to solve problems. Teachers need to become aware that these same time-tested steps can be used to solve the academic, emotional, and social problems of children with emotional and behavioral disorders. Consequently, Dewey's approach to solving problems, that is, the scientific method, can be viewed as a metaparadigm for applying and integrating the interventions that have been presented.

In his book, *How we think,* Dewey set forth the stages of his approach as follows:

1. A "felt difficulty" occurs in which we sense that there is a problem.
2. We "establish its location and definition."
3. We formulate "suggestions of possible solutions" or hypotheses.
4. "Development by reasoning of the bearings of the suggestions, reflecting on the possible outcomes of acting on these suggestions or," in other words, we think about and ask ourselves what would probably happen if we tried out or tested particular hypotheses.
5. "Further observation and experiment leading to its acceptance or rejection", i.e., we test the hypotheses to see if the action taken provides a solution to the problem. (pp. 102-118)

What Dewey presented in detail is a step-by-step approach for solving problems. Without Dewey's prose, these steps might be reworded as follows:

1. There is a problem.
2. Identify, define, and describe the problem.
3. Generate possible plans for solving the problem.
4. Evaluate the plans and decide which plan is best.
5. Test the best plan by trying it out.

Although these steps are presented in an orderly sequence, they are not independent and do not necessarily occur in a given order, that is, they can occur so that the various steps interact with one another. For example, in the process of completing step 5 and determining that what was first viewed as the best plan of action was unsuccessful, additional information might suggest that the original definition of the problem was faulty. This new information might lead to either (a) seeking greater clarity with regard to the exact identity of the problem, that is, going back to step 2, or (b) deciding that the newly acquired information requires varying the original plan only slightly and testing the new amended plan immediately. The feedback obtained after implementing the plan will help with the assessment of its success or failure and provide additional information for solving the problem.

A Scientific Approach to Integrating Interventions

How can the scientific method be used to select an appropriate intervention for a particular behavioral problem? The steps of the scientific method and an example of how these can be used to select an intervention follow.

1. There is a Problem

Dewey used the phrase "felt difficulty" to describe the sense individuals might have which would motivate them to began to think about a problem. For special educators who teach children with emotional and behavior disorders, establishing that a problem exists usually will not be difficult. Problems such as teasing, crying, fighting, screaming, showing off, and talking out will most certainly attract our attention. However, because some students have problems of anxiety and avoidance or covert behaviors such as stealing, teachers have to be careful not to ignore problems which do not affect them directly. Teachers will have to determine whether "there is a problem." Therefore, an example of one intervention that step 1 of the scientific method might suggest would be active listening. The intervention will help teachers uncover covert problems and acquire insight into their nature.

2. Identify, Define, and Describe the Problem

In this step of the scientific method, not only active listening but other interpersonal skills are important. Teachers often define the problem too quickly, defining only superficial symptoms of the problems. In step 2, teachers should reflect on Gordon's problem ownership rectangle to make certain that they have correctly identified problem ownership (Gordon, 1974). Determining problem ownership is a necessary prerequisite for the next step, step 3, "generating possible plans for solving the problem." For example, if the student owns the problem, examples of interventions to consider might include active listening or Rational-Emotive Therapy, whereas if the teacher owns the problem, sending I-Messages or using a behavior-reduction technique such as time out (TO) might be advised. If the problem is a student-owned one, the teacher will be able to use listening skills in two major ways. First, the teacher can apply her skills to demonstrate that she understands, empathizes and accepts the student. Second, she can apply her listening skills as Carkhuff (1980) would advise, in either personalizing the problem or personalizing the meaning, to get the student to own the problem. In any case, the teacher's interpersonal listening skills represent one intervention for identifying, defining, and describing students' problems.

Other examples of intervention for identifying, defining, and describing student problems, would include the assessment techniques described in Chapter 3. In cases in which the problem is primarily academic, formal and informal assessments can be used to determine precisely what academic skills a student possesses. When the problem is social or emotional, the teacher can augment her listening skill by using anecdotal records, tests, interviews, self-ratings, and informant reports. The measurement strategies, for example, defining behavior, taking baselines, and trend projections, mentioned in Chapter 7 are useful also. These assessment techniques complement the interpersonal listening techniques described in Chapter 6.

3. Generating Possible Plans For Solving the Problem

The intervention plans described in Chapters 6, 7, and 8 are appropriate for a variety of academic, social, and emotional problems. Additionally, many of these interventions can be used in combination with one another. To generate possible intervention plans as rapidly as possible, each of the interpersonal skills, behavioral, and cognitive-learning interventions discussed in Chapter 6, 7, and 8 have been identified in Table 9-1. Further, interventions are matched with each of the major behavioral dimensions in Quay's (1987) dimensional classification system in Table 9-2. This latter table, however, should be interpreted with caution and used as a guide only in generating possible intervention plans.

Conduct Disorders

For conduct disorders, interventions were selected to reduce the frequency of the many inappropriate behaviors associated with this category. Because this disorder is characterized primarily by either annoying or hostile overt behavior problems, interventions were selected primarily from the behavioral model. Cognitive social problem solving and cognitive social skill training were also selected because of the possibility that some of the inappropriate behaviors associated with conduct disorders might be the result of a failure to learn appropriate social skills. Finally, Rational-Emotive Therapy (RET), Rational-Emotive Education (REE), and Rational-Emotive Group Counseling (REGC) were included for children whose behavioral problems were clearly the result of faulty cognition.

Socialized Aggression

For socialized aggression, active listening and interchangeable statements were selected because of the covert nature of the behaviors associated with this disorder. These interpersonal skills should be valuable for identification, definition, and description, and also helpful in influencing children with these problems, for example, to cease associating with delinquent friends and bad companions. Modeling and cognitive social skills training were also selected as interventions for teaching skills which would receive positive reinforcement from mainstream peers.

Attention Problems/Immaturity

For the problems associated with the dimension of attention problems/immaturity, behavioral techniques were selected. Too often children with attention problems receive reinforcement for off-task behaviors (Hall, Lund, & Jackson, 1968; Walker & Buckley, 1971).

TABLE 9-1. An identification of the intervention plans associated with the three major intervention models.

Interpersonal Skills Interventions	Behavioral Interventions	Cognitive-Learning Interventions
Establishing problem ownership	Respondent Extinction	Cognitive Social Problem Solving
Avoiding roadblocks to Communication	Graduated Extinction	Cognitive Self-Monitoring
Active listening	Counterconditioning	Cognitive Self-Instruction
Responding to feelings	Group Countercondi-tioning	Cognitive Social Skills Training
Complementing feeling with meaning	Token Systems	Stress Inoculation
Personalizing mean-ing	Positive Reinforce-ment	Rational-Emotive Therapy
Personalizing the problem	Positive Punishment	Rational-Emotive Education
Initiating responding	Negative Punishment	Rational-Emotive Group Counseling
Sending I-Messages	Operant Extinction	
Shifting from I-Messages to active listening	Shaping	
The No Lose Method of Resolving Conflict	Modeling	
	Scheduling	
	Discrimination Training	
	Fading	
	Chaining	
	Combination Interven-tions	
	DRO	
	DRL	
	OC	
	RC	
	TO	

Teachers need to become more aware of the ways in which these children "bootleg" reinforcement by receiving attention for concentrating poorly, becoming distracted, and exhibiting a short attention span. It is possible, however, to turn this situation around. The use of a variable interval (VI) schedule, for example, can be an ideal way

TABLE 9-2. An guideline to help teachers match interventions with disorders associated with Quay's major behavioral dimensions.

DISORDERS	PLAUSIBLE INTERVENTIONS
I. CONDUCT DISORDERS Seeks attention, shows off, disruptive, annoys and bothers others, fights, has temper tantrums	Operant Extinction, Negative Punishment, DRO, DRL, OC, RC, TO, Cognitive Social Problem solving, Cognitive Social Skills Training, RET, REE, REGC
II. SOCIALIZED AGGRESSION Steals in company with others, loyal to delinquent friends, truant from school, has bad companions, freely admits disrespect for moral values and laws	Active Listening, making interchangeable statements, Modeling, Cognitive Social Skills Training
III. ATTENTION PROBLEMS/ IMMATURITY Short attention span, poor concentration, distractible, easily diverted from task at hand, sluggish, slow moving, lethargic, answers without stopping to think	Positive Reinforcement, Operant Extinction, DRO, DRL, Cognitive Self-Monitoring, Scheduling, Fading
IV. ANXIETY-WITHDRAWAL Self-conscious, easily embarrassed, hypersensitive, feelings easily hurt, generally fearful, anxious, depressed, always sad	Active Listening, making interchangeable statements, Graduated Extinction, Counter-conditioning, Stress Inoculation, RET, REE, REG
V. PSYCHOTIC BEHAVIOR Repetitive speech, says same thing over and over, expresses strange far fetched ideas	Positive Reinforcement, Operant Extinction, Negative Punishment, Shaping, Modeling, Scheduling, Discrimination Training, Fading, Chaining, DRO, DRL, OC, RC, TO
VI. MOTOR EXCESS Restless, unable to sit still, tense, over talkative	Positive Reinforcement, Operant Extinction, Shaping, Scheduling, DRO, DRL

to get students to keep their eyes fixed on the assigned material. Short quizzes can be used afterward to determine whether students have concentrated. By making attending pay off on a VI schedule, that is, if a student's eyes are directed appropriately they receive reinforcement, and by providing reinforcement for correctly answered questions, students can be taught to manage their distractibility, concentrate, and increase their attention span.

Anxiety/Withdrawal

Because the problems associated with anxiety-withdrawal are often overlooked, active listening and interchangeable statements were selected as interventions which would help teachers not only in going deeper into the nature of the problem, but also in uncovering the relationship between thinking, emotions, and behavior. Although for some students the use of interpersonal listening skills will be sufficient to provide the necessary means for helping them solve their own problems, for others these skills will serve as the initial phase of treatment only. Graduated extinction and counterconditioning were also included as interventions which can be used to help fearful children conquer their fear. Additionally, stress inoculation was selected because it can be used as preparatory intervention for students who will benefit by anticipating or planning for anxiety- and fear-provoking situations. Finally, RET, REE, and REGC were selected because they directly link thinking, emotions, and behavior.

Psychotic Behavior

For the dimension of psychotic behavior, behavioral approaches were selected. Generally, the practitioner will want to reduce or eliminate inappropriate excess behavior or increase and shape behaviors which are deficient. For inappropriate behaviors such as self-stimulation, the literature provides many examples of the successful use of such interventions as time out (TO), overcorrection (OC), response cost (RC), and differential reinforcement of other behavior (DRO). For increasing appropriate behavior such as language or self-help skills, the use of discrimination training, shaping, fading and backward chaining have been used frequently with great success.

Motor Excess

For the dimension of motor excess, behavioral techniques were selected. Too often teachers inadvertently reinforce restlessness, squirming, and talking too much. Walker and Buckley (1971) found that of the attention directed toward problem children, 89% was for inappropriate responding, whereas only 11% was for appropriate responding. Teachers need to find ways to reinforce sitting still, being relaxed, and so on. Also, relaxation training has been shown to be useful in solving some of the problems of children who have excess motor behavior (Raymer & Poppen, 1985).

4. Evaluate the Plans and Decide Which Plan is Best

After examining each of the possible interventions, teachers should consider the specific nature of the student problem and the probable outcome of implementing each specific intervention. For example, in the case of a student who exhibits temper tantrums frequently, the teacher might observe the behavior for several days before deciding that a plausible explanation for these tantrums is the attention received immediately following each tantrum. Based on this analysis, the teacher may decide to place the tantrum behavior under operant extinction and use a DRO to reinforce nontantrum behavior and to speed up the extinction process. However, before implementing this intervention and after considering the problem further, by observing the behavior and using interpersonal listening skills, the teacher detects that each tantrum episode occurs after a perceived injustice, for example, the student did not get to put a problem on the board, did not get red construction paper, and so on. Based on this evidence, the teacher may decide to include the student in an REE group and in REGC also. This will help the student explore and examine the impact of his cognition on his emotions and behavior.

Therefore, to decide on the best intervention plan(s): (a) consider the specific nature of the problem by continuing to observe and listen and (b) reflect on the most probable outcome of applying each specific intervention.

5. Test the Best Plan By Trying It Out

After deciding on the best intervention or combination intervention, try it out. This is the means by which feedback can be obtained on the analysis of the problem. Also, while implementing the intervention, continue to observe and listen to determine whether or not the intervention is effective. If observations have been recorded appropriately as baseline data, behavior changes can be measured accurately. If change does not occur, return to step 2 of the scientific method and reconsider the nature of the problem. Continue to listen and observe to determine what may have been overlooked in the original analysis and then repeat the steps of the scientific method again. To solve the problems of children with emotional and behavioral disorders, teachers must continually and systematically re-examine the nature of the problem, critically reflect on the problem solving steps of the scientific method, and implement reasoned interventions.

Summary

For too long, arguments have been presented over which model of intervention was the most helpful in solving the problems of children with emotional or behavioral disorders. It is past time for scientists representing different interventions to come together to consider integrating their efforts to help children.

Some degree of physical and psychological structure appears to be a necessary component of most interventions. Structure is inherent in the design of IEPs, individualized curricula, qualitatively phrased classroom rules, teacher expectations, engineered classrooms, and level systems. The interpersonal skills, behavioral, and cognitive learning interventions are practically compatible with one another and can be combined or integrated to provide solutions to the problems of children with emotional or behavioral disorders.

In the past, teacher educators have attempted to provide teachers with ready-made techniques which are presumed to provide the answers to difficult educational problems. These ready made techniques are generally in vogue for a time and then diminish in importance as teachers become disenchanted and began to believe they have failed. However, teacher failures can be avoided when teachers are taught how to solve problems. John Dewey, the American pragmatist, pointed out that education was not the application of specific ready-made ideas to the solution of problems, but instead the formation of the right mental attitude in attacking problems. John Dewey demonstrated how ideas can be used as tools in providing the solution to real problems. The problem-solving stages he outlined approximate the scientific method. John Dewey's approach, the scientific method, can be viewed as a metaparadigm for applying and integrating interpersonal skills, behavioral, and cognitive interventions. The stages in his methods can be paraphrased as follows: (a) there is a problem; (b) identify, define and describe the problem; (c) generate possible plans for solving the problem; (d) evaluate the plans and decide which plan is best; and (e) test the best plan by trying it out. The steps of the scientific method can be used to select and integrate appropriate interventions for a particular behavioral problem. Examples of how to use the steps of the scientific method to select and integrate interventions were provided. To generate possible plans for solving the emotional or behavioral problems, possible interventions were matched with the major behavioral dimensions in Quay's dimensional classification system.

Review Questions

1. Why is there a need to integrate or combine interventions?
2. Identify the three positions that have been generally taken with regard to the selection of an intervention.
3. How does the engineered classroom provide physical and psychological structure?
4. Identify the major purposes associated with the interpersonal skills, behavioral, and cognitive-learning interventions.
5. List the steps involved in solving problems.
6. In step 2, what things do you need to be able to do to identify, define, and describe the problem?
7. What interventions are suggested for solving the problems of psychotic youth?
8. What two things do you need to do to decide on the best intervention plan(s)?
9. What should you do when it appears that the intervention you selected is not working?

Learning Activities

1. Divide into groups of five to six and as a group identify, define, and describe the problem presented below on a student assigned to your class. After doing this, generate five possible intervention plans for solving the problem. Evaluate each plan and decide on which plan your group would implement first. Each group is to present its conclusions to the class with an accompanying rationale.

Robert liked to fight, especially when he was upset. His entire demeanor seemed to say stay away if you know what's good for you. He was experienced at intimidation and could win most of the fights he started. One of his favorite tactics was to approach his classmates either in the restroom or on the way home from school with an opened pocket knife and to demand to touch their genitals. He usually approached children who could be easily intimidated, thus he often got what he wanted. Another pastime was to identify an unsuspecting student absorbed in some peaceful playground activity. Starting from afar, he would zoom in and start running toward his target as fast as he could, making fighter plane noises. Elbows forward, he would slam into his victim at about rib level, knocking the student down, and usually knocking the wind out of him.

10
Crisis Management

T his chapter discusses how teachers can prevent potential crises from occurring and describes how to intervene when a crisis has already occurred so that the crisis can be used as a learning opportunity. Specifically this chapter emphasizes: (a) the need for crisis management, (b) common approaches to crisis prevention, (c) common elements in most crisis intervention strategies, and (d) the Life Space Intervention.

The Need for Crisis Management

For many, an awareness of the need for crisis management is apparent. The problems of divorce, drug abuse, acoholism, rape, incest, gang violence, violence at school, crime, depression, and suicide seem to be everywhere. In television commentaries and in newspaper editorials, the high levels of deterioration and disturbance in families and communities are constantly being reported. The question of family values which served as a Republican platform issue during the 1992 presidential campaign is a reminder of the pervasive feelings of uneasiness which are experienced today as a result of many social problems. Although social problems are not new to the American landscape, it is clear that many problems have increased dramatically over the past several decades. Many externalizing problems such as crime and violent delinquency have increased (Doke & Flippo, 1983) and among children and youth identified as having behavior disorders or as being at risk, aggressive and violent tendencies are increasing (Simpson, Miles, Walker, Ormsbee, & Downing, 1991). Similarly, internalizing problems such as suicide and suicide attempts have increased dramatically during the past several decades in both adolescent and younger children (Hawton, 1986). In comparing the incidence of suicides in 1950 to 1980, the 1980 figures represent a 300% increase in the 15- to 24-year-old category, and attempted suicide is even more common (Davis, 1988).

Although the exact reasons for these escalating emotional and behavioral problems are not known, some authorities, who prefer to study multiple structural changes which occur as the result of divorce and remarriage, suspect that these changes contribute to behavioral problems by making it likely that the family system experiences difficulty in providing nurturance, sustaining intimacy, and containing anxiety (King & Goldman, 1988). Other investigators focus more generically. They view these escalating problems as the interaction among the personal psychological resources of the parent, characteristics of the child, and the environment context, which they argue provides both sources of support and stress (Belsky, 1984).

In any case, it is clear that teachers of the emotionally or behaviorally disordered will increasingly have to be able to provide the kind of support required in managing crises. At times, this help will take the form of prevention, that is, teachers must anticipate problems and develop strategies to prevent crises from occurring.

Common Approaches to Crisis Prevention

According to Sandoval (1985) there are at least five general strategies that are commonly used to prevent crises. These are educational workshops, anticipatory guidance, screening, consultation, and research (Sandoval, 1985).

Educational Workshop

Sandoval (1985) views an educational workshop as an intensive course of study designed to generate emotions. The purpose of these workshops is to circumvent future emotional problems, that is, they are preventative. Accordingly, Rational Emotive Education (REE), referred to in Chapter 8, would serve as an example of such a preventative program. Virtually any classroom lesson which would help children deal with their feelings and discuss what was occurring in their lives would fall into this category.

Anticipatory Guidance

This second approach which Sandoval (1985) has variously referred to as anticipatory guidance or emotional inoculation, is referred to in Chapter 8 as stress inoculation. The principal purpose of anticipatory guidance is to help students prepare for events in the future that are likely to be stressful, that is, being ridiculed during recess.

Screening Programs

This technique has to do with identifying children who are at risk for educational failure or other kinds of social and emotional crises. Rating scales, interviews, direct observation, and many other screening devices can be used to identify potential candidates. Once these candidates are identified, preventative interventions such as anticipatory guidance, REE, or school counseling are advised.

Consultation

In this context, consultation implies that someone other than the teacher act to prevent potential crises. A consultant who works with the teacher and perhaps the parents may be able to help these significant adults avert a crisis. The implication for teachers is to enlist the aid of support professionals, such as school counselors and administrators, and to work collaboratively for the purpose of preventing crises.

Research

Although Sandoval (1985) admits that doing research is not usually viewed as a part of crisis prevention, he suggests that the more that is learned through research about crises, the better society will be able to prevent them from occurring. In this context, it is suggested that research will contribute to greater effectiveness in designing workshops, developing curricula, and so on.

While these five approaches to crisis prevention will not guarantee that all crises will cease to occur, they are anticipatory and should result in a decrease in number of emergency situations in which an actual crisis intervention is required.

Sometimes, however, emergency situations will have already occurred and teachers will have to intervene to provide help to the student in crisis. When this occurs, the teacher will need to listen and will have to talk. Handling crises will require using many of the interpersonal skills discussed in Chapter 6. Sometimes these skills will protect teachers from danger. Also, teachers should try to turn the crisis into a learning experience for the student. Although there are many differing approaches to crisis intervention, many of these approaches share common elements.

Common Elements in Crisis Intervention Strategies

According to Baldwin (1978) crises may be divided into classes. These classes are: (a) dispositional crises, in which the helper's intervention is not directed to the emotional level of the client, for example, helping a pupil learn about a weight-training program to build bigger muscles; (b) anticipated life transitions, for example, moving from a self-contained special class to a regular class, (c) traumatic stress, for example, sexual assault; (d) maturational/developmental crises, in which the principal issues include sexual identity, dependency, response to authority, and self-discipline; (e) crises reflecting psychopathology, for example, psychotic behavior; and (f) psychiatric emergencies, for example, a suicide attempt.

Although these classes reflect a diversity of the types of problems which are associated with crises, the literature related to crisis intervention appears to be much less diverse in offering suggestions for managing crises. Because teachers will be called on increasingly to intervene in crises, the principal common elements in crisis intervention strategies have been synthesized and set forth below. These principal elements have been adapted from the work of Caplan (1964); Rusk (1971); Sandoval (1988); Eddy, Lawson, and Stilson (1983); and Parad and Parad (1991). Although listed sequentially, in the order in which they may often occur, teachers may find themselves having to return to repeat earlier steps or to advance to a later step in the sequence prior to having completed an intermediate step. Therefore, the following common elements in crisis intervention strategies are not necessarily sequential.

Relax and Begin Helping Immediately

When in crisis, the student is by definition off balance and in a state of psychological disequilibrium or confusion. This implies that the student is experiencing psychological pain and hurt. The longer the student is allowed to exist in this state the more difficult it will be to help him return to normal adjustment. Therefore, the teacher must intervene immediately to assist in the restoration of psychological balance and should view the crisis as a counseling/learning opportunity for the student.

Demonstrate a Motivation to Help

Some authorities view this as the most important element in crisis intervention. If students know that teachers really want to help and are sincerely concerned, they will often overlook other mistakes that may accidently occur. It is very important that teachers communicate a genuine desire to help.

Provide Hope

Because students in crisis are shaken, they need to be able to believe that things are not hopeless and that there is hope. Basically, they are afraid and need a degree of reassurance that will make them feel safe and believe that things will work out. The teacher can promote this feeling by acting confidently and by demonstrating competence in problem solving.

Support the Student by Listening

As suggested in Chapter 6, it is extremely important to listen. Listening is one of the core ingredients in crisis intervention. Teachers must demonstrate to the student that they empathize and understand so that students will come to understand that feelings can be discussed and used as the basis for problem exploration. Additionally, the teacher must avoid either actively or passively supporting students in blaming themselves or others. Instead try to gather concrete information in sufficient detail to understand the nature of the problem.

Identify and Solve the Problem

This step and the preceding step of listening are the most important elements in crisis intervention. Although it is necessary to listen in order to identify and solve the problem, at some point teachers will need to understand and identify exactly what events brought the student to crisis and begin helping them to identify and develop a plan for dealing with these events and solving the problem. To do this, teachers need to keep the student's attention focused on the problem-solving issues associated with the crisis and prevent the student from becoming overly defensive.

Support a Healthy Self-Concept

When students react to crises by projecting blame or through self-criticism, it is important for the teacher to keep in mind that crisis situations often result in diminished self-esteem. Such defenses as projection are often an attempt to maintain a healthy self-concept. With this in mind, teachers must make certain not to design problem-solving strategies that ask too much of the student too soon. The student too must succeed and feel good about the progress being made. Even in looking back at the crisis, teachers should try to find and emphasize what the student did that was positive. In any case, make certain that the intervention strategy will have a positive effect on the student's self-concept.

Foster Self-Reliance

During crisis intervention, the student will often become dependent on the teacher. This often occurs because the teacher has provided a good deal of emotional support and has empathized with the student. Although this temporary situation is initially desirable and serves the purpose of restoring psychological equilibrium, the teacher must find ways to re-establish self-reliance prior to ending the counseling session. This may be accomplished by helping the student own much of the responsibility for solving the problem and by de-emphasizing the teacher's own contributions to the process.

The Life Space Intervention

Although the elements presented above appear in most crisis intervention strategies, the Life Space Intervention (LSI) is emphasized because of its extensive growth and history of over 40 years. Initially this approach was published in the fifties and up until very recently most often referred to as the "Life Space Interview." Although the origins of the approach can be traced back to the 1900s in Europe, its more recent history is generally associated with the work of Fritz Redl and David Wineman who in the 1950s attempted at Pioneer House to understand and treat aggressive and delinquent children who had difficulty developing inner controls over their aggressive impulses. Although many others have been associated with this primarily psychoeducational approach, the credit for recently documenting its effectiveness belongs to Naslund (1987) who published a study which analyzed the changes that occurred during an academic year while using LSI. Finally, and most recently, Nicholas Long and Mary Wood, whose involvement can be traced back to the 1950s and the 1970s, respectively have published *Life space intervention: Talking with children and youth in crisis* to draw attention to LSI as powerful technique for teaching children how to regulate their own behavior (Wood & Long, 1991). Because the purpose of LSI is to help children get through stressful experiences and to deal with the conflicts that create crises, the events which Wood and Long have termed the Conflict Cycle are discussed first.

The Conflict Cycle

Although Wood and Long (1991) explain that the Conflict Cycle could also be called the Stress or Crisis Cycle, they say that they decided to use the term Conflict Cycle to highlight the opposing forces which occur between the needs within a student and the expectations of others. The resolution or minimization of these forces result in healthy adjustment, whereas the continuation or escalation of these opposites lead to maladjustment.

In its most basic sense, the Conflict Cycle occurs as a spiraling cycle in which, because of stress, the student develops negative feelings and anxieties that cause him to produce excessively defensive behaviors that result in negative reactions by others. These negative reactions are then recycled producing more stress, anxiety, and defensive behavior and keeping the Conflict Cycle going around and around with an ever increasing and expanding intensity.

Because there are so many sources of stress in contemporary society (i.e., family problems, school problems, and problems of growing up), students store memories of thoughts, feelings, and anxieties which are potentially painful and assaultive. To protect themselves from re-experiencing these earlier pains, students often develop excessively defensive behaviors such as denial, escapism, and substitution as a means of coping. Because these defensive maneuvers, for example, "He took the money, I didn't," produce negative reactions from others which produce stress, the Conflict Cycle will continue to expand unless an adult who understands the cycle intervenes. For teachers to do this, they must understand what is occurring and make certain not to respond with the counteraggression that many of the student's defensive behaviors will tend to elicit. Long (1993) has explained that untrained adults often inadvertently reinforce self-fulfilling prophesies and irrational beliefs, such as "Nothing good ever happens to me," by allowing themselves to become seduced into a power struggle. To intervene successfully, Wood and Long (1991) explain that teachers need to become familiar with the six steps of the Life Space Intervention.

The Six Steps of the Life Space Intervention

While the Life Space Intervention is conducted at the time a crisis occurs to help students understand their feelings and manage their behavior, Wood and Long advise that its use occur only after preventative strategies, for example, the use of a token system, have already been tried. Additionally, they explain that although it is the teacher's responsibility to accept and understand feelings, the Life Space Intervention must move from the acceptance of feelings to clearly establishing that reality consequences will occur if students make the choice to engage in inappropriate behavior. Finally, effective LSI should result in both long- and short-term gains which are indicative of the student's needs and circumstances. Figure 10-1 depict the six steps of the Life Space Intervention.

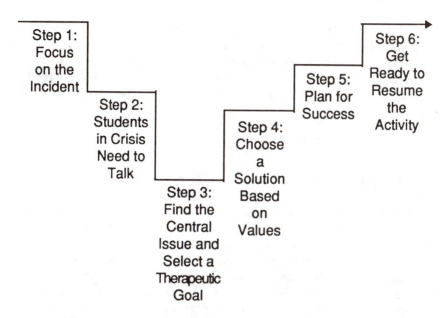

Figure 10-1. The six steps of Life Space Intervention. From *Life space intervention: Talking with children and youth in crisis* (p. 8) by M. Wood and N. Long, 1991, Austin: Pro-Ed, Inc. Copyright 1991 by Pro-Ed, Inc. Reprinted by permission.

Step 1. Focus on the Incident

In this step the teacher tries to get the student to start talking about the incident by showing empathy and a desire to help. Teachers often need to use their interpersonal listening skills while providing time for the students to express themselves and to get rid of intense emotional feelings. During this phase the event or incident that brought about the crisis should be identified. Wood and Long (1991) provide the following example of a statement a teacher may make during this step:

"This is a difficult situation, but we can work it out together." (p. 114)

Step 2. Students in Crisis Need to Talk

During this stage of the intervention, students need to continue to vent their emotions while developing a more rational grasp of the components of the incident. The teacher must continue to use listening skills and must also ask questions which will help the student understand the incident clearly. Additionally, the teachers must try to determine for themselves, whether the incident or some underlying anxiety is the paramount issue. Wood and Long (1991) provide the following example of a statment a teacher may make during this step.

"What happened before that?" (p. 118)

Step 3. Find the Central Issue and Select a Therapeutic Goal

In this phase, the teacher must continue to explore the incident in terms of both the student's surface behavior and underlying emotions. At this point, the teacher will have to influence the student to give up some of his overly defensive stances. This is necessary so that the teacher can state the central issue and determine what the therapeutic goal should be for the Life Space Intervention. Determining the therapeutic goal will be based in part on an assessment of the student's insights and desire to change. Wood and Long (1991) provide an example of a statement that a teacher may make during this step.

"It seems that messing with others leads to problems; and here you are, having a problem." (p. 126)

Step 4. Choose a Solution Based on Values

For there to be a degree of motivation on the part of the student to change his behavior, the teacher must attempt to get the student to own the solution to the problems by either identifying or helping to identify a solution which the student perceives as beneficial and valuable. This step is complete when the student chooses a solution that he can express in words. Wood and Long (1991) provide an example of a statement which a teacher might make in helping a student evaluate possible solutions.

"That would be really hard to do. Would it be worth the trouble?" (p. 136)

Step 5. Plan for Success

This is the step in which the student will have to practice and rehearse the behaviors that will have to be put into effect to implement the solution which was identified in the previous step. In this step, the student will need to anticipate potential problems and will require a good deal of encouragement to try out the new behaviors and to not rely on previous inappropriate and unsuccessful behaviors. Wood and Long (1991) provide the following example of a statement a teacher might make to encourage the student to rehearse responses in anticipation of problems.

> "You have a good idea here. What will you say to him when we leave here?" (p. 142)

Step 6. Get Ready to Resume Activity

In this step the teacher shifts from the incident and issue of how to implement the solution to helping prepare the student for re-entering the peer group. As this step ends, the student should be under rational control and be able to anticipate how others will react and how they will behave when he returns to rejoin the group.

Five Types of Therapeutic Goals

Once the issue has been formulated and the problem understood, Wood and Long (1991) discuss five particular therapeutic goals which will help students understand themselves and their behavior. These goals are to (a) organize reality when a student does not see an event as others do, (b) benignly confront unacceptable behavior when a student does not want to change, (c) build values that strengthen self-control, (d) teach new social skills, and (e) expose exploitation of students who are abused, isolated, or exploited by others.

Because almost every major issue can be resolved by organizing LSI around one of these goals, the teacher's task in step 3 of the LSI becomes one of selecting the goal which best represents the solution to the student's problem. In making this selection, teachers need to consider the student's motivation to change and current understanding of the incident. When teachers understand how the student perceives the incident, they enable themselves to more readily select a goal for the student that will facilitate student insight (Wood & Long, 1991). What follows is a condensed summary of each goal.

Organize Reality

These students feel they have been treated unfairly or gypped and that they are being falsely accused. In conducting a LSI around this goal, the teacher must attempt to correct the false perception and get the student to see his contribution to the problem. Wood and Long (1991) suggest that a potential new insight during step 3 for this goal might be "I only saw and remembered part of the problem. Now I see the part my own behavior played in the crisis" (p. 129).

Confront Unacceptable Behavior

These students feel that they have the right to engage in deviant behavior even at the expense of others. In this LSI, the goal is to make the deviant behavior uncomfortable by confronting rationalizations and using behavioral consequences. Wood and Long (1991) suggest that a potential new insight during step 3 for this goal might be "Maybe I'm not as smart as I tell myself. Maybe I've been cruel. Maybe I've been tricking myself" (p. 129).

Build Values to Strengthen Self-Control

These students lose control and later feel guilty. In this LSI, the teacher needs to emphasize the student's positive characteristics and through the use of listening skill help the student acquire insight into why he is losing control. By increasing student insight as well as confidence, students become better able to develop self-control. Wood and Long (1991) suggest that a potential new insight during step 3 for this goal might be "Even under tempting situations or group pressure, I have the capacity to control myself" (p. 130).

Teach New Social Skills

These students want to have friends, belong to a peer group, be approved of by the teacher, and so on, except their social behaviors tend to irritate and turn people away. The goal for this LSI is to help the students understand what they are doing wrong and teach new social skills that will pay off immediately. Wood and Long (1991) suggest that a potential new insight during stage 3 for this goal might be "I have the right intention, but I need help to learn the skills that will help me make friends, achieve, and get along with others" (p. 130).

Expose Exploitation

These students allow themselves to be used or manipulated by others because of their own emotional neediness. They are often abused, teased, and scapegoated. The goal for this LSI is to help the student understand how he is being manipulated and to support him in developing skills which he can use to acquire new and more genuine friends. Wood and Long (1991) suggest that a potential new insight during step 3 for this goal might be "A friend is someone who helps you solve problems and feel good rather than someone who gets you into trouble" (p. 131).

The Necessary Helping Skills

Wood and Long (1991) point out that for a teacher to effectively help a student during a LSI, the teacher must have a good foundation in the helping process. This implies that the teacher have a genuine desire to help and is able to avoid reacting personally to an incident. Wood and Long advise that helpers develop interpersonal skills similar to those discussed in Chapter 6. Table 10-1 lists the skills Wood and Long advise adults to possess in using LSI. Additionally, they identify "the potential pitfalls" in using LSI as:

1. beginning LSI when a student is not ready
2. getting off the subject
3. allowing an adversarial climate to develop
4. reflecting negatives
5. permitting a student to seduce you into counteraggression
6. treating complex feelings in trivial ways
7. failing to build LSI dialogue from a student's responses
8. invading a student's private space
9. interjecting personal comments about yourself
10. allowing students to reverse roles with you
11. failing to state the central issue simply and concisely
12. jumping to solutions prematurely
13. failing to consider negative solutions and consequences. (pp. 168-183)

TABLE 10-1. A list of skills for using the Life Space Intervention. From *Life space intervention: Talking with children and youth in crisis* (p. 160) by M. Wood and N. Long, 1991, Austin: Pro-Ed, Inc. Copyright 1991 by Pro-Ed, Inc. Reprinted by permission.

NONVERBAL BODY LANGUAGE	VERBAL STYLE	RELATIONSHIP
Convey support and alliance through body posture. Use eye contact or the opposite as needed to provide "space." Vary voice quality and volume as needed. Use physical stance to convey needed adult role and relationship. Avoid excessive touch. Maintain physical proximity or distance as needed. Stand or sit as needed to convey control. Convey interest, support, or other messages through facial expressions.	Use concrete words for clarity. Use imagery to motivate. Convey ideas clearly. Maximize student's talk. Use a time line to help student organize events. Assist student in clarifying an issue. Assist student in seeing cause-and-effect relationships. Use reflection effectively. Use interpretation effectively. Decode accurately. Use third-person form to generalize. Limit use of references to yourself. Limit use of negative statements.	Use active listening. Communicate respect for student. Communicate interest. Communicate calm self-control. Convey confidence and optimism. Convey focus and competence. Avoid intruding into student's private "space." Avoid value judgments. Avoid role reversals. Avoid counter-aggression.

Although teachers will make these mistakes occasionally, teachers should monitor themselves so that when mistakes are made they will know what to do to improve their next LSI (Wood & Long, 1991).

Summary

For many the need for crisis management is apparent. High levels of disturbance in families and communities are being constantly reported. Although the exact reasons for these escalating emotional or behavioral problems are not known, there are five general strategies used to prevent crises. These are educational workshops, anticipatory guidance, screening, consultation, and research.

Sometimes, however, emergency situations will have already occurred and teachers will have to intervene to help students in crisis. The literature related to crisis intervention suggests that teachers implement the following common principles in crisis intervention: (a) relax and begin helping immediately, (b) demonstrate a motivation to help, (c) provide hope, (d) support the student by listening, (e) identify and solve the problem, (f) support a healthy self-concept, and (g) foster self-reliance.

One particularly well documented approach to crisis intervention is called Life Space Intervention. Its purpose is to help children get through stressful experiences and deal with the conflicts that create crises. Stressful experiences often occur in cycles which have been called the conflict cycle. The conflict cycle occurs as a spiraling cycle in which, because of stress, students develop negative feelings and anxieties that cause them to produce defensive behaviors resulting in negative reactions from others. These negative reactions produce more stress, anxiety, and negative reactions, keeping the cycle of conflict revolving. In the Life Space Intervention, teachers attempt to help students break this cycle. The following six steps comprise a Life Space Intervention: (1) focus on the incident, (2) students in crisis need to talk, (3) find the central issue and select a therapeutic goal, (4) choose a solution based on values, (5) plan for success and (6) get ready to resume activity. During step three, teachers must organize the LSI around one of five therapeutic goals. They must select the goal which represents the best solution to the student's problem. The five therapeutic goals are: organize reality, confront unacceptable behavior, build values to strengthen self-control, teach new social skills, and expose exploitation. Teachers are advised to develop interpersonal skills similar to the ones discussed in Chapter 6.

Review Questions

1. Identify several reasons why teachers may need to manage crises.
2. Discuss the two major reasons the author gives for today's escalating emotional and behavioral problems.
3. Briefly describe five approaches to crisis prevention.
4. Give several examples of an educational workshop approach to crisis prevention.
5. Discuss the rationale for classifying research as a crisis prevention approach.
6. Identify and describe the classes into which crises are categorized.
7. Identify and describe the common element in crisis intervention strategies.
8. Identify the subject population that Fritz Redl and David Wineman first worked with and describe how their problem is viewed psychoeducationally.
9. What opposing forces are highlighted in the conflict cycle?
10. Describe a typical conflict cycle.
11. What is the purpose of the Life Space Intervention?
12. What must a teacher avoid doing to intervene successfully in a conflict cycle?
13. Identify and describe the six steps of the Life Space Intervention.
14. In what step in the Life Space Intervention does the teacher decide on a therapeutic goal?
15. Identify the five therapeutic goals and describe in what circumstances the application of each is appropriate.
16. Identify and describe the major kinds of interpersonal skill required by adults who use the Life Space Intervention.
17. Identify the potential pitfalls of using the Life Space Intervention.

Learning Activities

1. Divide into groups of five to six and based on a description of one of Robert's favorite activites, reproduced below, write a Life

Space Intervention plan. Include a detailed description of what your activities would be during each step of the intervention and what target responses you would attempt to elicit. Make certain to select the appropriate reality consequences and therapeutic goal.

> Another pastime was to identify an unsuspecting student absorbed in some peaceful playground activity. Starting from afar he would zoom in and start running toward his target as fast as he could, making fighter plane noises. Elbows forward, he would slam into his victim at about rib level, knocking the student down and usually knocking the wind out of him.

Appendix
Resources and Materials

Chapter One

There are several resources for the reader who wants further information regarding the characteristics, correlates, and consequences of major broad band disorders. Two of the most complete are:

Quay, H. C. & Werry, J. S. (Eds). (1986). *Psychopathological disorders of childhood* (3rd ed.). New York: Wiley.
Ollendick, T. H., & Hersen, M. (Eds.). (1983). *Handbook of child psychopathology*. New York: Plenum.

For individuals who would like to have a copy of DSM III-R, a copy can be obtained from the American Psychiatric Association. Correspondence can be directed to the Division of Publication and Marketing, American Psychiatric Association, 1400 K Street, NW, Washington, DC 20005.

Chapter Two

Most introductory special education textbooks will discuss service placement options. Two follow:

Hardman, M. L., Drew, C. J., Eagan, M. W., & Wolf, B. (1993). *Human exceptionality: Society, school and family* (4th ed.). Boston: Allyn & Bacon.

Hallahan, D. P., & Kauffman, J. M. (1991). *Exceptional children: Introduction to special education* (5th ed.). Englewood Cliffs, NJ: Prentice-Hall.

Further, most textbooks will discuss the services provided under PL 101-476 similarly to the manner in which they been discussed here. Students who have never seen an actual IEP, might want to obtain the forms used in composing one from a local school. Today some schools have computer generated IEPs.

A copy of Alternative Educational Delivery Systems: Enhancing Instructional Options for All Students, might be helpful to students interested in investigating emerging alternative educational services. The full reference is: Garden, J. L., Zins, J. E., & Curtis, M. J. (Eds.) (1988). *Alternative educational delivery systems: Enhancing instructional · options for all students.* Washington, D.C.: National Association of School Psychologists.

Chapter Three

Readers who are interested in obtaining a relatively reliable and valid achievement test, can obtain the Woodcock-Johnson-R Tests of Achievement, which is part of the Woodcock-Johnson Psychoeducational Battery, Revised, from DLM Teaching Resources, One DLM Park, Allen, Texas 75002. For an achievement test that covers a wide range of content areas, students might want to consider the Peabody Individual Achievement Test-Revised. This test covers six content areas and can be obtained from American Guidance Service, Publishers Building, P.O. Box 99 Circle Pines, MN 55014.

For readers interested in two excellent resources listing formal diagnostic assessment devices, for example, Woodcock Reading Mastery Tests-Revised, Gray Oral Reading Tests-Revised, Key Math-Revised, which survey subskills of broader academic areas, I recommend :

McLoughlin, J. A. & Lewis, Rena, B. (1990). *Assessing special needs students.* Columbus, OH: Merrill.

Sattler, M. (1988). *Assessment of children.* San Diego, CA: Jerome M. Sattler, Publisher.

For the reader interested in curriculum handbooks, *Teaching children basic skills: A curriculum handbook* by Stephens, Hartman, and Lucas (1982) provides tasks analyses for kindergarten through the eighth grade in reading, arithmetic, spelling, handwriting, and language arts. The Criterion Referenced Curriculum is another work by Stephens (1984) in which a complete curriculum is set forth for kindergarten through sixth grade in both math and reading. For readers interested in obtaining social skills curricula, four excellent programs follow:

Goldstein, A. P., & McGinnis, E. (1990). *Skillstreaming in early childhood.* Champaign, IL: Research Press.

Goldstein, A. P., & McGinnis, E. (1984). *Skillstreaming the elementary school child.* Champaign, IL: Research Press.

Goldstein, A. P., Sprafkin, R. P., Gershaw, N. J., & Klein, P. (1980). *Skillstreaming the adolescent.* Champaign, IL: Research Press.

Walker, H., McConnell, S., Holmes, D. Todis, B., Walker, J., & Golden, N. (1983). *The Walker social skills curriculum: The ACCEPTS program.* Austin, TX: Pro-ed.

For individuals interested in obtaining the personality tests or rating scales mentioned in this chapter, the names of each test and the accompanying address and telephone number of the publisher follow:

Personality Inventory for
Children
Western Psychological Services
12031 Wilshire Blvd.
Los Angeles, CA 90025
(310) 478-2061

Thematic Apperception Test
Harvard University Press
79 Garden Street
Cambridge, MA 02138
(617) 495-2600

Revised Behavior Problem Checklist
Psychological Assessment Resource
(PAR)
P.O. 998
Odessa, FL 33556
(800) 331-8378

Child Behavior Checklist
Department of Psychiatry
University of Vermont
University Associates in Psychiatry
1 South Street
Burlington, VT 05401
(802) 656-4563

Chapter Four

A thorough discussion of conceptual models which influence intervention is presented in *A study of child variance: Vol. 1. Theories* which was edited by Rhodes and Tracy in 1972. A companion work edited by the same authors, entitled *A study of child variance: Vol. 2. Interventions* was published in 1972 also. These works were originally published in Ann Arbor by the University of Michigan. For students who are interested in locating these volumes, a university library will probably be the best source. Full references for these works follow:

Rhodes, W. C., & Tracy, M. L. (Eds.). (1972a). *A study of child variance: Vol. 1. Theories.* Ann Arbor: University of Michigan.

Rhodes, W. C., & Tracy, M. L. (Eds.). (1972b). *A study of child variance: Vol. 2. Interventions.* Ann Arbor: University of Michigan.

Chapter Five

Discipline with dignity which was authored by Curwin and Mendler and published by the Association for Supervision and Curriculum Development is an excellent overview of current research on classroom management in general education.

Hewett's *The emotionally disturbed child in the classroom : A developmental strategy for educating children with maladaptive behaviors* which was originally published in 1968 and the more current book with Taylor, *The emotionally disturbed child in the classroom: The orchestration of success*, continue to be excellent sources for managing and educating children with emotional and behavioral disorders. These are cited in the references.

Chapter Six

Freedom to learn by Rogers is a classic and a book that should be read by students who would like to better understand some of the theoretical underpinning of the interpersonal skills approach. The following is a list of practical self-help books which will help students to acquire the interpersonal skills discussed in this chapter.

Gordon, T. (1974). *T.E.T.: Teacher effectiveness training.* New York: P. H. Wyden.

Carkuff, R. (1980). *The art of helping IV.* Amherst, Human Resource Development Press, Inc.

Carkhuff, R., & Anthony, W. (1979). *The skills of helping.* Amherst, Human Resource Development Press.

Carkhuff, R. Bereson, D., & Pierce, R. (1977). *The skill of teaching: Interpersonal skills.* Amherst, Human Resource Development Press.

Chapter Seven

Today there are many resources covering the behavioral approach. A couple of classics which students should be able to obtain from a university library are:

Skinner, B. F. (1968). *The technology of teaching.* New York: Appleton-Century-Crofts.

Whaley, D. L., & Malott, (1970) R. W. *Elementary principles of behavior.* Englewood Cliffs, NJ: Prentice-Hall.

These are very readable and the Whaley and Malott text provides numerous clinical and experimental examples which have occurred in both hospital and educational settings. Finally, a good behavioral text that is special-education oriented is:

Alberto, P., & Troutman, A. (1990). *Applied behavior analysis for teachers* (3rd. ed.). Columbus, OH: Merrill/Macmillan.

Information related to respondent conditioning can be found in *Treating children's fears and phobias: A behavioral approach* by Morris and Kratochwill which is cited in the references. In addition, an excellent source for teaching relaxation to disabled children is:

Cautela, J., & Groden, J. (1978). *Relaxation: A comprehensive manual for adults, children and children with special needs.* Champaign, IL: Research Press.

For individuals interested in practical how-to publications, a number of how-to booklets have been published by H. & H. Enterprises. These booklets are currently being distributed by Pro-Ed, 8700 Shoal Creek Boulevard, Austin, TX 78758.

Chapter Eight

There are many cognitive-learning resources. For readers who would like to look at a description of a problem-solving intervention see:

Weissberg, R. P., Gesten, E. L., Carnrike, C. L., Toro, P. A., Rapkin, B. D., Davidson, E., & Cowen, E. L. (1981). Social problem-solving skills training: A competence building intervention with second to fourth grade children. *American Journal of Community Psychology, 9,* 411-423.

For readers who would like to examine a practical social skills training program, the social skills training programs of Goldstein et al.(1980) will describe specific instructional steps for teaching prosocial skills.

There are many resources available for readers who are interested in understanding more about Rational-Emotive Therapy. *Reason and emotion in psychotherapy* by Ellis (1962) provides an excellent theoretical overview of this intervention. *Rational-Emotive therapy with children and adolescents* by Bernard and Joyce (1984) is a comprehensive presentation of both theory and practice.

At the level of practice only, *Thinking straight and talking sense* by Gerald and Eyman (1981), is comprised of numerous REE lesson plans. *Thinking, feeling and behaving: An emotional education curriculum for adolescents* by Vernon (1989) is full of activities for grades 7 through 12. All of the above are cited in the references.

In addition, the Institute for Rational-Emotive Therapy, 45 East 65th Street, New York , NY 10021 has a wide variety of materials including audio and video tapes. Also, the institute offers certification programs.

Chapter Nine

Because this chapter is somewhat unique the resources cited in the references will have to be sufficient. However, there are many excellent works that offer a discussion of the scientific method. One such text is:

Kerlinger, F. (1973). *Foundations of behavioral research.* NY: Holt, Rinehart, & Winston.

Chapter Ten

Two books which provide general guidelines regarding crisis counseling are *Crisis counseling, intervention, and prevention in the schools,* which has been edited by Sandoval and *Crisis intervention book 2: The practitioner sourcebook for brief therapy,* which was edited by Parad and Parad. These books discuss specific types of crises and are cited in the references.

For individuals who want to become proficient in the use of the Life Space Intervention, *Life space intervention: Talking with children and youth in crisis* by Wood and Long provides the reader with an in-depth analysis of the elements involved in each step of the intervention. This resource is cited in the references also.

Finally, a number of commercial materials and services including on site training programs are available from the National Crisis Prevention Institute, 3315-K North 124th Street, Brookfield, WI 53005.

Glossary

Academic Curriculum Profile. A profile indicating a student's academic strengths and weaknesses and comparing these to a normed reference group.

Active Listening. The interpersonal skill of decoding what another person is saying and mirroring or feeding back the results of this decoding to demonstrate understanding.

Anecdotal Records. A record which describes certain instances of behavior over long periods of time.

Anticipatory Guidance. A procedure designed to help students prepare for events in the future which are likely to be stressful.

Anxiety-Withdrawal. A dimensional classification category which describes children who are typically self-conscious, hypersensitive, and often have social skill deficits.

Attention Problems-Immaturity. A dimensional classification category which describes children who have cognitive and integrative problems and exhibit behaviors often typical of younger children.

Autonomic. Pertaining to the autonomic nervous system, the sympathetic and parasympathetic divisions of the nervous system, innervating glands, as well as smooth and cardiac muscle.

Backward Chaining. A technique in which a task made up of several responses is taught by conditioning the responses in a stimulus response chain in reverse order.

Baseline. A record of the operant level or pretreatment level of a behavior which exists during the initial phase of observation.

Behavioral Disputation. A technique that involves clients in the use of role play and homework assignments for the purpose of getting them to face directly and learn to cope with situations that cause them to have upsetting thoughts and feelings.

Cascade System. A classic pictorial representation of special education services which is shaped like an hour-glass to indicate the numbers of handicapped students served at various levels.

Chaining. A technique in which a task made up of several responses is taught by conditioning the responses in a stimulus response chain.

Childhood Schizophrenia. A childhood disorder that occurs in adolescence or early adulthood and refers to psychotic behavior characterized by a loss of contact with reality, and bizarre thought processes and behavior.

Clinical Teaching Design. Also referred to as an A-B design. This design evaluates student improvement and teacher effectiveness by including a baseline and intervention phase. Data from both phases are displayed graphically and evaluated visually.

Cognition. The process of knowing, thinking or perceiving.

Cognitive Behavior Modification. A number of interventions which have consolidated cognitive and behavioral treatment approaches.

Cognitive Disputation. A technique that involves identifying and disputing or helping clients to identify and dispute the irrational ideas that cause upsetting feelings and problem behavior.

Cognitive Self-Instruction. A cognitive learning intervention that teaches children how to use verbal self-talk to improve their behavior.

Cognitive Self-Monitoring. A cognitive learning intervention that attempts to get children to attend to specific behaviors in systematic ways.

Cognitive Social Skills Training. A cognitive learning intervention that helps children think correctly about their interpersonal social behavior so that they can solve interpersonal social problems when they arise.

Concrete Operational Children. Children who are developmentally able to understand their world in accordance with Piaget's concrete operational stage of cognitive development. These children are able to learn concepts, but they must be connected to specific situations.

Conduct Disorder. A dimensional classification category which describes children who are physically and verbally aggressive, noncompliant, intrusive, lack self control and have impaired interpersonal relationships.

Conflict Cycle. A description of a spiraling cycle of forces which occur between the needs of students and the expectations of others which cause them to produce defensive behaviors that result in negative reactions by others.

Congruence. Also referred to as authenticity, realness, or genuineness. Congruence or personal congruence implies that the thoughts and feelings a person is experiencing are available to awareness and able to be communicated if appropriate.

Consistency Criteria. A type of functional or mastery standard which complements a performance criteria and indicates the frequency with which performance must be demonstrated.

Content Analysis. The process of fractioning down a long-term goal through a number of subskills into short-term objectives.

Continuous Reinforcement. One of the two basic types of schedules of reinforcement. On this schedule, reinforcement is delivered immediately after each response.

Cooperative Group Learning. A group learning strategy in which students collaborate in learning exercises to stimulate learning and achieve group approval and rewards.

Counterconditioning. A respondent conditioning procedure in which an anxiety antagonistic response is paired with a negatively conditioned stimulus until the negatively conditioned stimulus loses its power to evoke an anxiety response.

Crisis Intervention. An intervention designed to help individuals get through crises and cope with the events that created them.

Crisis Management. A general term used to describe approaches by which crises can be handled. The term includes crisis prevention and crisis intervention.

Crisis Prevention. A term used to describe one or more of several approaches designed to prevent the occurrence of crises.

Diagnostic and Statistical Manual of Mental Disorders-Revised (DSM III-R). A comprehensive classification system of mental disorders, which is published by the American Psychiatric Association.

Dimensional Classification System. A highly reliable classification system based on the statistical technique of factor analysis in which clusters of highly intercorrelated behaviors are identified under six dimensions.

Discrimination Training. The procedure of conditioning a response in the presence of one stimulus and extinguishing it in the presence of another.

Duration Recording. A method of recording which requires a measurement of how long a response last.

Emotional Disputation. A technique that involves procedures designed to get students to connect their emotions to their newly acquired rational cognition.

Engineered Classroom. A classroom which is supported by a floor plan in which curricular tasks have been designed to complement each student's developmental level.

Fading. A procedure for increasing the probability of success in mastering a task. Antecedent stimuli which assist the student are added and then gradually removed.

Fixed Interval. A schedule of intermittent reinforcement in which the first response after a fixed time period measured from the last reinforcement yields reinforcement.

Fixed Ratio. A schedule of intermittent reinforcement in which reinforcement is delivered after a fixed number of responses occur.

Formal Assessment. A form of indirect measurement in which academic or social and emotional behavior are assessed by means of a standardized norm referenced test.

Formal Operational Children. Children who are able to understand their world in accordance with Piaget's cognitive developmental stage of formal operations. These children are able to think abstractly and hypothetically.

Frequency Recording. A method of recording in which the number of times an event occurs per unit time is recorded.

Full Inclusion. An approach to the delivery of educational services in which all students, regardless of whether they are at risk or disabled, receive services in the regular classroom.

Graduated Extinction. A respondent procedure in which a negatively conditioned response is made to undergo extinction by either modifying the distance or the features of the negatively conditioned stimulus.

Group Counterconditioning. Implementing the respondent procedure of counterconditioning with a group of children who share the same or a very similar anxiety response.

I-Messages. A nonjudgmental message which helps individuals communicate their real feelings effectively to someone whose behavior is negatively affecting them.

Individualized Education Program (IEP). An individualized instructional plan required under PL 101-476 which must include specific components. Every disabled student must have an IEP.

Infantile Autism. A serious childhood disorder which begins in infancy or childhood and is characterized by an impairment in social interaction, verbal and nonverbal communication, and a restricted repertoire of activities and interests.

Informal Assessment.   A form of direct measurement in which academic, social, and emotional behavior are assessed directly by observation.

Interchangeable Statement.   A response provided by a helper that demonstrates a complete understanding of what the helpee has communicated.

Intermittent Reinforcement.   One of the two basic schedules of reinforcement. On this schedule reinforcement is delivered intermittently.

Interval Recording.   A method of recording data in which a session is divided into an equal number of small intervals and a record is made of the number of intervals in which responding occurs.

Level System.   A system which provides physical and psychological structure in an environment by ensuring that as progress is made from one level to another the expectations and privileges are increased. Conversely, when a regression occurs from one level to another the expectations and privileges are decreased.

Life Space Intervention.   A particular type of crisis intervention in which children are taught how to regulate their behavior.

Modeling.   Observational learning in which the learner acquires responses as the result of observation.

Motor Excess.   A dimensional classification category which describes children who exhibit excess activity and are typically restless, unpredictable, flighty distractible, impulsive, irritable, and destructive.

Negative Punishment.   A procedure in which a response subtracts a stimulus and becomes less probable.

Negative Reinforcement.   A procedure in which a response subtracts a stimulus and becomes more probable.

No-Lose Method.   A method of resolving interpersonal conflicts in which all parties get their needs meet.

Operant Conditioning.   The procedure of presenting a positive reinforcer immediately after a response which results in an increase in the frequency or strength of the response.

Operant Extinction.   The procedure of withholding reinforcement from a conditioned response, which results in a decrease in the response rate, until the response occurs no more frequently than it did prior to conditioning.

Peer Tutoring.   A strategy for structuring learning opportunities in which teachers design and monitor activities or lessons which allow older more competent students to provide instruction to younger less able students.

Performance Criterion.   A type of functional or mastery standard which indicates the accuracy level of the performance of a skill.

Positive Punishment. A procedure in which a response adds a stimulus and becomes less probable.

Positive Reinforcement. A procedure in which a response adds a stimulus and becomes more probable.

Preoperational Children. Children who are developmentally able to understand their world in accordance with Piaget's preoperational stage of cognitive development. These children will have difficulty understanding things from another's point of view and cannot easily consider two important things at the same time.

Pre-referral Intervention. An intervention which attempts to facilitate general education's capability for serving all students by developing collaborative strategies designed to reduce or eliminate the formal referral of students to general education.

Primary Reinforcer. A reinforcer for which a history of conditioning is not required.

Psychotic Behavior. Behavior exhibited by individuals who are psychotic which is characterized by an impairment in social interaction, verbal and nonverbal communication, loss of contact with reality, and bizzare thought processes.

Rational-Emotive Education (REE). An educational and preventative program based on the theory underlying Rational-Emotive Therapy which has been designed to anticipate problems by teaching children to eliminate the irrational thoughts that cause negative feelings.

Rational-Emotive Group Counseling (REGC). A therapeutic treatment approach based on the theory underlying Rational-Emotive Therapy which has been designed to treat target problems which group members share.

Rational-Emotive Therapy (RET). An individual therapeutic treatment approach based primarily on the twin premises that (a) illogical thinking leads to emotional and behavioral problems and (b) when faulty thinking is corrected, emotional and behavioral problems will diminish.

Regular Education Initiative. A educational reform movement whose proponents believe that all students regardless of whether they are at risk or have a disability should be provided with services in the regular classroom.

Respondent Conditioning. The procedure of pairing a neutral stimulus with an unconditioned stimulus until the neutral stimulus becomes conditioned and as such evokes a conditioned response.

Respondent Extinction. A respondent procedure in which a negatively conditioned response is made to undergo extinction by causing the response to occur in the presence of the negatively conditioned stimulus.

Schedules of Reinforcement. The exact manner in which reinforcement is delivered according to the number of responses, the time between responses, or both.

Secondary Reinforcer. Reinforcers which depend upon a history of stimulus pairing with other stimuli which already have reinforcing properties.

Shaping. A method of teaching a behavior that is not exhibited in the organism's repertoire. It employs the method of successive approximations in which successive approximations of the terminal behavior are reinforced sequentially until the terminal behavior is made to occur.

Social Behavior Profile. A profile indicating a student's social strengths and weaknesses. This profile may be based on various assessment sources and provides a starting point for the direct observation of specific social behaviors.

Socialized Aggression. A dimensional classification category which describes children who exhibit aggressive behavior, but conform to the norms and rules of their own often delinquent subculture.

Straining the Ratio. The procedural error, associated with schedules of reinforcement, of making the ratio too high too quickly so that a response undergoes operant extinction.

Stress Inoculation. A cognitive learning intervention that teaches children to prepare for events in the future that are likely to be stressful.

Task Analysis. The process of fractioning down a short-term objective through a number of subskills into instructional objectives.

Task Sampling. A method of recording in which an assessment is made of either a student's ability to (a) complete a task correctly or (b) complete a series of graduated steps which comprise a task.

Time Sampling. A method of recording data in which sessions are divided into small intervals and a sample of each interval is taken to determine whether responding occurred during this sampling time. A record of the number of samples in which responding occurred is recorded.

Token System. A system for managing the delivery of reinforcement which is based on the concept of secondary reinforcement. Tokens are secondary reinforcers which can later be exchanged for more powerful back up reinforcers.

Trend Projection. A method of projecting from baseline data what future behavior can be expected. Trend projections can be used to determine whether intervention is appropriate and necessary.

Unconditional Positive Regard. An interpersonal attitude in which the therapist or teacher prizes and values the client or student unconditionally.

Variable Interval. A schedule of reinforcement in which the first response after an average period of time receives reinforcement.

Variable Ratio. A schedule of reinforcement in which reinforcement is delivered after an average number of responses occur.

References

Achenbach, T. M. (1991). Manual for the *Child Behavior Checklist/4-18 and 1991 profile*. Burlington, VT: University of Vermont, Department of Psychiatry.

Achenbach, T. M., & Edelbrock, C. S. (1981). Behavior problems and competencies reported by parents of normal and disturbed children aged four through sixteen. *Monographs of the Society for Research in Child Development, 46,* (1, Serial No. 188).

Achenbach, T. M., & Edelbrock, C. S. (1984). *Child Behavior Checklist—Teacher's Report*. Burlington, VT: University Associates in Psychiatry.

Ager, C. L., & Cole, C. L. (1991). A review of cognitive-behavioral interventions for children and adolescents with behavior disorders. *Behavioral Disorders, 16,* 276-287.

American Psychiatric Association. (1987). *Diagnostic and statistical manual of mental disorders* (3rd ed., revised). Washington, DC: American Psychiatric Association.

Baldwin, B. A. (1978). A paradigm for the classification of emotional crises: Implications for crisis intervention. *American Journal of Orthopsychiatry, 40,* 538-551.

Bandura, A. (1977). *Social learning theory.* Englewood Cliffs, NJ: Prentice-Hall.

Bandura, A. (1986). *Social foundations of thought and actions: A social cognitive theory.* Englewood Cliffs, NJ: Prentice-Hall.

Bandura, A., & Walters, R. (1963). *Social learning and personality development.* New York: Holt, Rinehart and Winston.

Bard, J. A. (1980). *Rational-emotive therapy in practice.* Champaign, IL: Research Press.

Bauer, A., Shea, M., & Keppler, R. (1986). Level systems: A framework for the individualization of behavior management. *Behavioral Disorders, 12,* 28-35.

Baumrind, D. (1971). Current patterns of parental authority. In J. E. Brophy & J. G. Putnam (Eds.), *Classroom management.* Chicago, IL: University of Chicago Press.

Bellack, A. S., & Hersen, M. (1977). The use of self-report inventories in behavioral assessment. In J. D. Cone & R. P. Hawkins (Eds.), *Behavioral assessment: New directions in clinical psychology.* New York: Brunner/Mazel.

Belsky, J. (1984). The determinants of parenting: A process model. *Child Development, 55,* 83-96.

Bernard, M. E., & Joyce, M. R. (1984). *Rational-emotive therapy with children and adolescents: Theory, treatment strategies, preventative methods.* New York: John Wiley & Sons.

Bower, E. M. (1981). *Early identification of emotionally handicapped children in school* (3rd ed.). Springfield, IL: Charles C. Thomas.

Bower, E. M. (1982). Defining emotional disturbance: Public policy and research, *Psychology in the Schools, 19* (1), 55-60.

Brophy, J. E., & Putnam, J. G. (1979). Classroom management in the elementary grades. In D. L. Duke & K. J. Rehage (Eds.), *Classroom management: The seventy-eighth yearbook of the National Society for the Study of Education* (pp. 182-216). Chicago, IL: University of Chicago Press.

Camp, B. W., & Bash, M. A. (1981). *Think aloud: Increasing social and cognitive skills, a problem solving program for children.* Champaign, IL: Research Press.

Caplan, G. (1964). *Principles of preventative psychiatry.* New York: Basic Books.

Carkhuff, R. R. (1980). *The art of helping IV.* Amherst, Human Resource Development Press.

Carkhuff, R. R., Berenson, D. H., & Pierce, R. M. (1977). *The skills of teaching: Interpersonal skills.* Amherst, Human Resource Development Press.

Carpenter, R. L., & Apter, S. J. (1988). Research integration of cognitive-emotional interventions for behaviorally disordered children and youth. In M. C. Wang, M. C. Reynolds, & H. J. Walberg (Eds.), *Handbook of special education: Research and practice. Volume 2: Mildly handicapped conditions* (pp. 155-169). Oxford, Great Britain: Pergamon Press.

Cartledge, G., & Milburn, J. F. (Eds.), (1980). *Teaching social skills to children: Innovative approaches.* New York: Pergamon Press.

Center, D. (1989). *Curriculum and teaching strategies for students with behavioral disorders.* Englewood Cliffs, NJ: Prentice-Hall.

Center, D. B. (1990). Social maladjustment: An interpretation. *Behavioral Disorders, 15,* 141-148.

Cohen, A. S., & Van Tassel, E. A. (1978). A comparison: Partial and complete paired comparisons in sociometric measurement of preschool groups. *Applied Psychological Measurement, 2,* 31-40.

Coleman, M., Pieffer, S. & Oakland, T. (1992). Aggression replacement training with behaviorally disordered adolescents. *Behavioral Disorders, 18,* 54-66.

Cullinan, D., Epstein, M. H., & Kauffman, J. M. (1984). Teachers' ratings of students' behaviors: What constitutes behavior disorder in schools? *Behavioral Disorders, 10,* 9-19.

Curtis, M. J., & Meyers, J. (1988). Consultation: A foundation for alternative services in the schools. In J. L. Garden, J. E. Zins, & M. J. Curtis (Eds.), *Alternative educational delivery systems: Enhancing instructional options for all students* (pp. 35-48). Washington, DC: National Association of School Psychologists.

Curwin, R. L., & Mendler, A. N. (1988). *Discipline with dignity.* Alexandria, VA: Association for Supervision and Curriculum Development.

Davis, J.M. (1988). Suicide and the schools: Intervention and prevention. In J. Sandoval (Ed.), *Crisis counseling, intervention, and prevention in the schools.* Hillsdale, NJ: Lawrence Erlbaum.

Deno, E. (1970). Special education as developmental capital. *Exceptional Children, 37(3),* 229-37.

Dewey, J. (1933). *How we think.* Boston: Heath.

Doke, L. A., & Flippo, J. R. (1983). Aggressive and oppositional behavior. In T. H. Ollendick & M. Hersen (Eds.), *Handbook of child psychopathology.* New York: Plenum.

Eddy, J.P., Lawson, D.M., Jr., & Stilson, D.C. (1983). *Crisis intervention: A manual for education and action.* Lanham, University Press of America.

Elias, M. J. (1983). Improving coping skills of emotionally disturbed boys through television-based social problem solving. *American Journal of Orthopsychiatry, 53,* 61-72.

Ellis, A. (1962). *Reason and emotion in psychotherapy.* New York: Stuart.

Ellis, A. (1971). *Rational-emotive therapy and its application to emotional education.* New York: Institute for Rational Living.

Ellis, A. (1973). *Humanistic psychotherapy: The rational-emotive approach.* New York: McGraw-Hill.

Ellis, A. (1974). Rational-emotive theory. In A. Burton (Ed.), *Operational theories of personality* (pp. 308-344). New York: Bruner-Mazel.

Ellis, A. (1977). The basic clinical theory of rational-emotive therapy. In A. Ellis & R. Grieger (Eds.), *Handbook of rational-emotive therapy.* New York: Springer.

Ellis, A. (1992). My current views on Rational-Emotive Therapy (RET) and religiousness. *Journal of Rational-Emotive Therapy & Cognitive-Behavior Therapy, 10,* 37-40.

Etscheidt, S. E. (1991). Reducing aggressive behavior and improving self-control: A cognitive-behavioral treatment program for behaviorally disordered adolescents. *Behavioral Disorders, 16,* 107-115.

Fagan, S. A., & Long, N. J. (1979). A psychoeducational curriculum approach to teaching self-control. *Behavioral Disorders, 4,* 68-82.

Forness, S. R. (1988). Planning for the needs of children with serious emotional disturbance: The national special education and mental health coalition. *Behavioral Disorders, 13,* 127-133.

Fuchs, D., & Fuchs, L. (1988). Mainstream assistance teams to accommodate difficult to teach students in general education. In J. L. Garden, J. E. Zins, & M. J. Curtis (Eds.), *Alternative educational delivery systems: Enhancing instructional options for all students* (pp. 49-70). Washington, DC: National Association of School Psychologists.

Fuchs, D., & Fuchs, L. (1991). Framing the REI debate: Abolitionists versus conservationists. In J. W. Lloyd, N. N. Singh, & A. C. Repp (Eds.), *Regular education initiative: Alternative perspectives on concepts, issues, and models* (pp. 241-255). Sycamore, IL: Sycamore.

Fifer, F. L. (1986). Effective classroom management. *Academic Therapy, 21,* 401-410.

Gartner, A., & Lipsky, D. K. (1989). *The yoke of special education: How to break it.* Rochester, NY: National Center on Education and the Economy.

Gerald, M., & Eyman, W. (1981). *Thinking straight and talking sense.* New York: Institute for Rational Living.

Ginott, H. (1959). The theory and practice of therapeutic intervention in child treatment. In H. Dupont (Ed.), *Educating emotionally disturbed children: Readings.* New York: Holt, Reinhart and Winston.

Goldstein, A. P., & Glick, B. (1987). *Aggression replacement training: A comprehensive intervention for aggressive youth.* Champaign, IL: Research Press.

Goldstein, A. P., Sprafkin, R. P., Gershaw, N. J., & Klein, P. (1980). *Skillstreaming the adolescent.* Champaign, IL: Research Press.

Good, T. L., & Brophy, J. E. (1987). *Looking in classrooms* (4th ed). New York: Harper and Row.

Good, T. L., & Brophy, J. E, (1991). *Looking in classrooms* (5th ed). New York: Harper and Row.

Gordon, T. (1974). *TET—Teacher effectiveness training.* New York: Wyden.

Green, E., & Green, A. (1983). General and specific applications of thermal biofeedback. In J. V. Basmajian (Eds.), *Biofeedback: Principles and practices for clinicians.* Baltimore: Williams & Wilkins.

Greenwood, C. R., Walker, H. M., & Hops, H. (1977). Some issues in social interaction/withdrawal assessment. *Exceptional Children, 43,* 490-499.

Grieger, R. M., & Boyd, J. D. (1983). Childhood anxieties, fears and phobias: A cognitive-behavioral psychosituational approach. In A. Ellis & M. E. Bernard (Eds.), *Rational-emotive approaches to problems of childhood* (pp. 211-239). New York: Plenum.

Halford, K. (1983). Teaching rational self-talk to help socially isolated children and youth. In A. Ellis & M. E. Bernard (Eds.), *Rational-emotive approaches to the problems of childhood* (pp. 241-270). New York: Plenum.

Hall, R. V., Lund, D., & Jackson, D. (1968). Effects of teacher attention on study behavior. *Journal of Applied Behavior Analysis, 1,* 1-12.

Hallahan, D. P., & Kauffman, J. M. (1991). *Exceptional children: Introduction to special education* (5th ed.). Englewood Cliffs, NJ: Prentice-Hall.

Hardman, M. L., Drew, C. L., Egan, M. W., & Wolf, B. (1993). *Human exceptionality: Society, school, and family* (4th ed.). Boston, Allyn & Bacon.

Haring, N. G., Liberty, K. A., & White, O. R. (1980). Rules for data based strategy decisions in instructional programs: Current research and instructional implications. In W. Sailor, B. Wilcox, & L. Brown (eds.), *Methods of instruction for severely handicapped students* (pp. 159-192). Baltimore: Paul H. Brookes.

Harris, K. R., & Pressley, M. (1991). The nature of cognitive strategy instruction: Interactive strategy construction. *Exceptional Children, 57,* 392-404.

Hogan, S., & Prater, M. A. (1993). The effects of peer tutoring and self-management on on-task, academic, and disruptive behaviors. *Behavioral Disorders, 18,* 118-128.

Hawryluk, M. K., & Smallwood, D. L. (1988). Using peers as instructional agents: Peer tutoring and cooperative learning. In J. L. Garden, J. E. Zins, & M. J. Curtis (Eds.), *Alternative educational delivery systems: Enhancing instructional options for all students* (pp. 371-389). Washington, DC: National Association of School Psychologists.

Hawton, K. (1986). *Suicide and attempted suicide among children and adolescents.* Newbury Park, CA: Sage.

Hewett, F. M. (1968). *The emotionally disturbed child in the classroom: A developmental strategy for educating children with maladaptive behaviors.* Boston, Allyn & Bacon.

Hewett, F. M., & Taylor, F. D. (1980). *The emotionally disturbed child in the classroom: The orchestration of success* (2nd ed.). Boston, Allyn & Bacon.

Hewitt, L. E., & Jenkins, R. L. (1946). *Fundamental patterns of maladjustment: The dynamics of their origin.* Springfield, IL: State of Illinois.

Ianacone, R. N, & Stodden, R. A. (1987). Transition Issues and directions for individuals who are mentally retarded. In R. N. Ianacone, & R. A. Stodden (Eds.), *Transition issues and directions* (pp. 1-7). Reston, VA: Council for Exceptional Children.

Idol, L. (1988). A rationale and guidelines for establishing special education and consultation programs. *Remedial and Special Education, 9(6),* 48-58.

Idol, L., Paolucci-Whitcomb, P., & Nevin, A. (1986). *Collaborative consultation.* Rockville, Aspen.

Jensen, B., & Haynes, S. (1986). Self-report questionnaires and inventories. In A. R. Ciminero, K. S. Calhoun, & H. E. Adams (Eds.), *Handbook of behavioral assessment.* New York: John Wiley & Sons.

Jones, V.F. (1992). Integrating behavioral and insight-oriented treatment in school-based programs for seriously emotionally disturbed students. *Behavioral Disorders, 17,* 225-236.

Karon, B. P. (1981). The Thematic Apperception Test (TAT). In A. I. Rabin, (Ed.), *Assessment with projective techniques: A concise introduction.* New York: Springer.

Kauffman, J. M. (1989). *Characteristics of children's behavior disorders* (4th ed.). Columbus, OH: Merrill.

Kauffman, J. M. (1991). Restructuring the sociopolitical context: Reservations about the effects of current reform proposals on students with disabilities. In J. W. Lloyd, N. N. Singh, & A. C. Repp (Eds.), *The regular education initiative: Alternative perspectives on concepts, issues, and models* (pp. 43-56). Sycamore, IL: Sycamore.

Kauffman, J. M. (1993). *Characteristics of emotional and behavioral disorders of children and youth* (5th ed.). Columbus, OH: Merrill.

Kauffman, J., Lloyd, J., Cook, L., Cullinan, D., Epstein, M., Forness, S., Hallahan, D., Nelson, M., Polsgrove, L., Sabornie, E., Strain, P., & Walker, H. (1991). Problems and promises in special education and related services for children and youth with emotional or behavioral disorders. *Behavioral Disorders, 16,* 299-313.

Kauffman, J. M., Lloyd, J. W., & McGee, K. A. (1989). Adaptive and maladaptive behavior: Teachers' attitudes and their technical assistance needs. *Journal of Special Education, 23,* 185-200.

Kazdin, A. E. (1978). *History of behavior modification.* Baltimore: University Park Press.

Kendall, P. C. (1981). Assessment and cognitive-behavioral interventions: Purposes, proposals and problems. In P. C. Kendall & S. D. Hollon (Eds.), *Assessment strategies for cognitive-behavioral interventions.* New York: Academic Press.

King, M.J., & Goldman, R.K. (1988). Crisis intervention and prevention with children of divorce and remarriage. In J. Sandoval (Ed.), *Crisis counseling, intervention, and prevention in the schools.* Hillsdale, NJ: Lawrence Erlbaum.

Kirk, S. A. (1972). *Educating exceptional children* (2nd ed.). Boston, MA: Houghton Mifflin.

Kounin, J. S. (1970). *Discipline and group management in classrooms.* New York: Holt, Rinehart and Winston.

Larson, K. A., & Gerber, M. M. (1987). Effects of social metacognitive training for enhancing overt behavior in learning disabled and low achieving delinquents, *Exceptional Children, 54,* 201-211.

Lazarus, R. (1966). *Psychological stress and the coping process.* New York: McGraw-Hill.

Libet, J., & Lewisohn, P. (1973). Concept of social skill with special reference to the behavior of depressed persons. *Journal of Consulting Psychology, 40,* 304-312.

Lipsky, D. K., & Gartner, A. (1991). Restructuring for quality. In J. W. Lloyd, N. N. Singh, & A. C. Repp (Eds.), *The regular education initiative: Alternative perspectives on concepts, issues, and models* (pp. 43-56). Sycamore, IL: Sycamore.

Long, N. (1993, April). *Expanding the power and effectiveness of Life Space Interview: An essential skill for professionals in the nineties.* Paper presented at the annual meeting for the Council of Exceptional Children, San Antonio, TX.

Lovaas, O. I. (1987). Behavioral treatment and normal educational and intellectual functioning in young autistic children. *Journal of Consulting and Clinical Psychology, 55,* 3-9.

Mastropieri, M. A., Jenne, T., & Scruggs, T. E. (1988). A level system for managing problem behaviors in a high school resource program. *Behavioral Disorders, 13,* 202-208.

McCarl, J. J., Svobodny, L., & Beare, P. L. (1991). Self-recording in a classroom for students with mild to moderate mental handicaps: Effects on productivity and on-task behavior. *Education and Training in Mental Retardation, 26,* 79-88.

McDonnell, J., Wilcox, B., & Hardman, M. L. (1991). *Secondary programs for students with developmental disabilities.* Boston: Allyn & Bacon.

McGinnis, E., & Goldstein, A. (1984). *Skillstreaming the elementary school child.* Champaign, IL: Research Press.

McMahon. R. J., & Forehand, R. (1988). Conduct disorders. In E. J. Mash & L. G. Terdal (Eds.) *Behavioral Assessment of Childhood Disorders.* New York: Guilford Press.

Meichenbaum, D. (1977). *Cognitive-behavior modification: An integrative approach.* New York: Plenum.

Miller, J. A., & Peterson, D. W. (1987). Peer influenced academic interventionists. In C. A. Maher & J. E. Zins (Eds.), *Psychoeducational interventions in the schools: Methods and procedures for enhancing student competence.* Elmsford, NY: Pergamon.

Morse, W. C. (1985). *The education and treatment of socioemotionally impaired children and youth.* Syracuse, NY: Syracuse University Press.

Morris, R. J., & Kratochwill, T. R. (1983). *Treating children's fears and phobias: A behavioral approach.* New York: Pergamon.

Muro, J. J., & Dinkmeyer, D. C. (1977). *Counseling in the elementary and middle schools.* Dubuque, IA: Wm. C. Brown.

Murray, E. J. (1964). *Motivation and emotion.* Englewood Cliffs, NJ: Prentice-Hall.

Murray, E. J., & Jacobson, L. J. (1978). Cognition and learning in traditional and behavioral therapy. In S. L. Garfield & A. E. Bergon (Eds.), *Handbook of psychotherapy and behavior change* (2nd ed., pp. 689-722). New York: Wiley.

Naslund, S. R. (1987). Life space interviewing: A psychoeducational interviewing model for teaching pupil insights and measuring program effectiveness. *The Pointer, 31,* 12-15.

Ollendick, T. H., & Hersen, M. (Eds.). (1984). *Childhood behavioral assessment: Principles and procedures.* New York: Pergamon.

Parad, H. J., & Parad, L. G. (1990). *Crisis Intervention book 2: The practitioneer's sourcebook for brief therapy.* Milwaukee, WI: Family Service America.

Patterson, G. R. (1980). Mothers: The unacknowledged victims. *Monographs of the Society for Research in Child Development, 45* (5, Serial No. 186).

Prater, M. A., Hogan, S., & Miller, S. R. (1992). Using self-monitoring to improve on-task behavior and academic skills of an adolescent with mild disabilities across special and regular settings. *Education and Treatment of Children, 15,* 43-55.

Prior, M., & Werry, J. S. (1986). Autism, schizophrenia and allied disorders. In H. C. Quay & J. S. Werry (Eds.), *Psychopathological disorders of childhood* (3rd ed., pp. 156-210). New York: Wiley.

Pullen, P. L., & Kauffman, J. M. (1987). *What should I know about special education? Answers for classroom teachers.* Austin, TX: Pro-Ed.

Quay, H. C. (1979). Classification. In H. C. Quay & J. S. Werry (Eds.), *Psychopathological disorders of childhood* (2nd ed., pp. 1-34). New York: Wiley.

Quay, H. C. (1983). A dimensional approach to behavior disorder: The revised behavior problem checklist. *School Psychology Review, 12,* (3), 244-249.

Quay, H. C. (1986). Conduct disorders. In H. C. Quay & J. S. Werry (Eds.), *Psychopathological disorders of childhood* (2nd ed., pp. 35-72). New York: Wiley.

Quay, H. C. (1987). Patterns of delinquent behavior. In H. Quay (Ed.), *Handbook of juvenile delinquency* (pp. 118-138). New York: Wiley.

Quay, H. C., & Peterson, D. R. (1987). *Manual for the Revised Behavior Problem Checklist.* Coral Gables, FL: Author.

Raymer, R., & Poppen, R. (1985). Behavioral relaxation training for hyperactive children. *Journal of Behavior Therapy and Experimental Psychiatry, 16,* 309-316.

Redl, F., & Wineman, D. (1952). *Controls from within.* Glencoe, IL: The Free Press.

Repp, A. C. (1983). *Teaching the mentally retarded.* Englewood Cliffs, NJ: Prentice-Hall.

Reiher, T. C. (1992). Identified deficits and their congruence to the IEP for behaviorally disordered students. *Behavioral Disorders, 17,* 167-177.

Robin, A., Schneider, M., & Dolnick, M. (1976). The Turtle Technique: An extended case of self-control in the classroom. *Psychology in the Schools, 13,* 449-453.

Rogers, C. R. (1951). *Client centered therapy.* Cambridge, Riverdale Press.

Rogers, C. R. (1969). *Freedom to learn.* Columbus, OH: Merrill.

Rogers, C. R. (1980). *Freedom to learn: For the 80's.* Columbus, OH: Merrill.

Rossi, A. S. (1977). RET with children: More than child's play. *Rational Living, 12,* 21-24.

Rosenthal, R., & Jacobson, L. (1968). *Pygmalion in the classroom.* New York: Holt, Rinehart and Winston.

Rubin, R. A., & Balow, B. (1971). Learning and behavior disorders: A longitudinal study. *Exceptional Children, 38,* 292-299.

Rusk, T. N. (1971). Opportunity and technique in crisis psychiatry. *Comprehensive Psychiatry, 12,* 249-263.

Rutter, M., & Schopler, E. (1987). Autism and pervasive developmental disorders: Concepts and diagnostic issues. *Journal of Autism and Developmental Disorders, 17,* 159-186.

Sandoval, J. (Ed.). (1985). Mini-series on crisis counseling in the schools. *School Psychology Review, 14,* 255-324.

Sandoval, J. (Ed.). (1988). *Crisis counseling, intervention, and prevention in the schools.* Hillsdale, NJ: Lawrence Erlbaum.

Schacter, S. (1966). The interaction of cognitive and physiological determinants of emotional state. In C. Spielberger (Ed.), *Anxiety and behavior* (pp. 193-224). New York: Academic Press.

Sharan, S. (1980). Cooperative learning in small groups: Recent methods and effects on achievement, attitudes and ethnic relations. *Review of Educational Research, 50,* 241-271.

Shores, R. E., (1993, April). *General classroom management strategies: Are they effective with violent and aggressive students?* Paper presented at the annual meeting of the Council of Exceptional Children, San Antonio, TX.

Shores, R. E., Gunter, P. L., & Jack, S. L. (1993). Classroom management strategies: Are they setting events for coercesion? *Behavioral Disorders, 18,* 92-102.

Simpsom, R. L., Miles, B. S., Walker, B. L., Ormsbee, C. K., & Downing, J. A. (1991). *Programming for aggressive and violent students.* Reston, VA: The Council for Exceptional Children.

Slenkovich, J. (1983). *P.L. 94-142 as applied to DSM III diagnoses: An analysis of DSM III diagnoses vis-a-vis special education law.* Cupertino, CA: Kinghorn Press.

Smith, S. W., & Simpson, R. L. (1989). An analysis of individualized education programs (IEP's) for students with behavioral disorders. *Behavioral Disorders, 14,* 107-116.

Smith, C. R., Woods, F. H., & Grimes, J. (1988). Issues in the identification and placement of behaviorally disordered students. In M. C. Wang, M. C. Reynolds, & H. J. Walberg (Eds.), *Handbook of special education: Research and practice* (vol. 2, pp. 95-123). New York: Pergamon.

Spivak, G., & Shure, M. B. (1974). *Social adjustment of young children: A cognitive approach to solving real-life problems.* San Francisco CA: Jossey-Bass.

Stainback, W., & Stainback, S. (1990). *Support networks for inclusive schooling: Interdependent integrated education.* Baltimore: Paul H. Brookes.

Stainback, W., & Stainback, S. (1991). Rationale for integration and restructuring: A synopsis. In J. W. Lloyd, N. N. Singh, & A. C. Repp (Eds.), *The regular education initiative: Alternative perspectives on concepts, issues and models* (pp. 225-240). Sycamore, IL: Sycamore.

Swap, S. M. (1991). Ecological theory and practice. In J. L. Paul & B. C. Epanchin (Eds.), *Educating emotionally disturbed children and youth: Theories and practices for teachers* (pp. 243-272). New York: Macmillan.

Sweeney, D. P. (1993, April). *A model for the determination of eligibility and assessment requirements for the proposed new definition of SED.* Paper presented at the annual International Convention for the Council of Exceptional Children, San Antonio, TX.

Thoresen, C. E., & Mahoney, M. J. (1974). *Behavioral self-control.* New York: Holt, Rinehart and Winston.

Thousands, J. S., Villa, R. A., Paolucci-Whitcomb, P., & Nevins, A. (1992). In W. Stainback & S. Stainback (Eds.), *Controversial issues confronting special education: Divergent perspectives* (pp. 223-232). Boston: Allyn & Bacon.

Thurer, S., & Hursh, N. C. (1981). Characteristics of the therapeutic relationship. In C. E. Walker (Ed.), *Clinical practice of psychology* (pp. 62-82). New York: Pergamon.

Vernon, A. (1989). *Thinking, feeling, behaving: An emotional education curriculum for adolescents grades 7-12.* Champaign IL: Research Press.

Walen, S. R., DiGuiseppe, R., & Wessler, R. L. (1980). *A practitioner's guide to rational-emotive therapy.* New York: Oxford University Press.

Walker, H., & Buckley, N. K. (1971). Investigation of some classroom control parameters as a function of teacher dispensed social reinforcers. *Journal of Applied Behavior Analysis, 5,* 209-224.

Walker, H., McConnell, S., Holmes, D., Todis, B., Walker, J., & Golden, N. (1983). *The Walker social skills curriculum: The ACCEPTS program.* Austin, TX: Pro-Ed.

Wang, M. C., Reynolds, M. C., & Walberg, H. J. (1988). Integrating the children of the second system. *Phi Delta Kappan, 70,* 248-251.

Wang, M. C., Peverly, S. T., & Catalano, R. (1987). Integrating special needs students in regular classes: Programming, implementation, and policy issues. In J. Gottlieb & B. W. Gottlieb (Eds.), *Advances in special education* (vol. 6, pp. 119-149). Greenwich, CT: JAI Press.

Watson, J. B., & Rayner, R. (1920). Conditioned emotional reaction. *Journal of Experimental Psychology, 3,* 1-4.

Weissberg, R. P., & Gesten, E. (1982). Considerations for developing effective school-based social problem-solving (SPS) training programs. *School Psychology Review, 11,* 56-63.

Wessler, R. A., & Wessler, R. L. (1980). *The principles and practice of rational-emotive therapy.* San Francisco, CA: Jossey-Bass.

Whaley, D. L., & Malott, R. W. (1971). *Elementary principles of behavior.* Englewood, Cliffs, NJ: Prentice-Hall.

Will, M. (1986). Educating children with learning problems: A shared responsibility. *Exceptional Children, 52,* 411-415.

Wolpe, J. (1973). *The practice of behavior therapy* (2nd ed.). Elmsford, NY: Pergamon Press.

Wood, F. H. (1990). Editorial. *Behavioral Disorders, 15* (3), 139.

Wood, M. M., & Long, N. J. (1991). *Life space intervention: Talking with children and youth in crisis.* Austin, TX: Pro-Ed.

Zins, J. E., Curtis, M. J., Garden, J. L., & Ponti, C. R. (1988). *Helping students succeed in the regular classroom.* San Francisco: Jossey-Bass.

Index

biophysical, 68-69
cognitive-learning, 74-76
ecological, 70-71
humanistic, 71-73
psychodynamic, 66-68
psychoeducational, 69-70
Motor excess, 210-211

N

National Mental Health and Special
Education Coalition, 6-7

O

Operant conditioning, 129-130
strategies
chaining, 160-161
discrimination training, 156-159
extinction, operant, 150-151
fading, 159-160
modeling, 152
punishment, 149-150
reinforcement schedules, 152-156
reinforcers, 147-148
shaping, 151
token systems, 148
Overcorrection (OC), 163-164, 210
Overcorrection Through Positive Practice
(OC-P), 163
Overcorrection Through Restitution
(OC-R), 163
Overcorrection through the Full Use of
Both Methods (OC-F), 164

P

Peabody Individual Achievement Test-
Revised, 44, 45
Peer-assisted learning (PAL), 37
Pica, 11
PL. *See* Public Law
Program design assessment, 43-53
Psychosis, 17-19, 210. *See also* Autism;
Schizophrenia
Public Law 85-926 (PL 85-926), 3-4

Public Law 88-164 (PL 88-164), 3-4
Public Law 94-142, Education for All
Handicapped Children Act, 1975 (PL 94-
142), 3, 23, 29, 37
Public Law 99-457, 1986 (PL 99-457), 38.
See also Individual Family Service Plan
(IFSP)
Public Law 101-476, Individuals With
Disabilities Education Act, 1990 (PL
101-476, IDEA), 4, 5, 23, 28, 39. *See
also* Individual education program
(IEP); Least restrictive environment
(LRE)

Q

Quay's dimensional classification, 10-20,
207, 209

R

Rational-Emotive Education (REE),
184-186
anxiety/withdrawal, 210
conduct disorders, 207
Rational-Emotive Group Counseling
(REGC)
anxiety/withdrawal, 210, 211
characteristics, group, 189-190
characteristics, teacher/therapist,
186-187, 189
conduct disorders, 207
stages, 190-196
Rational-Emotive Therapy (RET), 206, 207
ABC theory, 180-181
anxiety/withdrawal, 210
behavioral disputation, 184
cognitive disputation, 181-183
conduct disorders, 207
emotional disputation, 183-184
theory, 179
Regular education initiative (REI), 33-34,
39-40
Respondent conditioning, 127-129
strategies
counterconditioning, 142-146, 229
group, 147
extinction